Handing on Christ

Handing on Christ

Rediscovering the Gift of Christian Doctrine

Richard Clutterbuck

✚ EPWORTH

British Library Cataloguing in Publication data

A catalogue record for this book is available
from the British Library

978 0 7162 0621 7

First published in 2009
by Epworth
Methodist Church House
25 Marylebone Road
London NW1 5JR

Typeset by Regent Typesetting
Printed and bound in Great Britain by
MPG Books Ltd, Bodmin, Cornwall

Contents

Preface		vi
1	Christian Doctrine and How We Got There	1
2	The Gift of Christ	32
3	The Uncherished Gift	48
4	Giving Doctrine a Good Name	74
5	How Christian Doctrine Works	95
6	Recovering the Gift: The Rehabilitation of Doctrine in Recent Theology	114
7	Using the Gift: Doctrinal Communities	138
8	Unearthing the Buried Treasure: Rediscovering Neglected Doctrines	153
9	Handing on Christ: The Future of Christian Doctrine	182
Index of Subjects and Names		209

Preface

As a defence of the importance and role of doctrine in the life of the Christian community, this book is going against much that we now take for granted. My hope is that it will encourage readers to think again about the value of doctrine and to question the assumption that doctrine is no more than an intellectual straitjacket from which all sensible people would wish to be free.

Contemporary western culture is largely concerned with the present. L. P. Hartley's famous line, 'The past is another country; they do things differently there'[1] sums up its attitude to the past. As for the future, for all the talk of saving the planet, there is little sign of us amending our lives to ensure that a habitable world is handed on to our children's children.

But there is no present without a past to precede it or a future to follow it. For Christianity, the present makes sense and can be lived out well only if it is seen in the context of a past from which we receive and a future to which we give. Because the Christian God is active in human history, learning about God will mean receiving the story of Jesus Christ from those who have gone before us. Because the Christian God holds the world's future, being faithful to God will mean handing that story on to those who follow us. 'Doctrine' describes both the process of handing on the teaching about Christian belief, and the content that is handed on.

My own interest in this area goes back to my initial theological education in the 1970s. As an adolescent I had conformed to a rather simplistic version of evangelical Christianity. A university

---

1 The opening sentence of L. P. Hartley's novel *The Go Between*, Penguin Classics, 2004.

chaplain, no doubt wanting to prick my bubble of certainty, handed me a copy of John Robinson's *Honest to God*,[2] then regarded as a rather radical attack on traditional Christian doctrine. Some old certainties did crumble, but I was fortunate in my teachers and came to realize that Christian faith could be both dynamic and traditional. A course on the development of doctrine, while I was studying at the Irish School of Ecumenics, was especially helpful. It introduced me to John Henry Newman's essay on development, with its subtle interplay between change and faithfulness in Christian teaching. Since then I have moved between pastoral ministry and theological education, finding myself called to share the task of interpreting and handing on the faith. I am not the first person to find that my own understanding of Christian doctrine has been immensely enriched by the experience of teaching it to others. The impetus to develop more of my own thinking came through the invitation to deliver the 1997 Fernley Hartley Lecture. There I explored the origins and implications of the term 'our doctrines', so characteristic of the Methodist dialect of Christian speech, and so difficult to define. Since then, I have come to realize that the place and status of doctrine is an issue for all Christian traditions, and not just my own. As a result, this book has a much wider scope and will, I hope, be relevant to readers from many different backgrounds.

It is impossible to write about 'handing on Christ' without being conscious of a debt to the many communities and individuals who have handed on Christ to me: my parents and the people of Coddington and Hawtonville Methodist Churches; teachers at the Queen's College, Birmingham University and the Irish School of Ecumenics; and a host of friends, colleagues, authors, preachers and speakers. And behind them the two thousand years of Christian teaching and writing, from St Paul to Rowan Williams. To share in their labour, even in a minor role, is both awesome and joyful.

Finally, this book is dedicated to my daughters Elizabeth and Miriam. Whatever ineptness there has been in the way my wife,

---

2 John Robinson, *Honest to God*, SCM Press, 1963.

Diane and I have handed on Christ to them, their participation in the community and life of faith is a sign of hope for the future.

Richard Clutterbuck

Belfast
The feast of Mary, Martha and Lazarus, 2008

I

Christian Doctrine and How We Got There

Beginning after the beginning

I intend to start this journey into the story of Christian doctrine not at the beginning (thereby ignoring the advice given by *Alice in Wonderland* to the distressed dormouse), but at a point several centuries later. Sometimes it is only in an episode in the middle of a long and complex epic that we begin to see the shape of the story as a whole.

This part of the story focuses on the obscure Syrian town of Cyrrhus during the fifth century, towards the end of that formative era in the development of Christian doctrine that is traditionally called the patristic period.

The debates (perhaps a more accurate term would be 'conflicts') that led to the formation of Christian doctrine are usually associated with the great centres of power and learning in the late Roman Empire: Rome, Alexandria, Antioch, Constantinople and Jerusalem.[3] Yet the human and theological interest often emerges in the far-flung corners of the Roman Empire. Take, for example, the town of Cyrrhus and the diocese named after it. From 423, for at least 30 years, its bishop was a man called Theodoret. He was born to wealthy parents in Antioch, but as a young man had dedicated himself to a life of monastic poverty. His intellectual, spiritual and administrative gifts led him to the role of bishop. The town of Cyrrhus is now known by the Arabic name of Nabi

---

3 These five cities were regarded as having the metropolitan Christian churches, whose bishops were sometimes designated 'patriarch'.

Huri and it lies about 50 miles north of Aleppo. Then, as now, it was a frontier town. It had been occupied at various times by the Persians and Armenians as well as the Romans, and its heyday was well in the past. Its public buildings and amenities had suffered from long neglect, and only the intervention of Theodoret himself, in an early example of a church's support for its wider community, provided the means to rebuild bridges and raise civic pride.

Only about 30 years old when made bishop, Theodoret began his episcopate with zeal. He was particularly concerned that his far-flung diocese of about 800 parishes was ridden with both Christian heresy and the remnants of Paganism. Against the latter he wrote one of the last great apologetic works of the early Church.

Before long Europe and the Byzantine Empire would be so uniformly Christian that no such arguments would be thought necessary. For Theodoret, though, there was still a need to set out reasons for the truth of Christianity against the scepticism of those who held to the old religions of Rome and Greece or to the philosophies of Plato and the Stoics. Against heresy, Theodoret took a different line. He found that many of the churches in the diocese, instead of using the four canonical Gospels, were making use of a compendium of all four. This harmony of the Gospels of Matthew, Mark, Luke and John was known as the *Diatessaron*, from the Greek for 'through four'. It was attributed to the second-century author Tatian, and although it may have been originally compiled in Greek, it was particularly popular in Syriac-speaking areas, such as the diocese of Cyrrhus. As a young bishop Theodoret boasted of having destroyed 200 copies of the *Diatessaron* (an act that has not earned him the gratitude of later historians!), and of having made sure that complete copies of all four Gospels were supplied instead. His motive in this (to modern eyes) destructive act of censorship was doctrinal. He believed that Tatian was tainted with heresy, which is short-hand for saying that his opinions and teachings were at variance with the traditional teaching of the Christian Church. The *Diatessaron* gave people, under the guise of scripture, the opinions of just one person, whose compilation was bound to be influenced by his own theology and culture. Groups loyal to

Tatian[4] and Marcion (another second-century 'heretic', famous for teaching that Christians should ditch the Old Testament) were still active in the area. By using the same book as these groups, churches were, in Theodoret's eyes, risking heresy by association. In particular, Theodoret saw the *Diatessaron*'s removal of the genealogies of Matthew's and Luke's Gospels as a slur on the humanity of Christ.

However, in the autumn of 449, Theodoret was – to say the least – an unhappy man. A synod in Ephesus (since nicknamed 'The Robber Synod') had condemned him as a heretic and deposed him from his bishopric. Theodoret was one of many players in a doctrinal controversy about the person of Christ that was to reach a resolution of sorts at the Council of Chalcedon in 451. For the time being he had fallen foul of a potent mixture of theology and politics. As part of a campaign to regain his position he wrote to Leo, the Bishop of Rome, regarded even then as the pre-eminent Christian leader. His letter[5] bristles with righteous indignation. How could he, Theodoret, be accused of heresy when for over a quarter of a century he had worked tirelessly to deliver the 800 churches of his diocese from heresy and error? His writings from all those years, he says, are open for all to read and show him to have been consistent in his teaching and consistently hostile to such heresies as Marcionism, Arianism and Eunomianism.[6] Now he was being condemned on the instigation of the Bishop of Alexandria, without any opportunity to defend himself.

It is interesting that the letter from Theodoret to Pope Leo (and Leo's reply also survives) defends not only his doctrinal orthodoxy, but also his record as a pastorally dedicated and meticulously honest bishop, who used his position to serve the communities in his diocese and not to acquire anything for himself. For Theodoret, personal and doctrinal integrity went together and reinforced one other.

---

4 Tatian seems to have left the 'mainstream' Church to found his own group. His rejection of marriage was one of the areas that pitted him against traditional Christian teaching.

5 Letter CXIII, *The Nicene and Post-Nicene Fathers*, Vol. III, p. 293.

6 Marcionism pitted a vengeful Old Testament god against a redemptive Christian one. Arianism (and its later variant, Eunomianism) argued that the Son was created by the Father and did not share fully in the divine life.

What kind of things were at stake for Theodoret and his opponents? In 449 the hot issue concerned the relationship between the human and divine natures of Christ. One position, usually associated with the bishops of Alexandria[7] and their supporters, emphasized the absolute unity of the person of Christ, so that nothing could be said of Christ's humanity that could not be said about his divinity, and vice versa. Hence, they were happy to refer to Mary as *Theotokos* (a Greek word meaning 'Godbearer') because the human embryo she carried was also God incarnate. Theodoret, however, belonged to a tradition that is popularly associated with Antioch and with bishops of Constantinople such as John Chrysostom and Nestorius. Their emphasis was on what they saw as the proper integrity of both the humanity of Christ and his divinity, with a concern lest the two be improperly confused. As a result they were suspected of splitting Christ into two in a way that undermined the truth of the incarnation. Both sides to this debate had their extreme representatives and (as judged by later Councils of the Church) heretical tendencies. If, in the Antiochene tradition, Nestorius was in danger of splitting Christ into two, the Alexandrian Eutyches seemed to be replacing the human personality of Christ with the Divine nature.

By this time Christianity had for over 100 years not only been tolerated but promoted as the religion of the Roman Empire, East and West. One consequence was that the emperors often took sides in debates about Christian belief, using the sanctions of the state to promote or to proscribe doctrines and those who taught them. Through the 440s the emperor of the East, Theodosius, was a strong supporter of the position now called Monophysitism – the belief that there is in Christ only one, divine nature, rather than both a human and divine nature. It was through his influence that Theodoret found himself deposed from his position as bishop.

Theodoret's story had (at least for him) a happy ending. At the Council of Chalcedon, held in 451 a year after Theodosius' death

---

7 I am aware that common division of eastern theology in the fourth and fifth centuries into the Alexandrian and Antiochene schools of thought is crude and can be misleading. Nonetheless, it does retain value as a way into the discussion of the often complex variations on the doctrine of the person of Christ.

in a riding accident (as one historian puts it 'now, not for the last time in history, an important part was played by a horse'),[8] he was able to assert his orthodoxy and gain recognition of his place as bishop. The records of the Council show that this did not happen without some controversy (Egyptian bishops, in particular, kept up a barrage of heckling as Theodoret tried to speak) and that Theodoret had to make a public, and humiliating, condemnation of the views of his lifelong friend, Nestorius. Yet his acceptance at Chalcedon was a mark of the doctrinal breadth of the Church and the desire to find a formula that would enable Christians from a number of different traditions to affirm their belief in Christ and recognize the orthodoxy of others. Chalcedon, to be sure, did not accept all current theological positions as true to Christian doctrine. A significant number of churches (primarily in Egypt and in the east) went their own way, founding two distinctive doctrinal traditions, the Monophysite and the Nestorian.[9] Nonetheless, the 'Chalcedonian Definition', as the Council's main document is usually called, remains a classic expression of Christian belief in the complete humanity and divinity of Christ, and one that the overwhelming majority of Christians shared until quite recently. Theodoret was able to return to his diocese and resume his ministry.

Of course, this is just one story among many, and told from just one perspective. It does, though, point us towards some of the factors that will be important in thinking about the place of doctrine in the Christian community. Here are some of the more obvious.

First, Christian doctrine is a passionate subject that arouses strong feelings and reactions. While not all these reactions are positive or healthy, it is important that this passionate engagement is

---

8 Blomfield Jackson, *The Nicene and Post-Nicene Fathers*, Vol. III, p. 9.

9 These churches came to be known as the 'Oriental Orthodox Churches'. The Monophysite tradition, with its emphasis on the absolute unity of Christ's person, has been represented most prominently by the Coptic Church of Egypt. The Nestorian tradition, with its insistence on the integrity of Christ's human and divine natures, became a vibrant missionary church, spreading eastward as far as India, Mongolia and China. The Assyrian Church of Iraq would be its most prominent representative today. It is now generally acknowledged that both of these Christian traditions should be regarded as essentially orthodox in their doctrine.

recognized and taken seriously. Far too often, Christian doctrine is depicted (by its friends and opponents alike) as dry and entirely cerebral, remote from the flesh and blood concerns of real life and its emotional effects. The discussions about the true and appropriate form of Christian teaching about Christ was anything but a matter of dry formality for Theodoret and his contemporaries. Doctrines were worth living for and, if need be, dying for.

Second, Christian doctrine has a history. Its presentation at any one time and place is part of a process of handing on teaching that goes through the centuries and touches more than one place. Theodoret (in his removal of the *Diatessaron* from the churches) was concerned with the legacy of doctrinal debates already going back several centuries.

Third, notice the focus on the role of the bishop. Theodoret, undoubtedly an able administrator of church affairs and an effective pastor, also sees himself charged with doctrinal teaching. In fact, teaching the truth about the Christian faith and defending it from damaging error is at the heart of his understanding of the role of the bishop. Through his writing, speeches and preaching, he sets out to hand on what he understands as the Christian faith that has been handed down to him and given into his charge. This is why he is so indignant when charged with being untrue to the gospel himself: the accusations seem to undermine his whole identity as a bishop and Christian leader.

Fourth, there is the role of debate and councils. Christian doctrine is essentially corporate rather than individual. And this corporate dimension also implies that Christian doctrine is never entirely static: there will always be discussion, diversity and debate. Theodoret lived (perhaps like us) at a time when the differences between Christians over fundamental issues of faith were deeply divisive and expressed in passionate (and sometimes less than gracious) terms. But this period also saw the Council of Chalcedon, a coming together of Christian leaders and teachers, from different churches and with different theological points of view, seeking to find a way of expressing Christian truth that all could recognize and that none would find an unacceptable compromise.

Why doctrine?

This snapshot from the much larger story of the early development of Christian doctrine has already raised a number of questions. Among them are: What really is doctrine? Who decides what it is? Where do you find it? Can people differ on points of doctrine and still remain in the same Church? As well as flagging up these questions, the story of Theodoret suggests that the answers are not necessarily simple.

But one word that does need to be faced at the beginning of a book on Christian doctrine is 'Why?' Why is it important to take seriously something so apparently at odds with the world-views that dominate most modern culture? That is the key question this book tries to answer.

Let me move from fifth-century Syria to a more contemporary example, one drawn from my own Methodist tradition. A little more than halfway through the 800-plus pages of that masterpiece of ecclesiastical bureaucracy, *The Constitutional Practice and Discipline of the Methodist Church* (Volume 2!), in the midst of instructions on the role of the Circuit Minister, you will find the following gem of aspiration:

> There is urgent need that the main doctrines of the Christian faith should be more plainly and systematically set forth in public preaching, so that the Methodist people may be established in the faith and better defended against error and uncertainty.[10]

I have no idea when that clause was inserted, but I suspect that its presence follows the general principle that the urgency of a rule's proclamation is in direct proportion to its current neglect. In other words, the very fact that doctrinal preaching needs to be advocated is good evidence that it is not currently happening to any great extent.

Much of this book will try to argue that doctrine (as part of a balanced diet) is good for us and much more central to the life

---

10 *The Constitutional Practice and Discipline of the Methodist Church*, Vol. 2, 2007 edition, Methodist Publishing House, Standing Order 524.

of the Church than contemporary wisdom suggests. I believe that good doctrinal teaching is essential for the healthy development of Christian worship and life. But before plunging into the issues that have made doctrine such a term of suspicion, it will be helpful to say something about what Christian doctrine is and how it came about. This opening chapter attempts to do just that. I will sketch out a working definition of doctrine and a short (and by no means impartial) history of its origins. From there we should be well equipped for a first look at some of the major issues that surround the topic of doctrine and are the main theme of the remainder of the book.

What doctrine is

The *Concise Oxford Dictionary* defines the word 'doctrine' as 'a set of beliefs held and taught by a Church, political party, or other group'. Though brief, this is a very helpful definition and highlights a number of important aspects of doctrine. First, it talks about a set of beliefs. Later in the book I argue that Christian doctrine is much more than a set of beliefs, but it is important to say at the outset that it is nothing less than a set of beliefs about the truth revealed by God through Jesus Christ. In other words, doctrine is not just about an attitude to the world, or a set of values to live by, or the report of a certain kind of experience. It really does involve a claim about what is true and important. Second, the definition talks about something that is 'held and taught'. Christian doctrine is about teaching (that is, literally, what the Latin and Greek origins of the word mean), but it is the teaching of what is deeply rooted in the life of the Christian community. Doctrine is no mere passing on of information, it is a handing on of what is the deepest identity of Christianity, of what makes us Christian. The final aspect of the definition tells us that doctrine is a feature of groups (it is not a matter of individual belief) and that Christian churches are not the only ones to have it! In later chapters I give an account of how the modern world has come to associate Christian doctrine with something oppressive and outmoded. But we need to remind ourselves that there are plenty of other groups who compete for our belief and commitment. In fact, if you enter 'doctrine' into an internet search engine a large proportion of 'hits' will refer to political beliefs, for example the 'doctrine' of the Bush government on the Middle East.

What about a more specifically Christian definition? Three Greek words from the New Testament feed into the Christian understanding of what doctrine is. There will be opportunity later on to look at them in more detail. Here we can simply note the way they help us understand what doctrine is. *Didache* is a word that means 'teaching'. It is used by Matthew to describe the teaching of Jesus but in Acts it refers to the teaching of the apostles about what God has done through Jesus, and in Paul's letters it points to his teaching of the gospel of Christ. In later New Testament books, for example the Letter to the Hebrews, *didache* has more of a sense of a body of doctrine, while a work composed about the same time as the end of the New Testament period is called simply *The Didache* or *The Teaching of the Twelve Apostles*.

A second New Testament term is *kerygma*, meaning 'proclamation'. Biblical study in the twentieth century drew particular attention to this word, pointing out that although it refers to the action of proclamation, it can also mean the message that is proclaimed. So, for example, in Romans 16.25, when Paul talks about 'the proclamation of Jesus Christ' it is clear that he means 'the things we proclaim about Jesus Christ' as well as 'the act of proclaiming about Jesus'.

The final key word, and one to which I give much more attention in the next chapter, is *paradidomi*, 'to hand over'. This is a rich word, with many shades of meaning, but one important way in which it is used in the New Testament is in the sense of 'the tradition about Jesus Christ that has been handed down to us, and that we hand on to you'.

'Teaching about God's work in Jesus Christ', 'the content of our proclamation of the good news', 'the tradition of faith we pass on': all these phrases help us get a sense of how Christian doctrine came into being and what it means.

So, to get back to the question of what Christian doctrine is, we can say that it is 'the characteristic teaching of the Christian community throughout its history'. In doctrine (the word 'dogma' fits just as well), a community summarizes its core beliefs and presents them to its own members and to the wider world. So doctrine can be a description of what is believed, an invitation to believe, and an indication of where the limits of belief lie for this religious community. Not all religious traditions[11] have a strong emphasis on this kind of teaching, but chief among those that do are the so-called Abrahamic faiths: Judaism, Christianity and Islam. The story of Christian doctrine (and that is the focus of this book) therefore needs to begin with Judaism and with the Hebrew scriptures.

This emphasis on doctrine as teaching that reflects a community's belief and understanding is important. It means, for example, that doctrine has to be distinguished from theology. Theology (literally, thinking and speaking about God) can be practised by individuals who may or may not identify themselves with a particular religious tradition. In practice, most theology emerges from strands of thought within one religion or another, or at least from a culture that has been deeply influenced by one. And, of course, theological thinking often involves reflection on the content of doctrines. But this should not be confused with the teaching that forms the core beliefs of a community of people. You cannot have doctrine without theology, but you can certainly have theology without doctrine.

Where can doctrine be found?

If doctrine is about normative teaching, setting the characteristics of Christian belief and its boundaries, where is it to be found? The answer is: in quite a number of places, some of them obvious and some of them less expected.

---

11 There is quite a debate about whether we can talk about 'religions' or 'religious traditions' as if they were all slightly different examples of the same human phenomenon. I would not want to subscribe to the belief that all religions are fundamentally the same. Nevertheless, it is reasonable to talk about the 'doctrines' of Islam or Buddhism, as long as we remember that the word 'doctrine' will not mean exactly the same thing in different religions.

Scripture

The first, most obvious – and most important – answer is 'scripture', which for Jewish people means the Hebrew scriptures and for Christians means these plus those books we now call the New Testament. Almost all Christian traditions would link their key doctrines to the reading of scripture, often using such phrases as 'the Bible teaches'. Yet scripture is not to be identified with doctrine in a straightforward sense. Its combination of story, law, prophecy, letter, prayer and proverb means that it cannot be read simply as a textbook of Jewish or Christian belief. In fact, one of the mistakes that Christians sometimes make is to imagine that all that is needed is a rearrangement of the Bible into neater sections in order to make such a textbook. In my first term at university I was persuaded to buy just such a book, *In Understanding Be Men*,[12] which listed those Bible passages the author believed expressed each area of Christian doctrine in turn. I have come to the conclusion that this method distorts both scripture and doctrine. It distorts the Bible because scripture is treated as a collection of proof texts, to be selected for whichever question comes to mind. Instead, it needs to be seen as a complex whole through which the story of God's work of salvation is expressed in a variety of ways. This approach also distorts doctrine because it turns it into something static and lifeless, as if the words of the Bible give the last word on every topic.

Of course, it is difficult to envisage any proposed Christian doctrine that is not firmly related to the Christian Bible. Clergy in most Protestant denominations are asked to affirm that the Bible contains 'all things necessary to salvation',[13] while the *Constitution on Revelation* of the Second Vatican Council insists that the Church is under the authority of scripture.[14] But the controversial

---

12 T. C. Hammond, *On Understanding Be Men: A Handbook of Christian Doctrine*. Originally published in 1936, it is still in print and published by Inter-Varsity Press, 1968. The title has not been updated to reflect inclusive language.

13 See, for example, the service for 'The Ordination of Presbyters', in the (British) *Methodist Worship Book*, Methodist Publishing House, 1999, p. 303.

14 'Yet this Magisterium [teaching authority of the Church] is not superior to the Word of God, but is its servant.' 'The Dogmatic Constitution on Divine Revelation', in Austin Flannery (ed.), *Vatican II, The Conciliar and Post Conciliar Documents*, Dominican Publications, 1975, p. 756.

nature of some aspects of doctrinal history suggests that the key is in the way scripture is read and interpreted by the community of faith. One helpful way of expressing this was developed by the great Swiss theologian Karl Barth (1886–1968). He was surely right when he suggested that when we use the expression 'the Word of God' we are referring to three things. Primarily, 'the Word of God' refers to the eternal Word, the Son who becomes incarnate in Jesus of Nazareth, whose life, death and resurrection are God's definitive word to us. When we speak of the Bible as 'the Word of God' we do so in a secondary sense; scripture is the foremost witness to Christ, inspired words about the Word. Third, 'the Word of God' refers to the proclamation of the Christian Church in the present, as it hands on the gospel of Christ in words that are both faithful and relevant.

Barth's understanding of the Word of God implies that doctrine and scripture are mutually related. While we cannot pass on Christian teaching without close attention to the witness of scripture, we cannot make proper use of scripture unless we already have some understanding of that most characteristic doctrine of Christianity, the incarnation. This does not mean that doctrinal reasoning is entirely circular. But it does suggest that doctrine is more to do with the understanding of a faith that is already present than it is a means of arguing for that faith from a position of intellectual neutrality.

The relationship between the second and third of Barth's senses of the Word of God is also important. In looking for a model for the proclamation of Christian teaching we find that scripture itself, though not a compendium of doctrine, does contain doctrinal statements. These are summaries of belief that are offered as witness to core Jewish and Christian faith. This is something to explore as we look at the story of how Christian doctrine developed.

Creeds

'A concise, formal and authorized statement of important points of Christian doctrine' is how *The Oxford Dictionary of the Christian Church* defines the word 'creed'. The two that are now commonly used in the life of many churches are the Apostles' Creed and the Nicene Creed. Both have reached their present form through a long process of development. The Apostles' Creed, in spite of a legend that it had been jointly composed by the apostles themselves, seems to have developed from the statements of faith made by baptismal candidates in the early centuries of Christianity. It is used primarily in the churches of the West (the Roman Catholic Church and the churches of the Reformation), where it is associated both with the baptism service and (in some denominations) with daily prayers.

The origin of the Nicene Creed is rather easier to pin down. The Council of Nicaea, called in 325 to tackle the so-called Arian controversy over the doctrine of the person of Christ, produced a creed that was probably based on the baptismal creed of Jerusalem. It explicitly stated that the Son shared in the eternal life of God and was not, like human beings, a creature who came into existence at a point in time. This creed was expanded at the later Council of Constantinople (381) to a form very similar to the Nicene Creed we know today. The one main difference lies in an addition to the creed made in the sixth to tenth centuries in the Western Church. This inserts the words that have come to be known as the *filioque* clause: the Spirit proceeds from the Father *and the Son*. This difference forms the main doctrinal argument between the western and eastern forms of Christianity.

Both the Apostles' and Nicene creeds are quite short and neither encompasses the whole of Christian belief. However, they are important places where doctrine is focused and their use in worship and teaching means that they have been familiar to centuries of practising Christians. Those who recite them are identifying not only with the truth claims they contain but also with those who, through many centuries, have lived and died by them. The fact that they are shared by churches that are otherwise divided from each other in governance, theology and liturgy gives them a prominent place in ecumenical dialogue and the search for Christian unity.

One further point is worth making before we leave, at least for now, the topic of creeds. One popular use of the word 'creed' implies that a creed is any distinctive set of beliefs claimed by a group, or even by an individual. This implies that Christian traditions are divided by their creeds (which, with the exception of the *filioque* clause, is not the usually case). It also suggests that anyone can make up a creed for themselves, yet this contradicts the important element of community authorization in the definition of what a creed is. It is more helpful to see contemporary documents (and they are often produced as part of an order for worship or as an aid to teaching) not as creeds but as affirmations of faith for new generations of Christians to share.

Confessions

It is, then, best to reserve the term 'creed' for those short doctrinal statements originating from the early Christian centuries. Confessions, on the other hand, are those statements of doctrine that are seen as authoritative in individual churches, usually but not exclusively those of the Lutheran and Reformed traditions.[15] These confessions of faith imply that doctrine is an important part of the identity of a Christian community. There is a staggering number of them. The selection in volume two of Pelikan and Hotchkiss' *Creeds and Confession in the Christian Tradition* is substantial enough, but Pelikan reckons that the full texts of all the confessions in the post-Reformation period would run into thousands rather than hundreds of pages. Some of the best known examples are *The Augsburg Confession*, one of the foundation documents of Lutheranism; *The Westminster Confession*, which began as an attempt to move the Church of England in a more Calvinist direction, but continues to be a vital element in Irish Presbyterianism; and *The Thirty-Nine Articles of the Church of England*, to which those being ordained in the Church of England still have to subscribe. Each of these were forged in the fires of sixteenth- and seventeenth-century religious conflict, and their texts still show signs of the polemical world in which they were written.

---

15 Jaroslav Pelikan (*Credo*, Yale University Press, 2003, p. 458) points out that the distinction between creed and confession is somewhat arbitrary, but it does provide a logical way of referring to the authoritative doctrine of those Christian Churches wanting to defend their existence in the face of rival versions of Christianity.

Confessions of faith are not exclusively Protestant. Statements coming out of the medieval councils of the Catholic Church, especially on the nature of the Church, had a confessional quality. This became even more explicit in the post-Reformation *Tridentine Profession of Faith*, a document through which the sixteenth-century Council of Trent set out the doctrinal authority of 'Mother Church' over against (as the authors believed) its Protestant usurpers. Even the Orthodox churches came to issue confessional statements in response to the turmoil of western Christianity.

Because they embody distinctive teachings of Christian communities and emerge from times of controversy, confessions have needed careful handling where Christians from different traditions have tried to come together.[16]

It might be helpful to remember that the original use of the term 'confession' in the early Christian Church was rather different from this polemical tradition. It normally stood either for the profession of faith made by a martyr (or someone ready to face martyrdom) or for a church (or altar) built over a martyr's tomb. A 'confessor' was someone who had made a stand for their faith during a time of persecution and survived. It was not simply that (as is often said) the blood of the martyrs was the seed of the Church; the faith of the martyrs was made the foundation of places of Christian worship.

Catechisms

If, broadly speaking, creeds attempt to express the unified faith of all Christians, and confessions mark out the distinctive way in which a particular Christian body understands the faith, a catechism is an instrument of Christian instruction. In the early centuries the catechumenate (from a Greek word meaning to make someone hear, or to instruct) consisted of those who had expressed a desire for Christian baptism, but who needed to learn about the

---

16 One example of such confessional reconciliation is found in the document agreed in 1999 by the Roman Catholic Church and the World Lutheran Federation: *Joint Declaration on the Doctrine of Justification*. It can be found at: <www.vatican.va/roman_curia/pontifical_councils/chrstuni/documents/rc_pc_ chrstuni_doc_31101999_cath-luth-joint-declaration_en.htmln>.

faith and its practice before being initiated as full members of the Church. We still have some examples of the teaching given to the catechumens, such as the instruction given in the Jerusalem Church in the fourth century by its bishop, Cyril. These catechetical lectures, as they have been called, give a good picture of the way in which Christian doctrine was received by new converts to Christianity; only when they had digested this teaching and made a public profession of it themselves in baptism could they take their place in the body of Christian believers at the Eucharist. Even then, there were important areas of Christian life, such as the sacraments, that were only fully explained after the commitment of baptism. Catechumens, though, received their doctrine alongside a rigorous programme of prayer, liturgical preparation and the establishment of a Christian pattern of living. Clearly there was an intimate relationship between the doctrinal content of Christian faith and its living expression. It was no good learning about the doctrine of the incarnation but not being able to pray through Christ or to share in effective Christian discipleship.

Catechesis has been an important way of handing on Christian teaching throughout the Church's history. The Reformation, though, gave a fresh impetus to this movement. The development of printing and a concern that ordinary Christians should have a proper understanding of their faith came together and inspired the production of a series of catechisms for use in different traditions. Luther's *Little Catechism* became the standard for teaching the faith in Lutheran churches, while the *Heidelberg Catechism* did the same for Calvinism and the *Prayer Book Catechism* for the Church of England. Some catechisms are short, in a simple question-and-answer format (for example the current British *Catechism for the Use of the People Called Methodists*). Others (like the contemporary *Catechism of the Catholic Church*) are substantial works of doctrinal theology, designed to provide a resource for those who prepare programmes of instruction, rather than an introduction for those who are beginning to learn about Christian faith. The Roman Catholic Church, which reintroduced the catechumenate in the 1960s, now has a programme for the Christian Initiation of Adults which (like the catechumenate of the early

Church) combines doctrinal teaching with the development of liturgical and ethical life in the Christian community.

Councils

Acts 15 describes a crucial event in the life of the apostolic Church, as leaders in Jerusalem discussed with Paul the way in which the Christian faith was to be shared with gentiles as well as those of Jewish descent. It may be stretching the historical evidence to call this (as is sometimes done) 'the Council of Jerusalem', but it did foreshadow the gatherings, from the fourth century onwards, when bishops, as leaders of their Christian communities, came together to debate points of teaching and practice. For many (especially Eastern Orthodox) churches the gatherings known as the 'Oecumenical Councils' (from a Greek term that refers to the whole inhabited earth, and from which we get the English 'ecumenical') have a special authority. Their decisions, even if not summarized in creedal form, are normative. They are seven in number, starting with the first in Nicaea in 325 and ending with the seventh (also in Nicaea) in 787. The story of Theodoret has already made reference to the Council of Chalcedon, best known for its definition of the relationship between the humanity and divinity of Christ. These Oecumenical Councils were usually called by, or held on the authority of, the Roman or Byzantine Emperor. This has inevitably meant that they have been scrutinized in the light of the present concern for the use and abuse of power. To what extent, it is asked, do these Councils represent the guidance of the Holy Spirit and to what extent the political power struggles of the time? We will come back to this issue in a later chapter.

The Roman Catholic Church recognizes a much longer series of councils, the decisions of which are listed thematically in an encyclopaedic volume named after its original editor, *Denzinger*. The most recent is the Second Vatican Council (1962–65) which, with its documents covering most areas of Christian faith and practice, has had the biggest impact of any Christian council for centuries. Its documents are seen as decisive for shaping the life and teaching of the Roman Catholic Church in the contemporary world.

Protestants have generally been more cautious about recognizing councils as authoritative, emphasizing that for them scripture, rather than any human assembly, provides the norm for doctrine. Even so, the churches of the Reformation have drawn on the early councils for their doctrinal teaching, and even added some of their own. The Westminster Assembly (1643–49), for example, has had a lasting impact on Presbyterianism. In Methodist churches the practice of communally discerning the appropriate teaching of the faith is built into the very structure of the church. The annual conference has the final say in what counts as Methodist doctrine, alongside its guidance on the more structural work of the church. The very first question asked by John Wesley at the initial Methodist Conference in 1744 had a doctrinal concern: 'What shall we teach?'

Worship

Scripture, creeds, confessions, catechisms and councils are very much the usual suspects when it comes to locating doctrinal teaching. But the worship of Christian churches has also, from the early centuries, been intimately linked to the content of Christian doctrine. Where there have been important differences between Christians about doctrine (for example, at the time of the Reformation) there have usually been corresponding divergences in the forms of worship and in the language used for worship. Christian liturgy and worship has a unique place among sources of doctrinal teaching, for most human beings learn more by participating in actions and events than by only reading or listening.

This intimate relationship is classically expressed in the Latin slogan, *lex orandi, lex credendi*; literally, the rule of prayer is the rule of faith. What we say and do in acts of Christian worship is a guide to what we are to believe and teach. It points to the two-way traffic in this relationship. On the one hand, Christian worship has always been constructed so as to reflect the doctrinal convictions and understanding of the church in question. That is why, for example, most Protestant churches removed from their liturgies any suggestion of prayers for those who had died, intending to distance themselves doctrinally from the belief that such prayers could have any bearing on the eternal destiny of the deceased. It is also one of the reasons why the production of new liturgies and forms of worship are so controversial and arouse anxieties that key doctrinal emphases are to be altered or watered down. But it works the other way round, too. The prayer life of the Church is also a source that enables the Church to think through and discern the nature of Christian truth. This is especially so for the Eastern Orthodox churches, and one reason why they are liturgically the most conservative of Christian traditions. *The Divine Liturgy According to Saint John Chrysostom* has a special place in Orthodox life. Not only is it the baseline for the liturgical life of the churches; it serves as both source and expression of the distinctive orthodox understanding of Christian teaching.

Starting (after all) at the very beginning

So, having said something about the why, what and where of Christian doctrine, it is time to say rather more about the 'how'. A short sketch can hardly do justice to such a long and complex story, but there are plenty of textbooks that provide the details that would be impossible and inappropriate here. What we can do is get a sense of the process that gave the Christian Church the doctrinal standards that for centuries were taken for granted.

Jewish (and, later, Christian) people were a puzzle to their Greek, Persian or Roman rulers. Rather than bringing their own gods and rituals to add to the richness of the other nations, they perversely insisted on an exclusive form of worship. Worshipping just the one God and refusing to acknowledge the images of any other, they were marked out as a distinctive people and became the object, at different times, of curiosity, admiration, suspicion and persecution. That obstinate refusal to worship any other than the God of Israel was based on the Torah, the five books that form the core of the Tanach, the Jewish scriptures. Though Torah is often translated as 'law', 'instruction' is a better rendering. Through the

Torah and the other sacred writings Jews learned of the nature of their God and of the kind of worship and lifestyle that would be a proper response to this God.

Scripture as part of the story of doctrine

We might say that the Torah, interpreted by successive generations of teachers, provided a body of doctrine. But that doctrine has its core, a foundation (to change the metaphor) on which everything else depends. Jaroslav Pelikan, the greatest authority on the history of Christian doctrine in the last century, and therefore someone to whom this study is deeply indebted, makes this stark assertion:

> Behind and beneath all the primitive creeds of the apostolic and subapostolic era [of the early Christian church] there stands, as a monument and a fiery pillar, the primal creed and confession of the Christian church, *The Shema*: 'Hear, O Israel: The Lord our God is one Lord.'[17]

Found in a number of places in the (as Christians call it) Old Testament, the Shema brings into sharp focus the distinctive Jewish understanding of the nature of God and of that God's relationship to the Jewish people. It is also a point of continuity with Christian belief. Either it is taken for granted or it is explicitly quoted by many of the writers of the New Testament. It might be said that much of the early development of Christian doctrine has at its heart the need to square the Shema's 'the Lord our God is one Lord' with the fundamental Christian confession, 'Jesus is Lord'.

So, the first point to be made in this story is that the Christian scriptures (even though they need to be treated with care as a source of doctrinal teaching) are themselves concerned with doctrinal teaching and its content.

This is true for the person of Jesus himself, as he is presented in the Gospels. Not, of course, that we should imagine Jesus reciting

---

17 Jaroslav Pelikan and Valerie Hotchkiss (eds), *Creeds and Confessions of the Christian Tradition*, Vol. 1, Yale University Press, 2003, p. 7.

the words of the Nicene Creed to the crowds in Galilee. It does not make sense (and it is theologically dubious) to picture Jesus using the vocabulary and thinking of a later era. I am sure he did not introduce himself as 'God from God, light from light, true God from true God'. Nevertheless, there is compelling evidence that Jesus did substantially more than offer (as some liberal theologians of previous generations and some contemporary scholars suggest) sharp ethical challenges and wholesome spiritual guidance. Jesus is often addressed in the Gospels as *didaskalé* (teacher) and the content of his teaching includes the implication that in and through his own ministry God is making a decisive intervention in the affairs of the world, such as was connected with the Jewish hope of a messianic age.[18] He claims to speak in the name of God, to perform the works of God and to see the world and his fellow men and women as God sees them. Furthermore, even making allowance for the influence of later Christian thinking on the shaping of the Gospels, it seems that Jesus implied a significance to his death, a death that would be the inevitable result of such an uncompromising prophetic ministry. His death would actually help to bring about God's new kingdom. It is quite proper to point out the contrast between the words of Jesus in (especially) the Synoptic Gospels and the later doctrinal formulae of the Church, but it is naive to see Jesus as a simple peasant prophet whose down-to-earth message was distorted by later followers to become the metaphysical basis of a new religion.

Unless the Gospels are utterly misleading, Jesus intended to found a community that would express a new understanding of Israel and of its relationship to God. Jesus teaches, and his teaching expresses, that which is the core of this new community in terms of its belief and behaviour.

What is true of Jesus is true of the early generations that followed him. The apostle Paul, about whose approach to doctrine more will be said in later chapters, represents (so far as is known) the earliest Christian writing we have available. He writes as an evangelist, called to take Christianity beyond the boundaries of Judaism and

---

18 This view is expressed most persuasively by N. T. Wright in *Jesus and the Victory of God*, SPCK, 1996.

into the wider Roman and Hellenistic world, and he writes as a pastor, concerned with the health, faithfulness and practical living of those churches he has helped to found. But he also writes as a teacher of Christian doctrine. His doctrinal teaching does not arise because he has an insatiable need for intellectual speculation, nor because he wants to make the teaching of Jesus into something more interesting for Hellenistic consumption. For Paul getting Christian teaching right is a vital part of understanding the evangelistic task and of developing healthy Christian communities. As Ellen Charry has persuasively argued,[19] Paul is concerned with Christian formation, both individual and communal. Basic to this formation is our participation in Christ – especially in his death and resurrection. And this participation is only possible because of God's actions, actions which are the centre of any account of Christian doctrine. For that reason, Paul's letters are studded with doctrinal affirmation. Sometimes this seems to be in the form of a quotation from an already existing Christian expression of faith, for example the hymn to the self-emptying service of Christ in Philippians 2. In other places Paul appears to condense the gospel message he is expounding into a short, creed-like statement so as to convey the heart of it, for example in Romans 1.3–4:

> . . . the gospel concerning his Son, who was descended from David according to the flesh and declared to be the Son of God with power according to the spirit of holiness by resurrection from the dead, Jesus Christ our Lord.

It is through the person of Jesus Christ, understood in the light of the gospel story, that Paul has received the divine gift and calling for his ministry, 'to bring about the obedience of faith among all the Gentiles for the sake of his name'.[20]

If, as most commentators believe, the Gospels were written after the letters of Paul, they still bear witness to the faith of the earliest Christians. And that faith is, from the beginning, focused on

---

19 Ellen Charry, *By the Renewing of Your Minds: The Pastoral Function of Christian Doctrine*, Oxford University Press, 1997.
20 Romans 1.5

the person and significance of Jesus Christ. That it is not couched in the language of Nicene orthodoxy does not mean that it is not doctrinal in its expression. Recent New Testament study has suggested that a 'high Christology' (a strong belief in the significance and divine origin of Jesus Christ) was there at the very beginning of the Christian community and not a later development.[21] But do the Gospels teach the same thing about Jesus? After all, they seem to have rather different angles on Jesus. Yes, there certainly was diversity among the early Christians and the New Testament writers. But there was also a strong sense of a tradition that gave the early Christians more cohesion than might have been expected from such a scattered group.

The beginning of the story of Christian doctrine is, then, woven into the story of Israel as the people of God's ancient covenant; a people who, as an essential part of their identity, need to articulate the name and nature of their God. Similarly, it is woven into the story of Jesus. His whole leadership, ministry and teaching could not help but proclaim the meaning of God's kingdom and his significance within it. And in Paul, as well as the other writers of the New Testament, there is a concern to voice the content of Christian belief alongside the manner of Christian living.

Judaism and Christianity parting company

Doctrinal teaching, then, is a scriptural activity. It is also true that even within the New Testament we can discern the three concerns that lie at the heart of the development of Christian doctrine in the century or so after its completion. The first is the increasing need for the Christian community to distinguish itself from the Judaism out of which it had emerged. As N. T. Wright has pointed out, each of the Gospel writers is, in their own way, giving an account of the history of Israel that interprets it anew around the focal

---

21 See, for example, Larry Hurtado, *Lord Jesus Christ: Devotion to Jesus in Earliest Christianity*, Eerdmans, 2003; and J. D. G. Dunn, *Christology in the Making: A New Testament Inquiry into the Origins of the Doctrine of the Incarnation*, SCM Press, 2003, p. 996.

figure of Jesus of Nazareth.[22] The earliest Christians felt a strong continuity with their Jewish background, continuing to worship in the temple and to observe many of the regulations in the Torah. However, the increasing number of converts from outside Judaism, as well as the hostility towards the Christian movement from those Jews who saw it as a dangerous perversion, forced the Church to consider the relationship more clearly. On the one hand the answer to the question, 'Do Christian converts have to be circumcised and adhere to traditional Jewish dietary laws?' was a resounding 'No'. On the other hand there was the question of whether God had turned away from a covenant with one people in order to form a covenant with another, not to mention the dilemma of whether the Hebrew scriptures were still to be a source of Christian belief and practice. Romans 9—11 shows Paul agonizing about the status of Israel in relationship to God, but finally affirming both the old and the new covenants.

Later Christian reflection and teaching was not always as nuanced as Paul's. All too often it presented an unattractive form of what we now call supercessionism – the belief that Christianity has effectively replaced Judaism as the superior and final revelation of God. For Ignatius (Bishop of Antioch and living c.35–c.107), often called one of the 'Apostolic Fathers', the solution is to think of key figures in Judaism anticipating Christ. 'The divinely inspired prophets', he writes in his letter to the Magnesians, lived in expectation of Jesus Christ.[23] That they were often rejected and ill-treated by their contemporaries is for him an anticipation of the rejection of Jesus by his fellow Jews.

The discussion about the place of the Old Testament was an important one for Christian doctrine. There were those, the best known of whom was Marcion (died c.160), who argued that the Hebrew scriptures were no longer necessary, that because they spoke of a different and harsher god than that of the New Testament, they would be misleading as a source of Christian teaching. But it is clear from the writings that have survived from the second century that the dominant voice in the Church saw these

---

22 N. T. Wright, *Jesus and the Victory of God.*
23 Ignatius, in *Early Christian Writings*, Penguin, 1987, p. 72.

Jewish scriptures as essential to the development of sound Christian teaching. The God who was revealed through the Jewish scriptures was the same God who was encountered in Jesus Christ, and
these scriptures, when read through the eyes of faith, taught about
Christ himself.

In looking at this issue we have, incidentally, touched on another
aspect of Christian doctrine. As well as doctrines that express the
content of Christian belief (for example, 'Jesus is Lord', 'God created the universe out of nothing') there are also 'doctrines about doctrines'[24] that refer to the sources, principles and norms that govern
the way in which doctrines are developed and used. Discussions
about God's revelation and its relationship to scripture come in this
second category, and the fact that such debate began so early in the
history of Christianity points to an awareness of the many factors
involved in developing and presenting a religious faith.

Giving an account of the Christian hope

The second aspect of this early stage of development is the apologetic task of presenting the Christian gospel to those who were
still immersed in pagan religion and philosophy. Apologists try to
express the truth of Christianity in a way that will commend itself
to those who are currently hostile to it. It has a history as long as
Christianity itself and recent exponents of this difficult undertak-
ing have included C. S. Lewis and N. T. Wright. In some ways it
is a dangerous road to travel, as it means adopting aspects of the
vocabulary and world-view of the target audience. This is a procedure that has opened more than one apologist to the charge of
conforming Christian teaching to an alien philosophy rather than
commending the first and challenging the second. Apologetics,
therefore, is different from the teaching of doctrine: it is the Christian message for the world rather than for the Church alone.

Yet the apologetic demand that Christians clarify their language and develop ways of expressing their faith across a cultural

---

24 The expression comes from William Christian's *Doctrines of Religious
Communities: A Philosophical Study*, Yale University Press, 1987.

divide has been an important resource to the Church as a whole, for even those within the community of the Church are also part of the wider culture. The need to have something clear and coherent to say to those outside the Church fuelled the development of doctrinal teaching. This was especially so in the second and third centuries, with authors such as Justin Martyr, Athenagoras and Tertullian helping to develop the vocabulary that would become part of the creeds and the doctrinal teaching that expounded them. In fact, there was already more than a hint of this in some of the New Testament books. John's Gospel, to take what is perhaps the most obvious example, frequently speaks of Jesus Christ in language that seems designed to bridge the gap between Judaism and the world of Greek thought. Jesus is identified with the Word of God. He is the *Logos*, a word familiar to the Jewish readers of the Septuagint (the Greek translation of the Hebrew Scriptures, familiar across the Jewish diaspora), but also familiar to those with a background in Greek thought, where *Logos* referred to the organizing principle of the universe. In the second century Justin and others developed what has been called 'Logos Christology', which not only began to link the Christian doctrines of the incarnation and creation, but also opened up a route to talking with Platonic and Stoic philosophy.

Keeping faith with the truth

Third, and crucially for the development of Christian doctrine, there was a growing perception that the Church needed to discern between authentic and false interpretations of the faith. The New Testament books, when they explicitly mention 'doctrine' (usually with the Greek word *didaskale* or *didache* – translated 'teaching' in more recent versions) are often concerned with distinguishing between what is true or false, faithful or corrupt. For example, 1 Timothy 6.3–4 says that:

> Whoever teaches otherwise and does not agree with the sound words of our Lord Jesus Christ and the teaching that is in accord-

ance with godliness, is conceited, understanding nothing, and has a morbid craving for controversy and for disputes about words.

It is, of course, one thing to give stern warnings about the consequences of false teaching, but quite another to demonstrate how the true and the false can be told apart. In the second century Irenaeus, Bishop of Lyon, was concerned to defend what he saw as orthodox Christian doctrine from a version of Christianity that we have come to call Gnosticism. This movement, with its complex mythologies of salvation and its sharp contrast between the worlds of spirit and matter, proved extremely seductive then and has had a recent surge of popularity. But for Irenaeus it represented an illegitimate deviation from true Christian doctrine. He argued that there has to be consistency and faithfulness in Christian teaching; it is not something we can make up as we go along. The scriptures and the historic witness of the Church and its leaders provided him with the basis for deciding what is authentic Christian teaching and what is not.

The catholic tradition

This consistent and faithful pattern of teaching, on which Irenaeus insists, is often referred to as the 'catholic tradition'. That is, it is something universal, not confined to the Church in a particular place or at a particular time. It is because the first five centuries of the Christian Church were so formative for this teaching that they are regarded as having a unique place in the understanding of Christian doctrine. Not that Christian thinking stopped in the year 451 (clearly, and fortunately, it has not), or that the Church of the first centuries was completely of one mind (we have already seen that it never was), but during this time the Church came to a shared awareness of how scripture should be read and how the gospel should be expressed. Three things illustrate how this 'catholic tradition' developed.

A single canon of scripture

It was, of course, many years before the Bible as we know it was produced as a single book. Originally written as separate scrolls, the books of the Christian scriptures were gradually gathered together into codices, their pages bound together.[25] There were some minor differences in the lists of biblical books supplied by early Christian writers (for example, the book of Revelation was regarded with suspicion in some parts of the Church because of the way it had been used by fringe groups) but there is remarkable consistency in the books designated as 'scripture'. It is true that the earliest surviving list of books identical to the contents of the present Bible was only produced in 367, by Athanasius (Bishop of Alexandria). But there is no basis for the popular suggestion that until then there was only a chaotic medley of Christian literature. There was a common consensus on which books expressed the apostolic teaching about Christ, and therefore on which books should be read in order to develop an understanding of it.

A common creed

Part of the catholicity of the Church came from being a set of communities bound together by common literature – the canon of the Bible. Alongside this was an equally remarkable consensus about the story told by that literature. Even though it was several centuries before the creeds as we know them achieved their final form, the outline of Christian faith had a common shape: it was expressed in local creeds and in the preaching of the churches. Early Christian writers often talked about the 'rule of faith', a core of Christian teaching that had been handed down by word of mouth from the time of the apostles until the present. Irenaeus summarizes it in words that anticipate the first two sections of the later creeds:

> . . . this faith: in one God, the Father Almighty, who made the
> heaven and the earth and the seas and all the things that are in

---

25 Christians were among the first to adopt this form of book production, much easier that a scroll to transport and use.

them; and in one Christ Jesus, the Son of God, who was made flesh for our salvation; and in the Holy Spirit, who made known through the prophets the plan of salvation, and the coming, and the birth from a virgin, and the passion, and the resurrection from the dead, and the bodily ascension into heaven of the beloved Christ Jesus, our Lord, and his future appearing from heaven in the glory of the Father to sum up all things and to raise anew all flesh of the whole human race . . .[26]

A settled structure

Christians continue to debate the extent to which the Church should be structured and whether, for example, bishops are an essential (or even desirable) part of church authority. Nevertheless, it is clear that the development of a common approach to Christian teaching was related in the early centuries to the development of a common pattern of church organization and a common structure of Christian worship. This emerged during the second century, when the pattern of a threefold ministry of deacons, presbyters and bishops became the norm. Church structures seem very secondary to the truths of doctrine, but without them teaching is not going to have a viable context.

The story of doctrine or several competing stories?

In the next chapter I explore what it means to see doctrinal teaching in terms of a gift. Here, though, I want to emphasize its nature as story and to acknowledge the problems involved in making one story the norm.

We live, it is now commonly observed, in a 'story-shaped world',[27] but a world where it seems increasingly difficult to agree on the

---

26 Irenaeus, *Against Heresies*, X.1, in *Ancient Christian Writers: Against the Heresies*, Book 1, vol. 1, Paulist Press, 1997.

27 The first use of this precise phrase that I am aware of is in the title of Brian Wicker, *The Story-Shaped World: Fiction and Metaphysics: Some Variations on a Theme*, University of Notre Dame Press, 1975.

nature of the story. Living and working in Northern Ireland has brought home to me both the centrality of stories for understanding ourselves and others and the apparent impossibility of agreeing on what that story is. A local satirical television political cartoon has a regular feature in which politicians from the different sides of the nationalist and loyalist divide explain a recent event in totally different terms. The history of Christian doctrine often seems very similar. It does indeed tell a story. But it also has a story (perhaps more than one) and can be studied through stories. The classic story of Christian doctrine talks about the Holy Spirit at work in the writing, preservation and interpretation of the books we know as the New Testament. It sees the same Spirit moving in theological debates, in the results of Church Councils and in the formation of creeds. Doctrine, according to this story, is in some sense both revealed and normative.

This story has been exposed to challenge on a number of fronts, especially over the last 200 years, and a number of alternative stories have emerged. In the nineteenth century, for example, Ferdinand Christian Baur (1792–1860) suggested that the New Testament, far from depicting a united early Church, is actually testimony to a conflict between Jewish and Hellenistic elements in Christianity, each with their own understanding of Christian truth. Walter Bauer (whose influential *Orthodoxy and Heresy in Earliest Christianity* was published in 1934) took the discussion into the second century and argued that 'orthodoxy' only emerged out of a Christianity that was doctrinally much more varied than had previously been thought.

Another influential version of this challenge is currently represented by the work of the historian of religion Elaine Pagels. In a recent book she has given her own alternative story.[28] *Beyond Belief* is both the work of a professional scholar (though her conclusions would be disputed by many of her colleagues) and unashamed propaganda for a form of religion without dogma or authority. It centres around the Gospel of Thomas, the best known of the many so-called Gnostic works found at Nag Hammadi in Egypt in 1945.

---

28 Elaine Pagels, *Beyond Belief: Early Christian Paths Towards Transformation*, Macmillan, 2004.

Her alternative narrative goes something like this: early Christianity was built around supportive and egalitarian communities that were much more concerned with relationships and experience than with belief and hierarchy. There were many forms of Christian worship, many different writings treated as a source of Christian truth, and a wide variety of beliefs. Only with the increasing dominance of the Christian movement by bishops was there a demand for a fixed canon of scripture, a firm division between clergy and laity and an emphasis on correct and proper doctrine. Far from being the hero of orthodoxy (as traditional stories of Christian doctrine have described him), Bishop Irenaeus is for Pagels the author of a repressive uniformity in Christianity. She sees this in the (to her) regrettable determination to fix the canon of scripture and to discriminate between orthodox and heterodox beliefs in the Church. We have, she says, ended up with a form of Christian doctrine that represents the theology of the Gospel of John, but not the other sources of early Christianity.

Pagels' alternative narrative has found a ready-made audience in an intellectual atmosphere suspicious of authority, wary of normative stories and constantly on the look-out for conspiracies of domination. Perhaps this also accounts for the enormous success of Dan Brown's *Da Vinci Code*, with its own (though historically indefensible) story of Christian origins. I think there are good reasons for preferring a version of the traditional story of Christian doctrine's origins to the one propounded by Pagels and those like her, but I cannot deny that these other ways of telling the story exist.

Here, then, is a brief introduction to the topic of Christian doctrine. In this chapter I have focused mainly on the question of how doctrine developed from the biblical era through into the early centuries of the Christian Church. In the next chapters I look at the 'why' questions: why is doctrine so important, even though it seems to come from a different age? Why, if it really is important, has it come to be so despised and neglected? Eventually, I will turn from 'why?' to 'what?' and ask: What happens when Christians do take their doctrine more seriously?

2

The Gift of Christ

Why share the company of dead Christians?

I can imagine readers coming to the end of the last chapter and asking, 'So what? Why should it matter in the twenty-first century what went on in the first, second, third, fourth and fifth centuries? With all the pressing challenges to which Christians need to respond in a world that lurches from crisis to crisis, what possible relevance can there be in the study and defence of the doctrinal tradition?' It is a fair question, indeed the central question of this book. In the chapters that follow I will be defending the rather unfashionable idea that Christianity, and the churches and communities that represent it, have no future without a serious commitment to Christian doctrine. Furthermore, I will also claim that this commitment is possible without a descent into either zealous bigotry or narrow fundamentalism. This, I recognize, is something of a tall order, given the prejudice against 'doctrine', 'dogma' and 'tradition' in contemporary western culture. Nevertheless, it is a vital project. But before getting to grips with the detail of the arguments, it will be helpful to move on from our basic definition of doctrine and ask why it should be such a central aspect of the Christian movement.

Christian doctrine is, at its simplest and most literal, what is taught about Christianity by and through the Christian Church. To talk of Christian doctrine implies that there is about Christianity something that transcends the beliefs and experiences of individuals, or particular communities, or even whole generations. There is something given which, if not completely unalterable, nonetheless constrains those who wish to claim the name Christian. I use the word 'given' deliberately. It carries at least two implications. On the one hand it implies that which we cannot easily change, like the weather of the British Isles, or the annual budget for our organization. On the other hand it suggests a gift, something bestowed on us for us to receive and cherish.

This is a book about the 'givenness' of the gift that is God's love in Christ and the givenness of Christian teaching as it communicates that gift. Some of the earliest Christian documents speak of just such a givenness in relation to Christian belief and tradition. Writing to the Corinthian church,[29] St Paul says: 'For I received from the Lord what I also handed over to you, that the Lord Jesus Christ, on the night when he was handed over . . .'.[30] He is referring to the origins of the Christian service of Holy Communion in the meal celebrated by Jesus with his disciples 'on the night in which he was handed over' – what we have come to call 'the last supper' – and in the deep meaning of Jesus' death. Paul's use of language is very interesting. The Greek word *paradidomi* means both the handing on of belief, tradition and story, and the handing over of a person for punishment, torture or death. Paul uses the word in both these senses within a single sentence. He refers to the Christian teaching he has received and is passing on to the Corinthians, and to the person of Jesus who was given up to his enemies and to an ignominious death. This deliberate play on words has only recently been noted by commentators,[31] but is utterly typical of Paul's writing. The gift of God's very self, 'handed over' to us in the life, death and resurrection of Jesus, is intimately related to the way in which the story of, the beliefs about, and the practice of Christianity are 'handed on', or given, from one person and generation to another. According to the New Testament, the gift that is Jesus Christ was received and 'handed over' in one of two different and opposite ways. Paul expresses the positive way as he speaks of handing on Christ to others so that they may share the life he

29 I will use 'church' to refer to a particular local or denominational Christian grouping and 'Church' to refer to the universal Church of all times and places.

30 1 Corinthians 11.23. I have amended the NRSV text to reflect Thiselton's suggestion that 'handed over' is a preferable translation to 'betrayed'.

31 See the recent commentaries on 1 Corinthians by Richard B. Hays (John Knox Press, 1997) and by Anthony Thiselton (Eerdmans, 2000).

brings. The more negative way is represented by other characters in the New Testament drama, for example Pilate, who 'hands over' Jesus for humiliation and death.

We still have a trace of this play on words in English. The version of the Bible best known in Europe for over a thousand years, the Latin Vulgate, translates *paradōsis* with variations on *traditio* and *trado*, words which carry the same range of meaning: to hand over, to surrender, to communicate through teaching.[32] English sustains this wordplay through the words 'traitor' (someone who betrays their friends or country by handing over in a destructive way) and 'tradition' (the handing on from generation to generation). Interestingly, one of the uses of the expression 'to hand over' in the early centuries of the Church emerged in the context of Roman persecution. Those who sought to escape from the legal penalties of Church membership could do so if they handed over the books of the Church – the scriptures and service books. People in the North African Church who did so were called *traditores*, because they betrayed Christ, handing him over, so to speak, to the spiritual descendents of those who had crucified Jesus. The opposite of the *traditores* were the confessors and martyrs, those who handed on Christ by proclaiming him even at the cost of their own lives.

This sense of the gift of God which is to be honoured and handed on did not, of course, begin with Christianity. Even as Paul wrote of the 'handing over' of Jesus Christ, in all the richness of that phrase, he must have been conscious of his Jewish heritage with its emphasis on the gracious gift of God in history, law, covenant and promise. We saw in the opening chapter that in the Old Testament the Shema is the core statement of Jewish faith and practice. Deuteronomy 6.4–9 is its best-known version. It begins: 'Hear, O Israel: The Lord is our God, the Lord alone. You shall love the Lord your God with all your heart, and with all your soul and with all your might.'

The following verses make it clear that this understanding of the God of Israel, which carries with it such wide-ranging implica-

---

32 The Vulgate even introduces this word where the Greek text omits *paradō-sis*, speaking of the bread as Christ's body *'quod pro vobis traditor'* – delivered (or given up) for you.

tions for religious and ethical practice, is based on God's gifts of freedom from slavery and of a land with 'cities you did not build ... cisterns you did not hew, vineyards and olive groves that you did not plant'.[33]

Furthermore, this affirmation about the nature of Israel's God – the doctrine of God, in other words – is something to be handed on.

> Keep these words ... Recite them to your children and talk about them when you are at home and when you are away, when you lie down and when you rise. Bind them as a sign on your hand, fix them as an emblem on your forehead, and write them on the door posts of your house and on your gates.[34]

In fact, the words of the Shema are quoted by Jesus himself when he is challenged about his understanding of God and God's demands.[35] For all the radical challenges to the Judaism of his day that are part and parcel of the words and work of Jesus, there is no doubt that he saw himself in the tradition of handing on and interpreting anew the ancient word of God to Israel.

Christianity, then, has inherited from its Jewish roots a sense of the importance of the content of its faith. The nature of Israel's God has specific content that is expressed in teaching and confession as well as in story and ritual. Christianity and Judaism, therefore, share a confessional understanding of religion. This marks them out as rather unusual among religions, certainly over against the prevailing religious systems in the ancient Near East and in late antiquity. Ancient Greek religion, it is sometimes observed, was more a matter of doing certain things rather than saying certain words. In much the same way, Hinduism cannot be said to have a 'creed', a settled body of doctrine by which to test whether someone is or is not a true Hindu. To be a Hindu is first and foremost to participate in certain ritual actions. Similarly, ancient Greek religion had the myths of Homer, but no creed; it had patterns of religious performance, but no doctrinal confessions.

---

33 Deuteronomy 6.10–11.
34 Deuteronomy 6.6–9.
35 Mark 12.29.

By contrast, there has always been something 'given' about both Christianity and Judaism. They are about what is to be believed, as well as what is to be done. At some points in the New Testament, there is even a conscious expansion of the Jewish Shema into a Christian confession of faith. The first letter to Timothy puts it succinctly:

For there is one God;
there is also one mediator between God and humankind,
Christ Jesus, himself human,
who gave himself a ransom for all.[36]

Similarly, one of the most important doctrinal affirmations in the New Testament is to be found in Paul's letter to the Philippians.[37] It begins:

. . . Christ Jesus,
who, though he was in the form of God,
did not regard equality with God
as something to be exploited,
but emptied himself,
taking the form of a slave,
being born in human likeness.

Although this summary of Christian teaching, which probably began life as an early Christian hymn, does not use the word *paradosis* (the word for 'to hand over' that is so pivotal in 1 Corinthians 11), it carries the same sense of God in Christ coming to us as our greatest gift, so that by responding to the incarnate Word Christians might confess (and so hand on) the awesome truth that 'Jesus Christ is Lord'.

The Christian scriptures, then, no less than their Jewish predecessors, refer to a process of tradition, a handing on of the truth given by God. As the letter of Jude expresses it, Christians are called to 'contend for the faith that was once for all handed over

36 1 Timothy 2.5–6.
37 Philippians 2.6–11.

to the saints'.[38] Protestant Christians often contend for the principle of *sola scriptura*, believing that only the words of the Bible, rather than any tradition of Church teaching, can be given authority. Nevertheless, it is clear that even within scripture itself there is reference to the development of tradition and to a process of handing it down. In the chapters that follow I try to show that this process, which led to the formation of the historic creeds and the many confessions of Christian faith that have followed them, is an important part of the health of Christianity as a movement.

I have emphasized the element of *paradosis*, handing over, in the life of the Christian community. But, of course, something can only be handed on if it has first been received. Returning to 1 Corinthians 11, Paul writes there about handing on what he has first received. That reception, which was of the person of Christ as well as the message about him, came only after personal opposition and in the context of a dramatic conversion.

To speak of 'reception' as well as of 'handing over' is to emphasize that Christian doctrine and tradition exists within relationships. The relationships are both human–divine and human–human. Christians both 'receive from the Lord' and receive from those who hand on what they themselves have received. In fact, reception has come to be a key word in the understanding of Christian doctrine and I will return to it later. At this stage it is worth pointing out that for the first Christians, 'receiving from the Lord' involved a number of elements.

There was, of course, the reception of the person of Christ himself. The prologue to John's Gospel (in what is dramatic and intense doctrinal writing) speaks of God's eternal Word coming into the world where, 'to all who received him, who believed in his name, he gave power to become children of God'.[39] This reception of the truth of Christ is also a reception of all that Christ brings: 'From his fullness we have all received, grace upon grace.'[40] For Christians, divine revelation is never simply a matter of God

---

38 Jude 3. I have substituted 'handed over' for the NRSV's 'entrusted to', to bring out the root meaning of *paradotheisē*.
39 John 1.12.
40 John 1.16.

communicating information to human beings; it is communicating the nature and life of God. Receiving the message of Jesus is inseparable from receiving the person of Jesus.

Second, early Christians, both in the New Testament period and in the following centuries, had consciously to receive the Jewish scriptures as their own, as God's word of prophecy and promise in relation to Jesus Christ. This is evident in the constant allusion to, quotation from and commentary on the Old Testament. It occurs throughout the New Testament, but comes to a focus in such passages as 2 Timothy 3.1–17. Here the author (it does not matter for our purposes whether it is Paul or, as many commentators believe, a later writer) urges Timothy to continue to be faithful to the teaching he has received, with the particular note that 'all scripture is inspired by God and is useful for teaching'.[41]

Finally, the early Church had a sense of receiving revelation through the Holy Spirit. This certainly seems to be the case in Ephesians 3.1–6 where Paul (or a follower of Paul) talks of the mystery of God which has been revealed through the Spirit: 'the Gentiles have become fellow-heirs, members of the same body, and sharers in the promise in Christ Jesus through the gospel'.[42]

The New Testament sense of the gift of the Christian story and of the beliefs and practices that embody it continues in the following centuries. A few brief examples will illustrate the point. The *Didache*, a very early collection of Christian teaching, takes this sense of 'handing on' very seriously, in worship and behaviour as well as in belief. This was a time before a universal and settled pattern of Christian ministry had been established and wandering prophets and teachers might enter a Christian community and ask for an opportunity to stay and teach. Only those who were handing on the teaching of the apostles were to be received and heard by the community. For Irenaeus, as we have already seen, there is a 'rule of faith' that has been handed on through the authorized teachers of the Christian community. He argues that the very public nature of this teaching (especially from such authorized teachers as bishops) is an effective counter to those who want to turn

41 2 Timothy 3.16.
42 Ephesians 3.6.

Christianity into a set of esoteric beliefs and practices. Athanasius, Bishop of Alexandria, writing in the heat of fourth-century controversies over the person of Christ, speaks of 'the actual original tradition, teaching and faith of the Catholic Church, which the Lord bestowed, the apostles proclaimed and the fathers safeguarded'.[43] He saw this tradition represented in his own day by the creed agreed by the first Council of Nicaea in 325.

Of course, there are other ways of construing the history of Christian doctrine, and we have already seen how someone like Elaine Pagels has a much more negative attitude to this development, seeing it as a closing down of Christian options rather than as a consolidation of belief. That is a view that has to be taken seriously, though I believe that it displays more of a modern distaste for doctrine than an accurate historical assessment. At this stage, though, I simply want to point out how widespread this emphasis on authentic Christian tradition was. For these writers, and for many who followed them, the Holy Spirit was not only the divine power through which the gift of Jesus Christ reached us and by which his resurrection took place. Neither was it confined to the present gifts of Christian experience and Christian ministry. It was through the Holy Spirit that the gift embodied and expressed in Christian teaching was passed on, developed and interpreted. Indeed, for some early Christian theologians, like Gregory of Nazianzus, the Church is living in the age of the Spirit, and the Spirit ensures that the Church is gradually led into the full measure of the truth of God.[44]

The situation today, especially in the western world of the last two centuries, is very different. From being a cherished gift, the tradition of Christian teaching has become a disputed or neglected gift. My first purpose in this book is to indicate why this change has happened, how 'doctrine', 'dogma', 'tradition' and 'given' came to be understood in such negative ways. From an analysis of the symptoms I hope to outline a fresh way of understanding the value of Christian doctrine within the context of a pluralist and sceptical

---

43 Athanasius, *First Letter to Serapion.*
44 Gregory of Nazianzus, *Fifth Theological Oration: On the Holy Spirit,* 34.26.

world, and an appropriate way of receiving the gift anew. Finally, I try to give a picture of where such a doctrinal renewal might actually serve the present ministry and mission of the Church and how a 'handing on' of the Christian tradition might come about.

This may sound like an essentially conservative procedure and, indeed, there are conservative elements in what I am trying to do. Nevertheless it is important to emphasize at the outset that the intention is not merely conservative. My understanding of the gift that is given in Christ and which forms the 'givenness' of the Christian tradition is that it is received, held and passed on for a purpose. It is not a buried treasure to be kept safe; holding it, using it and passing it on will always involve an element of risk and (as I try to show) some change and development in the form the gift takes. Nevertheless it is still a gift to be treated as valuable and not lightly dismissed.

Signs that the handing over of the Christian gift (among many other 'givens') is subject to neglect and hostility are easy to find in the culture that currently dominates the West. This disparaging of tradition and doctrine is well exemplified in Dan Brown's international bestseller *The Da Vinci Code*. The plot of this novel is that the Christian Church, far from handing over a tradition of truth to successive generations, has actually conspired to cover up the true story of its origins and so perpetuate a falsehood. Jesus (so the story goes) was married to Mary Magdalene in a representation of the union of the male and female elements of the divine. Their blood line (the 'Holy Grail') has been the focus of this more feminine (and less world-denying) religion but has been consistently persecuted by the Church. The Christian scriptures, together with the doctrine and the preaching of the Church, have been designed to keep humanity repressed, to prevent the more liberating religion from taking hold and to maintain an oppressive power structure. There is no need to go into the details of Brown's historical claims: they have been widely discredited by scholars. The important thing is that such a message chimes so very easily with the world-view in the contemporary West. We will find later on in my story that much more sophisticated theses of this type have become popular within some contemporary Christian circles as well as with critics of Christianity.

To take another example: a contemporary popular song announces, 'Welcome to my truth',[45] a title that perfectly illustrates an increasingly common way of looking at the world. The social, cultural and intellectual changes of the last 40 years (sometimes summed up in the term 'postmodernism') have for many people undermined any confidence that truth is 'out there', whether in religious beliefs, political ideals or even scientific facts. In its place is an internal, self-generated truth that helps me to make sense of an otherwise chaotic and meaningless universe. The most that can be hoped for is a limited sharing of such internal truths in relationships and small groups. Though this view has only recently come to dominance, it is not at all new. It is in fact a move anticipated over a hundred years ago by Matthew Arnold in his famous poem, 'Dover Beach'. Written while on honeymoon, it compares the ebbing tide with the falling away of religious faith and looks to his marriage for a truth that the external world cannot provide:

Ah, love, let us be true
To one another! for the world, which seems
To lie before us like a land of dreams,
So various, so beautiful, so new,
Hath really neither joy, nor love, nor light,
Nor certitude, nor peace, nor help for pain;
And we are here as on a darkling plain
Swept with confused alarms of struggle and flight,
Where ignorant armies clash by night.

Now that even the most intimate of human relationships can seem no longer a place of enduring truth, but are widely suspected of trapping people into socially determined roles, the prospect seems even bleaker. In this way of looking at things, the Christian Church, whose 'sea of faith' is quickly drying out, has been reduced to no more than one of the 'ignorant armies' that clash by night. Its doctrinal tradition, so the postmodernists would say, is a discredited metanarrative. That is, it tries to tell a universal story

---

45 By the singer, Anastacia.

of the cosmos, and of humanity and their meaning, where no such story is possible. This kind of metanarrative, with its attempt at totality, forces (so it is said) what is particular and 'other' into a false and oppressive uniformity. Just as there is current suspicion of the 'canon of western literature', with its emphasis on the 'received' work of Shakespeare, Milton and their descendants, so there is also a suspicion of classical Christian texts and of the teaching associated with them: the Bible, the historic creeds, the traditional liturgies, hymns and confessions of faith. By contrast, the postmodern world-view argues that meaning is given to texts by those who use them. We choose to give them significance and we construct their meaning; they do not impose any meaning on us.

In the face of such hostility to tradition and, indeed, to normative teaching of any kind, the advocate of Christian doctrine may seem to face an uphill task. Even within Christian communities there has been a dramatic decline of confidence in the place of doctrine; the gift is less valued. A brief survey of official church websites showed that many failed to give any prominence to the beliefs and doctrines of Christianity, or of that particular church. To take my own Methodist denomination, for example, while the American United Methodist Church gave easy access to statements of belief and sources of doctrine (but was anxious to frame these alongside a number of other sources of theology), the British Methodist Church provided no guide to Christian or Methodist teaching beyond the church's own mission statement.[46] In between the two, the Methodist Church in Ireland website has a brief section on beliefs, centred around the Apostles' Creed and the 'four alls of Methodism'.[47]

But before getting further embroiled in these more detailed discussions, let me be as clear as I can about what I am trying to achieve, and what I am not trying to achieve, with this project. It may be helpful to begin with what I am not trying to do.

---

46 I am pleased to report that a recent revision of the website has improved the situation.

47 The 'four alls' are an early twentieth-century formula designed to sum up the distinctive doctrine of the Wesleys: All need to be saved. All can be saved. All can know they are saved. All can be saved to the uttermost.

I will not be advocating witch hunts against heretics. The cause of Christian truth has not been helped (to say the least) by the treatment its advocates have given to those they regarded as their opponents.[48] We will see in a later chapter that violent conflict over doctrine is one of the factors that led to its neglect. Nevertheless, I will want to suggest that there are some limits to what can be accepted as genuine Christian teaching and that there are real dangers involved in proclaiming as Christian something that is at odds with what has been received.

I will not be defending a wholly static approach to doctrine, one that is 'fundamentalist' in admitting no historical or cultural variation, no fresh development and no openness to interpretation. It is a matter of empirical fact that what has been taught as Christian doctrine has not, in every detail, been the same across all times and places. I will, though, want to argue that in Christian doctrine what is new is not necessarily what is best, and that what has been received through tradition is not necessarily outmoded.

I will not, I hope, be expressing a naive and unreflective Christian faith, which simply takes certain doctrines for granted and does not open them to discussion and critique. On the other hand I will argue that traditional Christian doctrine embodies certain claims to truth and that it is not in the Church's gift to dispense with these.

Finally, I will not be suggesting that we should focus on doctrine to the exclusion of other aspects of authentic Christianity: personal faith, corporate worship, active mission and social witness. But I do urge that none of these core elements of Christianity and Christian living are independent of a living tradition of doctrinal teaching.

More positively, I hope to develop a number of affirmations about the place of doctrine and tradition in the Christian community. I argue for what is sometimes called 'a generous orthodoxy'.[49] It is generous both in the sense of having a lot to give (hence the starting point of this chapter's biblical section) and in the sense

---

48 Well expressed in Sydney Carter's song, 'The Devil Wore a Crucifix'.

49 The phrase is becoming associated with a book of that title by the American author Brian McLaren (Zondervan, 2004), but it has been used for several years by a number of theologians, including Geoffrey Wainwright and George Hunsinger.

of being positive rather than negative in relation to the variety of views that surround it. In other words, alongside the close attention to authentic and faithful doctrine, there can and should be an openness to both the proper diversity and the authentic development of doctrine.

I will be arguing that Christianity, if it is to be practised well, requires a discipline of the mind as well as of the heart. In fact, it will be helpful to do away with any hard distinction (sadly, still commonly made) between the intellectual and emotional aspects of Christian faith. One of the helpful results of taking early Christian authors (such as Augustine of Hippo) seriously is an encounter with their sense that knowing, loving and enjoying God are inseparable aspects of a single human activity and relationship.

Doctrine, I will suggest, supports and enables the praise of God in a three-fold way. Most obviously it does so through properly directed and well-grounded belief. This would be close to the literal meaning of the term 'orthodoxy' and implies that the praise of God requires careful attention to the nature and action of the one we address in hymns, liturgy, prayer and devotional actions.

Second, doctrine supports the praise of God through that practice of Christian living and service which is inseparable from the life of prayer and worship. What is sometimes called 'orthopraxis'[50] (doing the right thing) is not, I am convinced, an alternative to 'orthodoxy', but closely related to it. Practices imply beliefs, and vice versa. For this reason I want to challenge the common slogan, 'doctrine divides but service unites'. There is no form of shared Christian action that does not imply some shared belief. Third, doctrine also supports the praise of God that is expressed in Christian experience, what we might call the affective dimension of Christianity. One recent author, reflecting on the traditional Methodist emphasis on Christian experience, has coined the term 'orthopathy' to refer to a sense of 'feeling the right thing' as a dimension of Christian living.[51] Such an emphasis on feeling and

---

50 In Christian circles, the term 'orthopraxis' is most often associated with liberation theology, with its central assertion that theology is a reflection on the liberating praxis of the grass-roots Christian community.
51 The term 'orthopathy' was coined by the American Methodist theologian

experience is by no means confined to Methodism. Again, I will argue that, contrary to assumptions that are commonly made, doctrine is supportive of personal Christian experience and growth in holiness. Doctrine, in other words, can and should be good for our souls.

At the heart of my belief in the necessity and worth of Christian doctrine is a conviction that Christianity is essentially a religion of community and history rather than a religion concerning what any individual believes in any one moment. In this I am questioning one of the main trends of European thinking, a trend often identified with the nineteenth-century Danish philosopher Søren Kierkegaard, and his existentialist manifesto, 'subjectivity is truth'. Instead, I am supportive of a different strand of modern thought, one that is inspired by a vision of living tradition, embodied in the life of communities and in the stories and practices they share.

Two warnings from fiction

To bring this chapter to an end, it may be helpful to enlist the help of two twentieth-century novelists in order to point up the twin dangers of taking doctrine too narrowly and treating it too lightly.

George Orwell's novel *1984* is a classic critique of the totalitarian control of human language and discourse. When written it was a futuristic vision of a nightmare society in which all individual thought and independent speech are not only forbidden but effectively erased. 'Big Brother' is the personification of a bureaucracy that controls every aspect of a person's life through the euphemistically titled 'Ministry of Truth' and its manipulative language, 'newspeak'. Winston Smith, the central character in the novel, falls in love with a young woman and through their relationship tastes the illicit independence and individuality. By the end of the novel, though, he has been brought to heel through the terrifying ordeal of 'Room 101' and the narrator can say of him, 'He loved Big Brother'.

Theodore Runyon, in *The New Creation: John Wesley's Theology Today*, Abingdon, 1998.

While *1984*, like Orwell's *Animal Farm*, is primarily an attack on political totalitarianism, it is easy to see how it can be seen as a critique of any attempt to make religious language and teaching so normative that no dissent, argument or criticism is possible or permitted. Undoubtedly these attempts have been made and continue to be made. There is a lingering suspicion that the very terms 'doctrine', 'dogma' and 'tradition' refer to just this kind of repression. Does that mean that any attempt, like this book, to rehabilitate these terms and to stress the need for Christian communities to be bound together by common teaching is doomed to represent the kind of control represented by the memory of the inquisition? I do not believe that it is. Nevertheless, it does need to reckon with the dangers this enterprise involves, and to be tested for its openness to criticism and dissent. It is important to emphasize my commitment to a vision of Christian doctrine that not only makes sense in terms of the life, experience and practice of the Christian community, but also takes account of proper criticism from both within its own constituency and beyond.

If *1984* is a story about the crushing of individual thought and independent discourse, my second example is more of a warning of the perils of allowing individualism untrammelled liberty within the Christian community. *Elmer Gantry* by Sinclair Lewis, published in 1927, is a scathing satire on American Christianity and particularly on the morality of its clergy. The anti-hero of the book, Elmer Gantry, is a self-obsessed young man with large sensual appetites and a gift for salesmanship. He drifts into training for Baptist ministry on the strength of a desire to be the centre of attention. Having seduced and made pregnant the daughter of a church deacon, Gantry leaves in disgrace, only to resurface as the assistant and lover of a flamboyant, and equally self-obsessed, itinerant evangelist. Her version of Christianity is a personal invention, remote from any orthodox teaching, and there is a serious disparity between her preaching and lifestyle, but the pair achieve apparent success until she is killed in a fire. Eventually Gantry becomes the outwardly respectable minister of a well-heeled Methodist congregation, apparently untroubled by any need either to modify his predatory behaviour or to submit himself to the wisdom and authority of a wider community. Christian teaching is here an individual activity, a vehicle for a person to achieve their own ambitions, a commodity to be shaped according to the needs of the market. Lewis makes his own position clear by contrasting Gantry and his willingness to assume any doctrinal guise that will advance his career with a fellow seminarian who resigns when he can no longer believe orthodox Christian teaching, devoting the rest of his life to social action.

Elmer Gantry is a crudely drawn and exaggerated figure, but represents a tendency and a danger, especially for Protestant churches in the market economy of America and Western Europe. I hope to show that a healthy attention to doctrinal teaching in Christian churches is a necessary element in countering this abuse of Christian ministry for personal gain.

3

The Uncherished Gift

So far I have been setting out the story of how the Christian community came to have the doctrinal teaching that has come down to us from the earliest centuries. In doing so, I hope I have been honest about the different ways in which the story can be told and construed. I have also tried to set out a case for the centrality of this kind of doctrinal teaching for a Christianity that takes its biblical and historical roots seriously. At the heart of the argument is a belief that the Christian God is by nature gracious. That is, the act of giving is a constant feature of God's engagement with humanity and that divine grace is at the heart of our experience of God. The Greek word usually translated as 'grace', *charis* (from which we get words such as charismatic and charisma), simply means 'gift'. When Christians, with Paul, affirm that 'by grace you are saved'[52] they are referring to the gift of Jesus Christ, 'handed over' for us in his life, passion and death, and handed on to us through the teaching and witness of the Church.

But, as I have already observed, Christian doctrine, in much of the Christian Church as well as in the popular imagination, has a similar status to an unwanted gift. There are various strategies for dealing with unwanted gifts and embarrassing legacies. They can be stored in the furthest recesses of cupboards and attics, perhaps brought out on the rare occasions when the giver pays a visit. Or they can be got rid of, sold on or dumped to make room for something more congenial. They can even be kept but largely ignored, like a picture in a dark corner, seen every day but never really noticed. So it has come to be with Christian doctrines.

---

52 Ephesians 2.5, 8.

Locked away, jettisoned or ignored by many Christians, they tend to arouse a mixture of puzzlement and anger in those outside the churches. William Abraham writes of the 'doctrinal amnesia' of the Church,[53] suggesting that it is stumbling about without any true idea of its identity. If the Christian doctrinal tradition really is a gift then it has become, in many quarters, one that is either despised or neglected. How and why has this happened? In this chapter I want to tease out some of the threads in the story of how the gift of Christian teaching became devalued and spurned. It would be foolish to suppose that a process that has taken place over several centuries, and in many different ways, can be captured in a short narrative. Nevertheless, I hope to provide a map of the territory that we will need to cross in the remainder of the book.

Doctrine and violence: can doctrine be bad for your health?

'Belief is something you die for; doctrine is something you kill for. There is all the difference in the world.' This remark, by the veteran left-wing British politician Tony Benn, sums up the misgivings that are frequently aired by critics of Christian doctrine or, indeed, of doctrine of any kind. Doctrine is easily associated with fanaticism, the violent suppression of those who think and speak differently, the willingness to wage war in order to make one form of religious belief dominant and another disappear.

In a more academically informed context, the historian Perez Zagorin can still write as the opening sentence of a work on religious tolerance, 'Of all the great world religions past and present, Christianity has been by far the most intolerant.'[54] Religious sceptics, from Voltaire to A. J. Ayer, have seen in the blood shed on behalf of Christianity and its doctrines one more reason for disbelieving its teaching. This association between Christianity and violence, even if not completely deserved, has led some to abandon Christianity altogether and others to lessen their interest in its doctrinal teaching.

---

53 William Abraham, *Waking from Doctrinal Amnesia: The Healing of Doctrine in the United Methodist Church*, Nashville, 1995.
54 Perez Zagorin, *How the Idea of Religious Toleration Came to the West*, Princeton University Press, 2003, p.1.

The key period for this reaction came in the wake of some of the most intense conflict Europe had known. The century and a half that followed the beginning of what we now call the Reformation was one of terrible violence throughout much of Europe, especially the Netherlands, France, Germany, Britain and Ireland. The religious aspect of this conflict, for example the St Bartholomew's Day Massacre of 1572 that dealt such a blow to the Protestant community in France, produced a response that was to question the tenets of those convictions for which people on all sides died. Zagorin proposes that the roots of religious toleration in the West lie in the response of certain radical and unorthodox Protestant writers who were active in the two centuries following the Reformation. In other words, he is saying, it is in those who do not share the doctrinal convictions of the main protagonists of the wars of religion (Catholic or Protestant) that we find the initial urge for religious tolerance. What emerges is that, for the most part, a development of religious tolerance in revulsion against the decades of violence was accompanied by a lessening sense of the importance of Christian doctrine.

Of course, conflict and violence were not simply about religious doctrine; in sixteenth-century Europe, as in late twentieth-century Northern Ireland, religion often served as the cover for settling old scores or pursuing ambitions of conquest. But in both cases religious differences, including conflicts over Christian doctrine, were at least part of the motivation for violent conflict. Conflict cannot be reduced entirely to matters of nationalism, or socio-economic change.

In England, for example, Henry VIII may not have had a doctrinal commitment to the Reformation; indeed, his personal beliefs inclined more to the Catholic tradition than to the Protestant. But that did not mean that the English Reformation, protracted and disputed through the reigns of his successors, did not involve genuine antagonism between supporters of different versions of Christian truth and the forms of worship based on them. What is the true nature of the Church? How does God bring about the salvation of human beings? What happens in the service of Holy Communion? These were just some of the questions that led to countless sermons, pamphlets and books. The violent suppression of the monasteries by Henry, the violence meted out to Protestant leaders under Mary and Catholic ones under Elizabeth, were seen at the time to be, at least in part, attempts to make one account of Christianity normative at the expense of another. Martyrs generally die for cherished beliefs, not for political expediency or economic advancement. The seventeenth-century English Civil War continued this mixture of social, political and doctrinal difference. Here again it is difficult not to find some disturbing association between doctrinal conviction and the willingness to wage war.

It seems that some of those who participated in the conflict drew this conclusion and that it began to sap their confidence in the importance and truth of Christian doctrine. One example is perhaps indicative of what happens when religious and political idealism both admit defeat. Edward Montagu, patron of the diarist Samuel Pepys, was as a young man a zealous and devout Puritan in the Parliamentary cause and played a leading role in the Civil War. As the Commonwealth crumbled, however, he found a way to make himself useful to the restored monarchy and was reinstalled by Charles II as Earl of Sandwich. Any devotion to puritan doctrine had evidently disappeared along with his loyalty to old comrades. Pepys records him on a number of occasions professing total indifference to religious matters, declaring himself to be a 'stoick and a skeptic' and wishing that sermons in church could be replaced by admonitions to political conformity.[55]

This could no doubt be repeated through many other examples, but for a more systematic reflection on the role of doctrine in the aftermath of religious conflict we need to turn to one of England's continental neighbours, Holland. It is here that we find a number of key thinkers asking whether doctrinal correctness might not be worth the high price of war and destruction. In the sixteenth century the Netherlands was under the control of Spain and its Catholic king, Philip (he of the Spanish Armada). He moved to crush the pockets of Calvinist resistance in the Netherlands, prompting a

---

55 Claire Tomalin, *Samuel Pepys: The Unequalled Self*, Penguin, 2003, pp. 113–4.

more general uprising against the Spanish. Philip sent the Duke of Alba with an army to quell the revolt in 1567 and to impose a tribunal, the Council of Troubles, to question and sentence Protestant heretics. This 'Council of Blood', as the Dutch called it, executed thousands of people before Alba was forced from the Netherlands. The long, bitter and (ultimately) successful campaign for Dutch autonomy did not, however, end the cycle of violence. Calvinists, in their turn, persecuted Catholics. Only gradually, after Dutch independence in 1648, were Catholics and those Protestant groups outside the dominant Dutch Reformed Church allowed freedom of worship and teaching.

In the wake of this bloodletting, and in the midst of an intolerant state church, a number of figures emerged who argued passionately for religious toleration. One of them, Arminius, gave his name to a whole tradition of Protestant theology that opposed many of the doctrinal tenets of Calvinism and argued for a much broader approach to Christian belief. Here I will focus on just one of this group, the educationalist and lawyer Hugo Grotius (1583–1645). He is today best known as the founder of much modern international law, especially the law of the sea. But he was also a religious thinker whose plea for tolerance was based on a critique of what he saw as a doctrine-centred Christianity. His short book, *True Religion*, is on the face of it an argument for the existence and goodness of God, and for Christianity as the best of all religions. Look closer, however, and Grotius can be seen to be doing something else. As he moves from a general commendation of Christianity to a consideration of some of its problems, he produces what he calls an 'Answer to an objection touching the controversies abounding among Christians'.[56]

He asks, does the existence of diverse 'sects and factions' among Christians count as evidence against its truth? No, he replies, such diversity is common in other fields of study, for human minds are not capable of perceiving all truth and so there are different perspectives on it. He believes that all Christians agree on cer-

---

56 Hugo Grotius, *True Religion*, a facsimile reprint of the English translation of 1632, held in the Bodleian Library, Da Capo Press, 1971, Section XIX.

tain basic foundations (what he calls the 'true doctrine of Christ'). The implication is that there is a minimum set of beliefs that constitutes Christian religion and that all others are, as it were, options adopted by this or that sect and not essential to the truth of Christianity.

The heart of Christianity, for Grotius, is following Christ's teachings. Grotius concludes his book with an exhortation to Christians to live holy lives, to eschew violence and to treat each other kindly. We are all baptized into one name – Christ – so there should be no conflicting sects. If we differ on the apprehension of truth, then we must patiently await the revelation of God. The proper way forward for Christians is to read scripture (preferably in the company of others) and to follow the precepts of Christ. Grotius gives us no Protestant or Catholic polemic and no sense that he is advocating one denominational form of Christianity over against another. Christianity, in the version commended by Grotius, is reduced to a small number of basic beliefs so as to bridge the gulf between different churches. In some ways Grotius seems to be anticipating the liberal Protestantism of the nineteenth century, with its preference for ethics rather than doctrine and for the teaching of Jesus rather than the teaching of the Church.

Here, then, is a voice that sounds quite contemporary, and indeed historians of the modern ecumenical movement sometimes claim Grotius as a founding member. Note, though, that while Grotius appears to be offering a doctrinally light version of Christianity as some sort of common denominator for all Christians, his own summary of Christian essentials inevitably contains a theological and doctrinal standpoint. What some call *adiaphora*, marginal matters of doctrine that make no substantial difference to Christian faith, others may see as more central – and vice versa. While there may be (as the documents of the Second Vatican Council put it) a hierarchy of truths, with some doctrines having a greater claim on us than others, it is never an easy matter to sort out the order in which doctrines should come. Take, for example, the proposals of Adolf von Harnack (1851–1930), who we will meet again in a later chapter. In 1899 this great German historian of doctrine gave an influential series of lectures to answer the question, 'What is Christianity?' His answer bears quite a strong resemblance to the one we have just heard from Grotius:

> The Gospel is no theoretical system of doctrine or philosophy of the universe; it is doctrine only in so far as it proclaims the reality of God the Father. It is a glad message assuring us of life eternal, and telling us what the things and the forces with which we have to do are worth. By treating of life eternal it teaches us how to lead our lives aright.[57]

Harnack believed that by stripping Christianity of its inherited doctrines (including the incarnation) he could present it as relevant for modern life and as the key to living well. The sad fact is that he achieved neither of these aims. In particular, his reduction of doctrine to a few general ethical principles did nothing to prevent the slide into the violence of twentieth-century warfare; indeed, Harnack himself played a leading role in the support of German aggression in World War One.

That, of course, is getting ahead of ourselves in the story. But the diversion to Harnack teaches us an important lesson: there is no easy short cut that avoids the difficulties of doctrinal decision and doctrinal language. Much as we may admire Grotius' tolerance and eirenicism (and they are admirable), he does not provide us with a long-term solution to the problem of Christian division.

Before we leave this moment in the history of Christianity, there is one further development to introduce, one that links the ideas of people like Arminius and Grotius with those of the pietists we come to next. It focuses on a saying that has become popular in the ecumenical movement and which is the motto of the Moravian Church: 'In essentials, unity; in non-essentials, liberty; in all things, charity.' This saying has been ascribed to a bewildering variety of authors, from Augustine of Hippo to John Wesley. However, its real origins are in early seventeenth-century Germany, the same period as Grotius and the Dutch remonstrants.[58]

---

57 Adolf von Harnack, *What is Christianity?*, New York, 1908, p. 146.

58 The term 'remonstrant' is generally used to describe those who opposed the prevalent strict Calvinism of the state church.

In 1629 Peter Meiderlin (also known as Rupertus Meldenius) produced a book called *A Prayerful Admonition for Peace to the Theologians of the Augsburg Confession*. What was wrong with the Lutheran church, so Meiderlin thought, was the concern of theologians to enforce a prescriptive orthodoxy that moved far beyond the bare essentials of doctrine to all manner of non-essential and contentious propositions. Not that he wanted to do away with doctrine altogether. He believed that there were basic doctrines that could be readily extracted from the Bible and applied to the core theological business (as he saw it) of personal salvation. But beyond this (and Meiderlin expressed his horror with descriptions of a vivid and violent dream in which the devil stirs up a militant group of doctrinal purists) lies all manner of speculation and sectarianism. The way of doctrinal excess is one of demonic violence. The way of doctrinal minimalism (to use a very un-seventeenth-century word) is one of peace. No wonder German theologians and church historians refer to this formula – 'in essentials, unity; in non-essentials, liberty; in all things, charity' – as the 'Peace Saying'.

There is little evidence that Meiderlin's plea had much influence among the Lutherans of his own day, though they prepared the way for the Pietists who would follow nearly a century later. In England the moderate Puritan divine Richard Baxter employed the saying in his own attempts to reconcile the warring factions in the churches before and after the Civil War.

While Grotius' arguments for tolerance and Meiderlin's peace saying strike us as commendable sentiments of the kind that might properly belong in a modern liberal democracy, the idea that fewer doctrines might mean less religious conflict and violence needs critical examination. A recent study of the role of religion in community divisions in Northern Ireland sees conflicting beliefs as relevant (and more relevant than some secular sociologists allow), but one of the less powerful factors at work.[59] It tends to be particular social circumstances, for example the national conflicts in post-reformation Europe, or the recent conflict over sovereignty

---

59 Claire Mitchell, *Religion, Identity and Politics in Northern Ireland: Boundaries of Belonging and Belief*, Ashgate, 2005.

in Ireland, that form the seedbed of violence. Religious doctrine is often abused as a weapon in the construction of campaigns of violence, but is rarely a root cause.

Doctrine and arid religion: can doctrine be bad for our souls?

If the legacy of religious wars made at least some people think that less Christian doctrine might mean less violent conflict, others came to the conclusion that less emphasis on correct doctrine might mean a more vibrant and authentic Christian faith. In other words, while the first suggested that doctrine might be bad for our physical health and survival, the second asked whether doctrine might not also be bad for our souls.

This approach is associated with one of the most important new developments in Christianity after the Reformation. It usually goes by the name of Pietism – a catch-all title that covers a large number of movements, individuals and groups.

General descriptions of movements that embrace many different groups, over a considerable period of time, are always dangerous. Nevertheless, according to the editor of a recent book on the theology of the pietists, Pietism involved a consistent 'emphasis that the Christian life is a walk, not a talk, a becoming not being, that heart religion opposes head religion, that life is over doctrine'.[60]

The seventeenth- and eighteenth-century pietists saw a forerunner of their movement in Johann Arndt (1555–1621), a German Lutheran theologian who was born at Ballenstedt in Anhalt. A preacher and teacher with mystical leanings, his book on the nature of *True Christianity* puts all the emphasis on the inner life rather than on truths that are apprehended by the mind. Becoming a Christian for Arndt consists of a new birth that comes about when Christ is, without reserve, admitted to the human heart. The truth lies in this relationship, in what he calls 'this deep trust and heartfelt assent', not in the intellectual assent to Christian teaching.

---

60 Carter Lindberg (ed.), *The Pietist Theologians: An Introduction to the Theology of the Seventeenth and Eighteenth Centuries*, Blackwell, 2005, p. 6.

Philipp Jakob Spener, the acknowledged founder of Pietism, was born at Rappoltsweiler, Upper Alsace, in 1635 and died at Berlin in 1705. His manifesto is set out in *Pia Desideria*, an introduction he wrote to Arndt's *True Christianity*. Spener's vision was for a Christianity freed from what he saw as the dry formalism of current Lutheran thinking and practice. The contemporary historian Mark Noll has summarized Spener's proposals under six headings:

(1) There should be 'a more extensive use of the Word of God among us.' The Bible, Spener said, 'must be the chief means for reforming something.'

(2) Spener called also for a renewal of 'the spiritual priesthood', the priesthood of all believers. Here he cited Luther's example in urging all Christians to be active in the general work of Christian ministry.

(3) He appealed for the reality of Christian practice and argued that Christianity is more than a matter of simple knowledge.

(4) Spener then urged restraint and charity in religious controversies. He asked his readers to love and pray for unbelievers and the erring, and to adopt a moderate tone in disputes.

(5) Next he called for a reform in the education of ministers. Here he stressed the need for training in piety and devotion as well as in academic subjects.

(6) Last he implored ministers to preach edifying sermons, understandable by the people, rather than technical discourses which few were interested in or could understand.[61]

Pietism had an enormous appeal. As well as the movement within Lutheranism, it led to the revival of the Moravian community under the leadership of Nicholas von Zinzendorf (himself a godson of Spener), it influenced the Jansenist movement in the Roman Catholic Church and led to the formation of missionary societies and Christian renewal movements as far apart as Siberia and North America. It had an early cultural expression in the cantatas and passion settings of Johann Sebastian Bach, thus giving it a hearing even

61 Mark Noll, <www.believe.net/>. Spener's *Pia Desideria* is available in an English translation by Theodore Tappert, Fortress Press, 1964.

today among those who otherwise would have no or little contact with Christianity. It led to the foundation of the universities of Halle and Tübingen as well as many other educational centres. Methodism, founded by the Anglicans John and Charles Wesley under the influence of Moravian piety, is perhaps the Christian denomination that has (at least until the more recent Pentecostal and charismatic movements) most effectively represented the pietist approach on the world stage. In the rapid spread of Methodism through Britain and America during the late eighteenth and early nineteenth centuries countless ordinary men and women came to identify themselves with a personal story of new birth in Christ and with the pursuit of holiness.[62] Through Methodism hymnody some of the best-known Christian hymns ever to be written have taken pietist sentiments into worship across the denominations and throughout the world.

Pietism (together with its evangelical, Pentecostal and charismatic successors) has perhaps been the most successful strand of Christianity in the modern era, still dominating American Protestant Christianity and, through the missionary activities of traditional denominations and the rise of indigenous churches, establishing strong footholds in South America and Africa. Because it has been so influential, and because of the nature of the objections it raised against a more doctrinal form of Christianity, it deserves more attention than some of the other oppositions to doctrine we are considering.

As a lifelong Methodist I have myself been nurtured in Pietism's emphasis on personal faith and holiness of life. I have committed to memory rather more of Charles Wesley's hymns than are now commonly sung. I am, in other words, a child of Pietism and can no more remove its influence from my life than I can stop being English. It is important to recognize its strengths and its appeal: the emphasis on personal responsibility, whether it is in the response of faith or the exercise of conscience; the important place it gives to the ordinary Christian and their story of faith; the appeal it makes to the affective side of human nature; the way it encourages openness to the new wind of the Holy Spirit.

---

62 The best account of this process is given in David Hempton, *Empire of the Spirit*, Yale University Press, 2005.

But there are serious problems around Pietism and its tendency to exalt the affective and denigrate the cognitive side of Christian faith. To tease them out, some more historical background is necessary.

Part of the clue to the success of Pietism and those strands of Christianity influenced by it lies in its adaptation of Christianity to the conditions of the modern world or (to be more neutral) its adoption of a form of Christianity to which people living within modernity could more readily relate. The eighteenth century was the era of the European Enlightenment. Its world-view included a new emphasis on the free individual, a denigration of tradition, and the beginning of a separation between the truths of reason, established by rational enquiry and empirical evidence, and the inner truths of personal belief. It saw the escalation of what has been called 'the turn to the subject'. In other words, there was increasing focus on the way human beings develop their own understanding and knowledge.[63]

As philosophers and scientists seemed to make ever more stringent attacks on a Christianity understood as truth established in the world of facts and reason, so there was a growing appeal to forms of religion that depended not on intellectual respectability but on the evidence of the human heart. It is surely significant that Immanuel Kant and Johann Wolfgang Goethe, respectively the outstanding philosopher and the greatest romantic poet of the immediate post-Enlightenment period, had both been influenced by Pietism in their youth. Kant's insistence that religion should not trespass in the realms of reason and Goethe's adoption of a self-made (though hardly Christian) religion both bear the imprint of the pietist turn towards the inner life for the evidence of faith.

Friedrich Schleiermacher (1768–1834), sometimes credited with founding the discipline of modern systematic theology, was also from a pietist background. Although he is often regarded as the first liberal theologian, his emphasis on experience, on the feeling of absolute dependence on God, meant that his theology reflected

---

63 For example, Locke's *Essay Concerning Human Understanding* (1690) and Kant's *Critique of Pure Reason* (1781).

the pietist agenda very well, and it would not be unfair to suggest that his approach to Christian faith has more in common with contemporary evangelicalism than most evangelicals would be prepared to admit. His greatest work was undoubtedly his *Glaubenslehre*, and while its English translation has the title 'The Christian Faith', the original German title implies that he is presenting a scheme of Christian doctrinal teaching. What he does is link the classic doctrines of the Christian faith (for example, the divine and human natures of Christ, or the atonement) to the experience of the believer and the believing community. The emphasis has shifted from doctrinal teaching that focuses on truth that is independent of human experience, to doctrines that express aspects of human experience.

What makes a movement strong can also indicate its weaknesses. There are a number of key problems with the pietist influence on Christianity, and particularly with its stance on doctrine. The first is that the opposition of a heart religion to a head religion distorts the nature of Christian faith. It produces a concentration on the faith by which the Christian believes at the expense of the faith that is believed in: what classical Christian thought has distinguished as *fides qua creditor* and *fides quae creditor*. In other words, the pietist emphasis is on the form of faith rather than on the content of faith. Faith is seen as the submission of the heart, an act of loving commitment, rather than as assent to a truth that has been given and handed on. The inner experience of the individual Christian is the touchstone of its authenticity. It is a point made in many traditional evangelical songs, such as in these words by Alfred H. Ackley:

He lives, He lives,
Christ Jesus lives today!
He walks with me and talks with me
Along life's narrow way.
He lives, He lives,
Salvation to impart!
You ask me how I know He lives?
He lives within my heart.

But the Jesus known principally through the witness of the heart rather than through the teaching and witness of the whole Christian community easily becomes a Jesus tailored to our own psychological needs, or (even worse) a Jesus in our own image. In its suspicion of any doctrine and theology that is not expressed through the direct experience of the believer, the pietist tradition risks a subjectivism and emotivism that neglects the cognitive aspect of human nature. The comment made by a Roman Catholic seminarian during an exchange visit when I was a theological student still has an uncomfortable ring of truth about it: 'Why is it that every time I ask a Methodist what they believe, they tell me how they feel?'

Speaking to us from the late fourth century, Augustine provides a helpful corrective. In some ways he shares many of the pietist preoccupations; his *Confessions* is essentially an autobiographical prayer that explores what God has been doing in his life up to the point of his full acceptance of the Christian gospel. His interest in what we would now call the psychology of faith strikes us as quite in tune with those same modern concerns that Pietism has addressed so effectively. But Augustine is not drawn into the pietist opposition of the head and heart. Rather, he sees the human mind as created in the image of God and created for communion with God. Knowing and loving God are inextricably bound together. So, then, when he later explored the doctrine of the Trinity in his great work *De Trinitate* he began with the scriptural story of God's mighty acts, together with the wisdom reflected in the earliest Christian writings. What he moved on to was neither an assertion of our inner experience of the Trinity nor a speculative leap into an abstract idea of God. Instead, he explored the ways in which our minds already reflect the Trinitarian nature of God, and the ways in which the Triune God seeks to reshape our lives through our intellectual perception.

What the pietist tradition tended to lose was Augustine's clear sense of the priority of God's action and God's nature over our perception of them, and of the need for Christians to employ their God-given powers of reason. Schleiermacher's focus on the inner experience of the believer in his discussion of doctrine could lead some people to the conclusion (certainly not intended by Schleier-macher himself) that there was no more to Christian belief than that. One nineteenth-century atheist thinker who exploited this was Ludwig Feuerbach. His *Essence of Christianity* attacked religion by claiming that what Christians say about God is nothing more than the projection of their deepest desire for humanity. Once we see that, he argued, we can jettison the false hope of religion and work to achieve humanity's full potential. There is an irony here. Part of the appeal of this aspect of the pietist tradition was its apparent offer of escape from philosophical criticism of religion. Yet this same strand in the pietist tradition opened the door for another attack on Christianity's credibility. If it is all about what is going on in my heart, why bother with the awkwardness of belief in a God beyond ourselves and the doctrines that accompany that belief?

The second problem with the pietist approach is the anti-intellectualism that has accompanied this exaltation of the heart over the head. This anti-intellectualism has prevented Christians engaging properly with the challenges of modern culture. There have, of course, been exceptions, and John Wesley (to name but one) had a passionate interest in the intellectual life of his day. But those Christian groups that are heirs to the early pietists have not, as a rule, valued scholarship or encouraged the life of the mind. Where they have (in the massive investment of American Methodism in higher education, for example) they have been perceived as drifting from their original character and have been challenged by newer movements more confident that the witness of the Spirit needs no intellectual embellishment. Early in the 1990s, Mark Noll (himself an evangelical Christian) observed: 'The scandal of the evangelical mind is there is not much of an evangelical mind.'[64]

The controversy that surrounded the founding of the first theological college for British Methodism, opened in Hoxton, London, in 1832, illustrates the point. Vigorous correspondence in the Methodist press debated whether the establishment of a college might not do more harm than good by diverting the spiritual fervour of

---

64 Mark Noll, *The Scandal of the Evangelical Mind*, Eerdmans, 1994, p. 3.

ministers into cool intellectualism. One wiser voice did eventually prevail, writing in the *Wesleyan-Methodist Magazine* in 1834, 'the time is coming when untutored piety may do more harm than has impious learning in the past'. Nevertheless, the word 'academic' is still frequently used in a pejorative way in contemporary churches and many theological students are impatient with doctrinal theology as a distraction from, rather than the basis of, ministerial practice. As a theological educator I have had to become used to comments (sometimes rather barbed) implying that my teaching is at best irrelevant and at worst an obstacle to sound Christian preaching. Clearly, 'untutored piety' (like 'impious learning') still has plenty of advocates!

Third, there is something disingenuous about the pietist disavowal of interest in doctrine. In practice such groups work with an implicit set of doctrines and doctrinal priorities even if they do not articulate them very clearly. Spener himself moved the emphasis in the doctrine of salvation away from Luther's focus on justification and instead concentrated more on the concept of regeneration. What in fact happens in Pietism, and the churches influenced by it, is that the emphasis is precisely on those doctrines that relate to the experience of the human heart, on those doctrines that reflect (to use John Wesley's phrase) an 'experimental divinity'. The conviction of sin, the desire for salvation, the acknowledgement of Jesus Christ as saviour, the new birth in the Spirit, the progress in Christian perfection: all these moments in the *ordo salutis* (order of salvation) had (and have) their counterparts in the teaching of churches in the pietist tradition. Pietist Christianity tends to dwell on this *ordo salutis* (with its emphasis on my story of salvation) at the expense of the *historia salutis* (the overarching story of God's ways with the world). The result is not so much a rejection of doctrine but rather a selective and uncritical use of doctrine. Doctrinal issues such as the eternal nature of God, or the relationship between God and creation, tend to get left out. Charles Wesley's corpus of hymns, for example, for all their scriptural allusions and creative presentation of God's work in Christ, treat the non-human creation as if it were merely the painted backdrop to a theatrical stage on which the only real business is that between God and the human soul. How different from the more literally scriptural hymns of Isaac Watts, with lines such as 'Nature with open volume stands, and spreads it maker's name abroad.'

A final, and unfortunate, consequence of the pietist approach to doctrine is an unwillingness to engage with the Christian tradition. While John Wesley may have urged his travelling preachers to read the great classics of Christian literature, which he abridged in his *Christian Library*, pietist movements and their descendants have had a tendency to look over the heads of the long succession of Christian teaching and thinking, appealing directly to God's historical revelation in scripture and God's current revelation in the hearts of believers. True, it can be argued that the Catholic and Orthodox streams in Christianity have so emphasized the role of the Holy Spirit in the development and passing on of the doctrinal tradition that there is insufficient scope for the Spirit's intervention and inspiration in the present. Nevertheless, the heirs of the pietists have gone too far in the opposite direction, virtually eliminating the work of the Holy Spirit in the historical life of the Church. It sometimes seems as if such groups imagine themselves to be alone on a desert island, breaking open a bottle washed up on the shore and finding a copy of the New Testament along with a note saying, 'Make yourselves a religion out of this!' The pietist tendency, with its proper emphasis on what God is doing in lives here and now, downplays the historical nature of Christianity, the way it has been sustained and passed on through visible human institutions. At worst, this involves an arrogant refusal to acknowledge what God has been doing in different times and places.

Doctrine and reason: can doctrine be bad for our minds?

If doctrine can be denounced as bad for our health and bad for our souls, it can also be attacked as a danger to our minds. This was the view of many of those caught up in the so-called Enlightenment of the eighteenth century.

Kant and the freedom of the human mind

Asked, in 1784, to explain what was meant by the (even then) tricky term 'Enlightenment', Immanuel Kant gave this pithy summary:

> Enlightenment is man's emergence from his self-incurred immaturity. Immaturity is the inability to use one's own understanding without the guidance of another.
>
> This immaturity is self-incurred if its cause is not lack of understanding, but lack of resolution and courage to use it without the guidance of another. The motto of enlightenment is therefore: Sapere aude! Have courage to use your own understanding!

Warming to his theme, Kant goes on to describe inherited dogmas as the intellectual equivalent of a ball and chain, preventing our free movement and making us unaware of how far we can walk and jump. How wonderful, he continues, to live in the time of Frederick the Great, whose indifference to religious matters makes it possible for clergy and scholars to say whatever they like, however incompatible it may be with inherited doctrine.[65]

Now, Kant is not saying that the content of inherited doctrine is necessarily wrong. It may well contain valid truth and it is true that Kant believed himself to be a good Lutheran. His point is that doctrinal statements (for example, 'God is immortal' or 'Jesus Christ is the Son of God') cannot be considered true (even if they are true), because they are taught by this or that authority, or included in a particular book. They can be acknowledged as the truth only because contemporary human beings have arrived at them themselves through the free use of reason. Yes, there are places that faith may reach, even though reason cannot go. *Religion Within the Limits of Reason Alone*, to use the title of another Kant volume, can only go so far. This may sound like an affirmation of religious faith, but such reaching out is emphatically not that firm knowledge of things beyond our sight that Kant takes to be the substance of traditional religious belief.

---

65 Kant's original essay was first published in the German periodical *Berlinische Monatsschrift*, in December 1784. It is frequently anthologized and can be easily accessed on the internet.

Thomas Paine and the imperative for human freedom

Unlike Kant, Paine did not consider himself to be a Christian. The revolutionary author of the *The Rights of Man*, who was also hugely influential in the development of the American constitution, was a deist. That is, he believed that while there may be a creator God behind the universe we inhabit, nothing further can be known about this God, and nothing should be expected by way of divine intervention. Deism, then, while not abandoning religious belief altogether, had no place for the traditional teaching of Christianity (or any other religion for that matter) and no role for scriptures or creeds. Defending deism, Paine describes it as the natural religion of humanity, shared by those who adhere to a myriad different faiths. Detailed doctrinal teaching, on the other hand, is a human invention, incapable of proof and inimical to reason. A rational and enlightened person must leave such nonsense behind:

> He may believe that Jesus was crucified, because many others were crucified, but who is to prove he was crucified for the sins of the world? This article has no evidence, not even in the New Testament; and if it had, where is the proof that the New Testament, in relating things neither probable nor provable, is to be believed as true?
>
> When an article in a creed does not admit of proof nor of probability, the salvo is to call it revelation; but this is only putting one difficulty in the place of another, for it is as impossible to prove a thing to be revelation as it is to prove that Mary was gotten with child by the Holy Ghost.
>
> Here it is that the religion of Deism is superior to the Christian Religion. It is free from all those invented and torturing articles that shock our reason or injure our humanity, and with which the Christian religion abounds. Its creed is pure, and sublimely simple. It believes in God, and there it rests.[66]

66 Thomas Paine, *Of the Religion of Deism Compared With the Christian Religion*. This is found in a number of places on the internet, including a site dedicated to promoting contemporary deism: <www.deism.com/paine_essay_deism_christianity.htm>.

If Kant was one of the most powerful intellects of the Enlightenment, and Paine one of its most strident voices, they were by no means alone in their scepticism about the value of Christian doctrine. For example, the Scottish philosopher David Hume wrote a devastating attack on the credibility of miracles, challenging people to believe the evidence of their own eyes rather than the testimony of ancient books. If the dead are not raised within the realm of our own experience, there is no reason to believe the stories of resurrection from the Gospels. Gotthold Ephraim Lessing, another member of the German Enlightenment, was if anything even more threatening. Even if it could be shown that Jesus Christ had risen from the dead (the foundation, after all, of one of the central doctrines of the Christian faith), that would not prove anything for people living in a different time or place. As Lessing put it in what has become one of the most famous challenges to traditional Christianity: 'the accidental truths of history can never become the proof of the necessary truths of reason' because there is 'an ugly broad ditch' placed between them.[67]

Here, then, are some of the roots of the intellectual contempt for doctrine that has steadily grown over the last 200 years. The critical, doubting human subject now became the arbiter of truth. Nothing was to be taken as 'given'; all was to be subject to rational enquiry. There is, in fact, little in the work of a contemporary advocate of atheism, such as Richard Dawkins, that does not have its basis in the eighteenth century. I have already suggested that one of its results was a tendency for Christianity to retreat from proclaiming doctrine as public truth to an emphasis on truth as inner experience. So Christians, even self-consciously conservative and evangelical ones, took on board more Enlightenment thinking than they realized.

Although many of the assumptions of the Enlightenment (for example, the essential freedom of the individual, the inexorable development of human knowledge and the existence of a common way of thinking for all human beings) have come to be questioned, we still live in a world largely shaped by the thinking of the eighteenth

---

67 *Lessing's Theological Writings: Selections in Translation*, trans. Henry Chadwick, University of Stanford Press, 1957, p. 55.

century. We are all the Enlightenment's children, growing up in a world where its results are all around us. Nor should Christians be entirely dismissive of its legacy. Few people do not value living in a democracy or having access to modern medicine and universal education. In retrospect, some of the Christian resistance against all things modern looks foolish and reactionary. Dietrich Bonhoeffer, writing from his Berlin prison cell in 1944, saw these modern developments as God's way of telling humanity to grow up, to be 'a world come of age'. Nevertheless, the Enlightenment has left us with an inheritance that has its tragic and inhuman side. We should not forget that much of the violence and totalitarianism of the twentieth century was in regimes, like Nazi Germany and Soviet Russia, deeply indebted to modernity and its Enlightenment creators.

The Enlightenment made assumptions about what counted as truth and what did not. It made a division between the facts that could be established through observation and the use of reason, and the values that were subjective and personal. On one side of the divide it placed scientific knowledge, on the other side religious opinions, ethical and aesthetic judgements. It made a sustained attack on tradition and left people cut off from their own past, expecting constantly to move on an upward curve of progress. It set up an ideal of education and civilization, denouncing as primitive those cultures that did not share them. In the next chapter I will draw on a number of recent thinkers who, without being at all reactionary, have tried to retrieve some of the human vision abandoned by modernity.

Doctrine and the call to action: 'Doctrine divides but service unites'

The last objection to the traditional place of doctrine in Christianity sees it as both a distraction and a barrier: a distraction from the primary purpose of Christianity, which is the expression of the kingdom of God through action in human society, and a barrier to Christian unity.

Like the pietist movement and its many descendants, this is an approach that sees Christianity more as a matter of 'walking the walk' than of 'talking the talk'. But while Pietism saw 'walking the walk' first and foremost in terms of an individual rebirth and only then as a life of Christian service, this newer movement sees co-ordinated Christian social action as the essential core of Christian life. Two prime examples of this approach to doctrine are found in the 'social gospel' and the 'Life and Work' movements of the early twentieth century.

The 'social gospel'

The social gospel movement is usually associated with the name of Walter Rauschenbusch (1861–1918), an American Baptist minister who was traumatized by his ministry in the Hell's Kitchen area of New York. He brought social and economic analysis to bear on a situation about which, he believed, Christians were all too complacent. Through a series of books and articles, and his later teaching as a seminary professor, Rauschenbusch argued that the focus of Christianity must be the kingdom of God and not merely the salvation of individuals. In the biblical prophets and the teaching of Jesus, Rauschenbusch found the moral values which he believed could answer the social malaise of inequality and poverty. The call is for Christ-like action that will bring the life of the human city into harmony with the life of heaven. Jesus is at the centre of Rauschenbusch's vision of Christianity, but it is Jesus the teacher and leader, not the Jesus of the traditional doctrines and creeds of the Church. He echoed the views of German liberal theologians, such as Adolf von Harnack, arguing that the history of doctrine was a history of restricted growth and increasing irrelevance. Writing on his reasons for being a Baptist, he highlighted a dependence on scripture rather than on inherited doctrines and creeds:

A creed contains sharply defined and abstract theology; the Bible contains a record of concrete and glowing religious life. A creed addresses itself to the intellect; the Bible appeals to the whole soul and edifies it. A creed tells you what you must believe; the Bible tells you what holy men have believed. A creed is religious philosophy, the Bible is religious history. A creed gives the truth as it looked to one set of clever men at one particular stage of human history; the Bible gives the truth as it looked to a great number of God-filled men running through many hundreds of years. The strength of a creed is in its uniformity and its tight fit; the beauty of the Bible is in its marvellous variety and richness. A creed imposes a law and binds thought; the Bible imparts a spirit and awakens thought.[68]

In essentials, then, Christianity is a matter of personal experience and social ethics.

The influence of Rauschenbusch and the social gospel has been far-reaching. It might be said that British Methodism is for the most part dominated by a combination of evangelical piety and social gospel, with some parts of the church putting the emphasis on one and other Methodists putting it on the other. In the Britain of the early part of the twentieth century, the social gospel was popularized in the Brotherhood Movement, an organization in the Christian socialist tradition of the Free Churches, aimed at the reform of society on Christian lines. The foundation of the Brotherhood was that 'Christianity is chiefly concerned with man's brotherly relation to man, and with the redemption through human effort of every sphere of man's activity on earth'. A slogan used by one Methodist city mission in Belfast might well sum up the social gospel: 'Need before Creed'.

Life and Work

If doctrine can be a distraction from the work of the kingdom of God, then it can also be seen as a barrier to collaboration and unity between Christians. One approach to Christian unity has taken exactly this perspective. The ecumenical movement of the early twentieth century led eventually to the creation of the World

---

68 Reprinted in *Christian Ethics Today*, 1995, Vol. 1, No. 1, April.

Council of Churches out of three originally distinct streams. One was the World Missionary Council, the impetus for which came from the Edinburgh World Conference on Mission in 1910. A second was the Faith and Order Movement, which through successive conferences sought to address the outstanding doctrinal differences between Christian traditions. The third was the Life and Work movement, associated with Archbishop Nathan Söderblom and the inaugural conference he organized in Sweden in 1925. In the aftermath of World War One, it was felt that the churches had done little to prevent the conflict and were ill-placed to address the social issues that dominated post-war Europe. A fresh commitment of the churches of the world to work together for social progress would, it was argued, not only be an immense service to the world; it would also unite the churches in a way that debate about doctrine had failed to do. The slogan of the movement was: 'Doctrine divides but service unites'. The implication was that the route of practical Christian action in service to the world provided a way to transcend the obstacles to Christian unity presented by centuries of doctrinal difference. If Catholics and Protestants, Lutherans and Baptists, Methodists and Anglicans could not sign up to a common set of doctrines, then at least they could be united around the compassionate response to a world and to people in trouble.

Now, it would be impossible not to affirm much of what has taken place in the name of the social gospel, or the Life and Work movement, or any one of the many relief and development agencies through which Christians of different backgrounds have sought to alleviate the suffering of the world and witness to the kingdom of God. It is easy to see why a doctor in a refugee camp, for example, would seem to be doing more good than someone (like me!) who is a teacher of doctrine in a denominational college, or why a group campaigning for political prisoners would seem more valuable than one hammering out an agreed statement on the doctrine of justification. That tradition of emphasizing Christianity as world-changing action rather than a set of beliefs remains, like the social gospel, popular and seductive. But action and doctrine are not as easily separated as these movements sometimes suggest.

As Geoffrey Wainwright argues in a recent article, 'all features of the ecumenical enterprise – evangelistic, humanitarian, moral, liturgical, sacramental, ecclesiological – bear a doctrinal dimension'.[69] In the Catholic Church it is common to speak of 'social doctrines',[70] implying that there is a unity between the Church's teaching on theological issues (such as the nature of God, the purpose of human life) and its teaching on social action. A recent example of this is the controversy over Amnesty International's decision to back the right of women to have access to abortions in certain circumstances. Many Catholics have withdrawn from Amnesty's work, which they had undertaken as Christian service, because of a conflict with their church's doctrine of human life. Churches cannot be united in service without some sense of unity in doctrine. The two movements I have described, and the many like them, have done immense good, but I want to argue that both movements have been at their best when, in spite of their own protests to the contrary, they have been theologically as well as socially active, and have taken Christian doctrine seriously.

Doctrine – a plea in mitigation

All this represents a formidable set of objections to doctrinal Christianity. The reader can be forgiven for thinking that the foregoing pages have completely undermined the intention of this book to bring doctrine to the centre of the Christian stage. Has not the cumulative effect of post-Reformation humanism, Christian Pietism, Enlightenment scepticism and Christian activism been to relegate doctrine to the dusty attic of religious history? Is it not guilty, as charged, of being the source of physical, spiritual, intellectual and social harm? Are we not better off without its baneful influence and stultifying restraint?

It would be foolish to deny that these are serious charges, and I have set them out in some detail because they are so seldom under-

---

69 Geoffrey Wainwright, 'Does Doctrine Still Divide?', *Ecclesiology*, 2005, Vol. 2, No. 1, pp. 11–34.

70 The term 'social doctrines' comes from the encyclical *Rerum Novarum*, published by Pope Leo XIII on 15 May 1891.

stood and weighed up. Certainly, they point to the dangers inherent in any doctrinal system and the possibilities of abuse that tempt those who develop and teach it. However, at each stage in the argument I have at least hinted at the problems created by these criticisms of doctrine. I think it can be shown that each of them creates more difficulties than it solves.

At the end of this chapter, I hope that we have a better understanding of the way doctrine came to be so neglected and derided in our present culture. In the following chapters I try to set out a more positive scheme. On the one hand there are arguments to be drawn from recent philosophy and theology to show the indispensability of a robust and dynamic system of Christian teaching. On the other hand there will be some pointers to the way in which closer attention to the doctrinal nature of Christianity can be a force for renewal.

4

Giving Doctrine a Good Name

How some recent thinkers make room for doctrine

It sometimes seems as if there are only two contemporary reactions to doctrine. People appear either to turn against the idea of doctrine as a vital and positive element in the life of the Christian community (and a great deal of both Christian and secular writing implies exactly that) or (as a trawl through internet sites featuring 'doctrine' suggests) they buy into a naive belief that the doctrinal standards of their own group are absolutely definitive and unquestionable. So, we might ask, is the present intellectual climate totally inhospitable to any defensible sense of authoritative tradition and shared doctrine? Not quite. In a later chapter we will encounter a number of Christian theologians who have been rehabilitating the notion of doctrine as central to Christianity. In this chapter, however, I want to introduce some of the figures who, as philosophers, enable us to see the role of doctrine in a more constructive and creative light. My selection is hardly comprehensive, but I have tried to show that the themes on which this book is based are not without intellectual foundation. Of course, I would not for one moment claim that any of these philosophers would enthusiastically endorse all that I am saying; nor would I be uncritical of their work. But here, I hope, is an introduction to some significant and suggestive thinking.

The modern attack on the whole concept of doctrine and dogma has been so thorough that it is tempting to think that no intellectually respectable defence of it can be made. In what follows I draw on the work of three leading mid to late twentieth-century philosophers: Michael Polanyi, Hans-Georg Gadamer and Paul Ricoeur. Each of them gives an alternative to some of the prevalent intellectual assumptions of modernity and each has been highly influential. Polanyi challenges the common assumptions about knowledge in an era dominated by science, while Gadamer and Ricoeur represent rigorous contributions to the discipline of hermeneutics, an activity best defined as 'what goes on when human beings engage in interpretation'.

Michael Polanyi (1891–1976)

Polanyi was a wide-ranging thinker who was successively professor of both physical chemistry and social studies at Manchester University. Educated in Hungary, he fled Germany as the Nazis tightened their grip on public life and made his university career impossible. He was as much disturbed by the (as he saw it) illusion of free and independent knowledge in modern liberalism as he was by the suppression of freedom in totalitarian regimes. He challenged the prevailing (and naive) belief that science had ushered in a time when coercive dogma and personal prejudice had been replaced by objective facts that were entirely independent of those who came to know them, and of the values they espoused. This view, he suggests, makes knowledge impersonal and denies the passionate involvement of the knower with the process of knowing. His 1951–52 Gifford Lectures (published as *Personal Knowledge*) are an extended critique of this approach and a careful exposition of his own alternative.[71] His aim was, as he put it, 'to achieve a frame of mind in which I may hold firmly to what I believe to be true, even though I know that it may conceivably be false'.[72] Here are a few of the ways in which his thinking can help our understanding of the debate about Christian doctrine.

---

71 Michael Polanyi, *Personal Knowledge: Towards a Post-Critical Philosophy*, Routledge and Kegan Paul, 1958. The Gifford Lectures are a prestigious series given for over 100 years in Scottish universities and focusing on the relationship between religious faith, philosophy and the natural world. Among the many outstanding books that have come out of the Gifford Lectures are William James' *The Varieties of Religious Experience* (1900–02), A. N. Whitehead's *Process and Reality* (1927–28) and Albert Schweitzer's *The Problem of Natural Theology and Natural Ethics* (1934–35).

72 Polanyi, *Personal Knowledge*, p. 214.

Tacit knowledge

According to its critics, one of the drawbacks of a system of doctrine, such as the Christian tradition, is its sheer presumption. It would suggest that we can know far more than human beings can, in reality, comprehend. Surely, it is argued (from the high Enlightenment philosophy of Immanuel Kant to the angry liberalism of Bishop Richard Holloway), the real truth of things is so far beyond human understanding and human language that only the most arrogant of men and women would claim that this or that set of words truly conveyed such profound mysteries. The truth, we must honestly conclude, is that we know far less than our words and statements suggest.

Polanyi takes the opposite view. Human beings, he says, actually know far more than they are able to articulate and express. A lot of knowledge is tacit; it arises from our use of language and our development of skills as we are nurtured in a particular community. Our explicit knowledge, be it a scientific theory or a religious doctrine, is not something that comes out of the blue and imposes itself on our mind. Instead, it is intimately related to that which we implicitly know from our sharing in human experience, language and activity. What Polanyi suggests is that human knowledge goes ahead of our theories, statements and agreed facts. We act as if things are true even before we can articulate that truth. If Polanyi is right, then it would be quite proper to see the fundamental doctrines of Christianity not as a form of collective arrogance, but as the careful summary of what Christians had been acting out from the beginning.

An example of this might be the doctrine of the Trinity. It is sometimes argued that because the Christian scriptures themselves do not explicitly spell out such a doctrine, this doctrine has actually been imposed on Christians as an alien and unfounded intellectual framework. But Polanyi's theory of tacit knowledge suggests something else. The writings of the New Testament, as well as other evidence from the first two centuries of Christianity, show people who are praying and living as if there was a triune and not an undifferentiated God. It was only after centuries of reflection on what the Church already, in a sense, knew, that the doctrine was explicitly articulated.

A passion for the truth

We saw that the pietist critique of doctrine centres on an opposition between the head and heart, between cool reason and warm passion. An emphasis on a passionate relationship with God seemed to the pietists (and seems to many contemporary Christians) incompatible with a keen interest in the doctrinal teaching of the Church. This division between the head and heart has become part of the popular imagination, with the romantic movement of the nineteenth century rebelling against the rationalism of science and more recent 'New Age' spirituality promoting an alternative to conventional medicine. In response, there are frequent protests in the intellectual press about a new superstition and the need to defend the rational advances of modernity.

But is it really the case that spiritual passion must keep itself clear of systematic teaching and carefully articulated claims to truth? And must genuine human knowledge dispense with any kind of passionate self-involvement and depend entirely on a dispassionate weighing of the evidence? Emphatically not, according to Polanyi. One of the recurring themes of *Personal Knowledge* is that all human knowledge depends on the passionate commitment and personal investment of the one who seeks to know. This is true for the scientist, who needs an intimate relationship with the questions and material under his or her investigation. It is equally true for the student of society and politics. And it is also true for the religious believer. Polanyi sees Christian doctrine as a form of passionate knowledge based on its intimate relationship with the passionate worship and service of God. On this view, Christian worship and service become, as it were, the laboratory in which the knowledge of God is both developed and shared.

Polanyi's insistence on the passionate nature of knowledge works two ways. On the one hand it helps to dispel the widespread and pernicious rumour that doctrine is a form of knowledge addressed

solely to the heads of Christian believers, having nothing whatsoever to do with the heart or with the passions. On the other hand
it offers a critique of any accounts of Christian doctrine (and there
have been far too many over the course of Christian history) that
have forgotten its essential relationship with the passionate commitment of a worshipping and serving community.

The fiduciary principle

What then of faith? Polanyi is aware that the modern world has
seen faith and scientific reason as opposite and opposing activities.
One, so it seems, deals with irrational prejudice, the other with
calm and disinterested facts. But, he says, nothing could be further
from the truth. In fact, there is no form of knowledge, scientific
knowledge included, that does not depend on some type of faith.
All knowledge depends on what he calls a fiduciary framework, a
bedrock of belief that cannot be proved, but on which we develop
our understanding. Whereas the Enlightenment philosopher John
Locke insisted on the rigid separation of faith and knowledge,
Polanyi suggests that we need to learn from Augustine's insight
that all knowledge is a gift of grace, accessed only on the basis of
human faith.

> Tacit assent and intellectual passion, the sharing of an idiom and
> of a cultural heritage, affiliation to a like-minded community:
> such are the impulses which shape our vision of the nature of
> things on which we rely for our mastery of things. No intel-
> ligence, however critical or original, can operate outside such a
> fiduciary framework.[73]

This, he admits, may sound like giving in to dogmatism. His response is to say that the naive trust in scientific objectivity has
already proved to be unworkable. The only alternative is for us to
admit that we cannot get away without holding certain unprovable
beliefs. He is even willing to provide room for those much-derided

---

73 Polanyi, *Personal Knowledge*, p. 266.

terms, 'dogma' and 'orthodoxy': 'dogmatic orthodoxy can be kept in check both internally and externally, while a creed inverted into a science is blind and deceptive'.[74]

Notice that while Polanyi insists that faith is personal and that knowledge is personal, it depends on commitment to a shared set of values and beliefs. There is an interesting link between Polanyi's views on knowledge and the approach to the Christian doctrine of George Lindbeck. As we shall see, Lindbeck's cultural-linguistic understanding of doctrine attempts to avoid what he sees as the twin errors of an over-objective account of doctrine and an over-subjective account. Polanyi is seeking to avoid both of these in his own account of knowledge.

The critique of doubt

Another feature of the modern critique of doctrine that comes under Polanyi's scrutiny is the assumption that doubt is inherently superior to belief. He notes that since Descartes in the seventeenth century doubt has been seen as the basic virtue for all critical thinking. Through sceptical questioning of inherited assumptions, modern humanity has (so it is commonly believed) freed itself from the tyranny of religious and political ideologies and from redundant and misleading beliefs about the universe. Polanyi acknowledges himself to be a product of this modern tendency. But he also points out that doubt – especially doubt as a principle of human thinking – is itself a form of belief. It is deceptive to suggest that doubt is an impartial agnosticism, a suspension of belief while the evidence is weighed, sorted and judged. Rather it is normally based on tacit, or explicit, ideas about what can and cannot be true. Doubt, just as much as belief, is an act of passion on the part of the person holding it.

Doubt, then, is no superhighway to the truth. On its own it is an intellectual cul-de-sac that yields no important insight. Instead, Polanyi looks for a 'post-critical' approach that, while acknowledging the important questions that need to be put to inherited

---

74 Polanyi, *Personal Knowledge*, p. 268.

ideas, takes intellectual risks by adopting a set of beliefs rather than doubting everything.

When it comes to religious doubt (and he notes that the engine driving modern scepticism has been the critique of dogma) there is a need to see the limits of what doubt can, and should, achieve. Christian doctrines are not objective statements of truth, completely independent of the experience and assumptions of those professing them. But then again, neither are the propositions of mathematics.

Polanyi's critique of doubt should make Christians rather less defensive about the truth-claims involved in expressing their faith. Tennyson's famous line, 'There lives more faith in honest doubt, believe me, than in half the creeds', is too often taken for granted. Christian doctrine is not, of course, immune from criticism, but criticism is not inherently superior to belief.

The necessity of a shared tradition

Polanyi is not, it should be emphasized, a conservative figure who believes that human thinking makes no progress or that individual beliefs and enterprises are insignificant. As a scientist he is excited by the prospect of new discovery and he is aware that knowledge is dynamic and never stands still. Knowledge, for Polanyi, is personal and so he constantly uses the language of personal relationship (such as 'commitment', 'passion') to talk about the process of knowing the truth. Nevertheless, he puts equal stress on the fact that human knowledge can never be an individual activity, separate from the business of living in society. Those who see religious societies, with their inherited traditions and their shared belief systems, as forms of coercion fail to understand the way in which all societies, of whatever kind, depend on a kind of orthodoxy. As Polanyi himself puts it:

The recognition granted in a free society to the independent growth of science, art and morality, involves a dedication of society to the fostering of a specific tradition of thought, transmitted and cultivated by a particular group of authoritative specialists, perpetuating themselves by co-option. To uphold the independence of thought implemented by such a society is to subscribe to a kind of orthodoxy which, though it specifies no fixed articles of faith, is virtually unassailable within the limits imposed on the process of innovation by the cultural leadership of a free society.[75]

Polanyi is insistent that those who claim to forge new knowledge independent of tradition and free from any authority are either mischievous or victims of an illusion. Such a thing is a human impossibility. If he is right, and I believe he is, this would imply that religious doctrine fits in with the way in which critical human knowledge normally and properly develops. It is not (as caricatures so often depict it) an aberration that holds us back from proper enquiry and critical thinking. Not that Polanyi himself was an uncritical adherent of traditional Christian doctrine. He saw the need for it to be expressed in new ways. Nevertheless, while doctrines have, indeed, been challenged by modern thinking and discoveries, such challenges do not, for Polanyi, mean that they rob them of their inherent truth.

I chose to begin with Polanyi, even though today he is a relatively little-known author, because he tackles, from the standpoint of an insider, many of the claims and misunderstandings of modernity and its resistance to tradition and doctrine. My own introduction to his thought came from Bishop Lesslie Newbigin, one of the great Christian leaders of the twentieth century. Newbigin, who had been one of the first bishops of the Church of South India and a leader in the ecumenical movement, spent his last years challenging British Christians to make a more robust defence of their faith and its tradition.[76] Coming from a long experience of service in the pluralist society of India, he found it difficult to understand how British Christians could be so tentative about their faith and so unwilling to see that it implies wide-ranging truth-claims. From Polanyi he was able to develop a response to the widespread assumption that

---

75 Polanyi, *Personal Knowledge*, pp. 244f.
76 For example, 'Dogma and Doubt in a Pluralist Culture', in Lesslie Newbigin, *The Gospel in a Pluralist Society*, SPCK, 1989.

modern thought had all but killed off the Christian claim to offer knowledge and truth through the gospel.

Hans-Georg Gadamer (1900–2002)

Gadamer, who lived through the whole of the twentieth century and witnessed Nazi and Communist regimes at first hand, was a philosopher who made a particular contribution to hermeneutics – the discipline of interpretation. His best-known book, *Truth and Method*,[77] is regarded as one of the seminal works in this field and has prompted both widespread interest and respectful criticism. There are several ways in which it helps us discuss contemporary attitudes to doctrine.

The two horizons

Recent generations have been particularly sensitive to the gap between themselves and previous historical periods. If our lives and our perspective on life are so radically different from those who produced the New Testament, or the historical creeds, or the confessions of Church Councils, how can they possibly speak to our condition? Is it true (as the New Testament scholar Rudolf Bultmann famously taught) that no one who uses electric light or a refrigerator can believe in the physical resurrection of Jesus? If so, then traditional Christian teaching is indeed highly problematic and of doubtful relevance as we try to work out what life (and death) means here and now. Taken to its extreme, this perspective would suggest that we are all trapped in our own isolated historical and cultural situation, unable to understand or learn from the situations of other times and places.

Gadamer (and let me emphasize again, he is not speaking directly about Christian doctrine) has an approach to hermeneutics that suggests a much more positive relationship between past and present than is proposed by Bultmann's argument (and by the argu-

---

77 Hans-Georg Gadamer, *Truth and Method*, Continuum, 1975.

ments of other historical relativists).[78] He claims that we live our life within a certain horizon that is defined by our time and place, our culture and experience. We are, as is often said in postmodern writing, 'situated'. What we see is dependent on where we are. But this life-horizon is not, of course, a static horizon. The historical situation we occupy is constantly on the move; it is as if we are at the edge of a glacier that is moving inexorably from mountain to sea. Day by day we watch ice that was once deeply embedded in the glacier's valley crumble and fall into the ocean. At the same time, ours is not the only horizon. The object we want to understand and interpret (be it a Greek tragedy, a book of the Bible or the Nicene Creed) also comes out of a horizon and that horizon is also a dynamic one. Aristophanes, the apostle Paul and the bishops who met at the Council of Nicaea, all wrote out of a particular horizon defined by history and geography. That is why it is wrong to imagine that we can simply take up something from another culture and understand it in the same way as those who produced it. However, we are not condemned to total incomprehension; we and the material we want to interpret are not on totally parallel tracks. Understanding and interpretation do happen, but in a more complex way than we often imagine. What is happening in a genuine act of understanding, says Gadamer, is that the two horizons come together and fuse. How does that happen? The key term for Gadamer is 'conversation'; we are engaged in a conversation with the text so that (and this is of central importance) we develop and extend our understanding of that reality to which the text points.

To move back to the topic of Christian doctrine, Gadamer's picture would suggest that we engage in a conversation with the teaching of the Christian tradition in order to develop and extend our understanding, here and now, of what that teaching refers to.

---

78 The relevance of Gadamer's ideas to Christian theology is particularly well developed in Anthony Thiselton's works: *The Two Horizons: New Testament Hermeneutics and Philosophical Description with Special Reference to Heidegger, Bultmann, Gadamer and Wittgenstein*, Paternoster, 1980; and *New Horizons in Hermeneutics: The Theory and Practice of Transforming Bible Reading*, HarperCollins, 1992. Thiselton's latest major work, *The Hermeneutics of Doctrine* (Eerdmans, 2007), addresses many of the issues that I deal with in this book, but it appeared after it was largely complete.

That, in short, is nothing less than the Christian gospel itself: the being and action of the God who is Father, Son and Holy Spirit. And the result of this conversation will be a fusing of our own horizon with that of the Christian tradition and its texts. In that way our own horizon changes for ever; it has gained a new shape because of the conversation.

Prejudice is not all bad

Just as Polanyi wants to rehabilitate passion as an essential dimension of human knowledge, so Gadamer wants to put in a good word for prejudice.[79] On the face of it that seems an even more difficult task than that of defending the role of dogma. Some explanation is therefore called for. Prejudice in popular usage tends to be most often used in the sense of judging people and situations in advance of learning the full truth about them, usually on the basis of their ethnicity, gender, age or sexuality. It is the kind of attitude that leads, at the time of writing, to passengers being asked to leave aircraft because their appearance and speech has led to the prejudiced view that they are young Muslims who just might also be terrorists. But this kind of prejudice, which we properly seek to overcome, is not really what Gadamer is thinking of. For him, prejudice is a reflection of the fact that we are finite human beings and that our engagement with texts and with reality has to start somewhere. Prejudice, then, becomes another way of saying that we do not approach anything with, as it were, a blank sheet of paper or a completely open mind. When we read the Bible or consider what Christian teaching is, we inevitably approach our task with a degree of advance understanding, with an idea of the questions we want to ask, the problems we want to solve, the things that we are going to find difficult. This is part of what Gadamer means by talking about our own horizon. As people of a certain kind, living at this or that time in a particular place, we cannot eliminate prejudice, though we can be open to the possibility that some of our prejudices are barriers to a critical understanding rather than

---

79 Polanyi, *Truth and Method*, pp. 246ff.

an aid to it. In fact, the nature of our prejudices will probably only become apparent once we open ourselves to the conversation that is central to interpretation. Our questions will themselves be questioned; our aims may well be diverted in a different direction; our pre-judgements, in short, will be revised.

If we apply this insight of Gadamer's to the question of doctrine and to authorized Christian teaching, two things emerge. The first is that there is no neutral place from which we can judge the truth or relevance of doctrine with disinterested logic. Sometimes commentators write with a tone that says, more or less, 'those who drew up the creeds thought such and such, but we now know differently'. But that is precisely what Gadamer insists we cannot do. We have our prejudices and assumptions, every bit as much as our forebears did in the first, fourth or eighteenth centuries. Our approach to the question of the nature of God, the person of Christ or the role of the Church does not involve a form of superior and unbiased judgement compared to those who framed those doctrines in the first place.

Second, and more positively, every approach to Christian doctrine, quite properly and legitimately, has certain questions and priorities in mind. To take one example, to which I will return, the recent damaging consequences of human domination of planet earth have prompted questions about the doctrine of creation. What is God's intention for the creation as a whole? What role has God given to humanity in relation to the rest of creation? How can we speak of creation being renewed and not simply of individual human beings being saved? What resources does the Christian doctrine of creation offer us as we seek a responsible and sustainable future for the earth? These questions constitute a very different set of 'prejudices' from, for example, the ones that motivated early Methodists in the eighteenth century. For them, the transforming work of the Spirit in the lives of individual Christians formed a doctrinal priority; interestingly, though, one of the sermons from John Wesley's old age was on the theme of the redemption of the whole of creation.

Another contemporary example relates to the issue of gender. What has the Christian doctrine of humanity to say to us as we reflect on the debates about the relationship between men and women in society and in the Church? Questions about the leadership of women are bound to reflect the 'prejudice' of our situation in a society where the equality and equal ability of women has become axiomatic. Like all prejudices, those brought in to the discussion of Christian belief will need to be criticized and revised as the conversation draws the two horizons together, but they provide a starting point that gives our understanding a practical relevance.

Tradition is a vital aspect of truth

We have seen that a central plank of the Enlightenment platform is that human freedom involves freedom from inherited tradition. It was a given for Immanuel Kant that the authority of the past has to be overcome if men and women are to think for themselves. Since then, the word 'tradition' has been burdened with a sense of an oppressive weight that drags people down, or an irrational and tyrannical authority that imposes alien structures on ideas and inhibits freedom of thought and action. The only exception to this completely negative connotation is the use of 'tradition' to designate a nostalgic space where we can escape from the harsh realities of modernity.[80] But even that implies that tradition has little to do with the business of real life in the here and now.

All that these definitions of tradition imply has been part of the negative attitude to Christian doctrine, of the sense of it as functioning either as an authoritative tradition of belief and practice or as an exercise in nostalgic escapism.

Alongside his determination to rehabilitate prejudice, Gadamer wants to point to the positive aspects of tradition. He believes that truth in the human sciences cannot simply follow the methodology of the physical sciences. We cannot conduct research as if we were starting from scratch and interpreting data entirely by ourselves. We should, though, note in passing that Polanyi would have told

---

80 An example would lie in the popularity of the British chain of shops called Past Times. The products they stock almost all reflect a nostalgic understanding of tradition.

him that the physical sciences, too, needed a wider definition and that they cannot follow a method of 'pure' observation. Instead of such a simplistic definition of understanding, truth has to be seen as having a communal dimension; it is not simply a matter of brute facts. Instead, it is embedded in a shared language that we need to both learn and inhabit. The discernment of truth requires a shared culture and the acknowledgement of a shared tradition that exercises a measure of authority over us.

All this implies that we can never stand apart from history; we ourselves are part of the reality we are trying to understand. This in turn leads Gadamer to talk about our solidarity with the tradition, our acknowledgement that we cannot have truth on our own, either as an individual or as a generation. He is emphatic that this is not just a conservative ideology offering stubborn, but ultimately futile, resistance to change. Rather it is an acknowledgement that all development and change is the development of an already existing tradition. Tradition is not merely restrictive, it can produce genuine creative freedom as we engage with it in that conversation that brings together our own horizon with that of the past. Gadamer's work on tradition provides us with a helpful route to discuss its role in Christian teaching.

Of course, Gadamer does not provide us with all that a Christian thinker requires for a discussion of doctrine. I would certainly want a more robust concept of truth, one that makes it more than a function of a shared language. Truth is not simply a matter of consensus, any more than it is simply a matter of the correspondence between our language and the 'facts' to which they refer. This is an area that Polanyi and Ricoeur, in rather different ways, help us to navigate. And, with some of Gadamer's critics,[81] I would acknowledge that traditions can produce distortions of truth as well as expressions of truth. To take one obvious example, the history of Christian anti-semitism is a stark reminder of the capacity of the Christian community to develop a distorted language that is alien to Christian truth and horribly sinful in its effects. Nonetheless, Gadamer is surely right in insisting that truth can never be

---

81 Chief among them has been the philosopher Jürgen Habermas, who entered into an intense debate with Gadamer on this very point.

separated from a shared language, a common history and a common canon of 'classics' that reach to us across the generations. The truth of Christianity claims us in precisely this way. It cannot be distilled into a set of metaphysical beliefs or ethical principles. It reaches us as we participate in a community that shares in the long history of reading the scriptures, reciting the creeds and reflecting on the gospel.

The theological writing of Archbishop Rowan Williams is especially strong in asserting this sense of solidarity with the tradition that has been given to us. A colleague once remarked that when reading Williams it was almost as if the past great teachers of Christian theology were sitting round the same table and joining in the discussion.[82] When we take Christian doctrine seriously, we are taking our place alongside those who have shared the faith in different times and places. We belong to them, we are saying, and they belong to us. The alternative is to imagine that we in the present can construct our own Christianity, without any regard for the 2,000-year history of the Christian religion.

Paul Ricoeur (1913–2005)

While Gadamer did not write with any explicit religious perspective (though his work has been extensively used by theologians), Ricoeur might well be regarded as the foremost Christian philosopher of the last century. Born in France, with a Protestant background, he held a variety of university posts including, in his later years, one in the Divinity School at Chicago. His writing reflects deep engagement with the literature and the problems of modern European thought, and although his work often focuses on language and the interpretation of texts he was not aloof from the great ethical questions of the day. Like Polanyi, he delivered a series of Gifford Lectures, but compared with Polanyi he was first and foremost a philosopher, primarily in the continental hermeneutic tradition, though with a keen interest in the more analytical phil-

---

82 Rowan Williams, *On Christian Theology*, Blackwell, 1999.

osophy of the Anglo-Saxon world.[83] While he writes as a believing philosopher, like other thinkers in this chapter he is not, for the most part, explicitly addressing the doctrinal concerns of Christian theology. We have to pay close attention to his philosophical discussion and listen for ideas and arguments that shed some light on the central theme of this book. No more than Polanyi or Gadamer does Ricoeur supply us with a ready-made framework or knock-down arguments. Instead, he helps us to challenge some of the assumptions of modernity and to chart a careful course through the icebergs of contemporary thinking.

Post-critical thinking and the hermeneutics of retrieval

The popular but annoyingly imprecise term 'postmodern' has been in vogue for many years. Polanyi, though, introduces us to the potentially more helpful phrase 'post-critical'. By this he means a way of thinking that seeks to move beyond the systematic scepticism of a good deal of modern thought so that we truly can affirm something, even though we do not have total proof for it.

Ricoeur develops this concept of the 'post-critical' as way of explaining something without explaining it away. In doing so he enables us to take seriously the modern criticisms of belief, without necessarily succumbing to them. Famously, he refers to pivotal and critical figures such as Karl Marx, Sigmund Freud and Friedrich Nietzsche as 'masters of suspicion'. In their work these giants of nineteenth- and twentieth-century thought explain human beliefs (including – perhaps especially – religious beliefs) so that they no longer have any value as statements of truth but are instead revealed as serving another function.[84] For Marx, religious doctrines are to be reduced to the unjust economic systems that underlie them and which (as the 'opiate of the masses') they seek to mask. For Freud, they are symptoms of psychological dysfunction, a sign of primitive tensions between human beings and their parents. For

---

83 *Oneself as Another*, 1985–86.
84 This approach is developed most fully in Paul Ricoeur, *Freud and Philosophy: An Essay in Interpretation*, Yale University Press, 1970.

Nietzsche, so influential in contemporary 'postmodernism', they are caused by biological factors and cultural weakness.

All these explanations, Ricoeur reminds us, are reductionist. That is, they explain the economic, psychological or social function of religious beliefs without giving us any understanding of their content. In this way they provide the basis for a 'hermeneutic of suspicion', a reading (in the case of Christianity) of scriptural and doctrinal texts that unmasks their real nature and subverts their claim to convey a picture of what is real and true. This form of interpretation has become widespread in western culture. We have already seen that scholars such as Elaine Pagels, as well as many more popular writers, understand doctrinal statements about the divinity of Christ as the means of exercising control over society in a repressive way. At the same time, the columns of broadsheet newspapers (usually written by people who assume Christianity to be false) gleefully seize opportunities to interpret Christian belief in one of these functional (or, more likely, dysfunctional) ways. And, of course, the hermeneutic of suspicion has been an important weapon for many of those within the Christian tradition who believe that doctrine needs to be revised or removed. To take just one example, the feminist theologian Elisabeth Schüssler Fiorenza has a section towards the beginning of her work *Jesus: Miriam's Child, Sophia's Prophet* called 'The Sociopolitical Location of Christological Doctrine'.[85] In this she attacks what she calls the 'kyriarchy' of the traditional doctrine of Christ as Lord, king and judge. This was produced (so she believes) as a function of the imperial desire for a Church that mirrored and legitimized the Roman empire. She is seeking to 'deconstruct' the apparently innocent claims of Christian doctrine to reveal the oppressive domination which (she thinks) it expresses.

Ricoeur, it is important to realize, does not deny that such explanations are necessary or legitimate. There is a real need for a hermeneutic of suspicion to unmask the idolatry that leads human beings to misplace their intellectual and spiritual commitment. There is a place for demystification and stripping away illusion; the critical role

---

85 Elisabeth Schüssler Fiorenza, *Jesus: Miriam's Child, Sophia's Prophet: Critical Issues in Feminist Christology*, SCM Press, 1995, p. 18.

of modern thought cannot be bypassed. Nevertheless, it is equally true that the hermeneutics of suspicion cannot be the end of the process of interpretation. It needs to be balanced by what Ricoeur calls the 'hermeneutic of retrieval'. Through this we are able to listen to what is being said in our inherited texts and then allow them to challenge and shape us. From suspicion, interpretation needs to turn to faith, to 'the manifestation and restoration of a meaning addressed to me in the manner of a message, a proclamation . . . a kerygma'.[86] In this way the interpretation of religious texts leads us to a genuine, though chastened understanding of reality, what Ricoeur, in another of his memorable phrases, calls a 'second naïveté'. This is why one commentator suggests that a characteristic of Ricoeur's work is that he seeks to combine 'both the unmasking function of explanation and the creative function of understanding'.[87]

This aspect of Ricoeur's thought, it is true, gives some encouragement to those who are critical of inherited doctrines and creeds and is a proper corrective to any who think that past beliefs can be repeated without any interpretation. But it also places a limitation on that criticism and provides compelling reasons for taking such teachings seriously, as we listen for the message they give us. For Christians this message is nothing less than the word of God.

Metaphor and symbol as truth

A frequent theme in Ricoeur's work is the importance of symbol, metaphor and narrative as bearers of truth. The tendency has been for these aspects of language to be seen as subjective, reflecting at best the personal experience, values and creativity of those who employ them. Metaphors, for example, tend to be seen as mere ornaments to language, having nothing to do with the reality to which language refers. On this basis it is argued that because doctrinal statements such as 'the risen Jesus sits at the right hand of the Father' or, 'Christ has redeemed us through his blood' are metaphorical they cannot convey anything of ultimate reality.

---

86 Ricoeur, *Freud and Philosophy*, p.27.
87 Thiselton, *New Horizons in Hermeneutics*, p. 344.

For Ricoeur, though, to say that something is expressed through symbol, metaphor or narrative (as so much Christian teaching is) in no way lessens its claim on us as reality and truth. In fact, it is vital that we learn to listen to symbols and myths. He says that 'symbols give, they are the gift of language; but this gift creates for me a duty to think'.[88] Taking a particular example from one of his earlier works, *The Symbolism of Evil*, Ricoeur points out that the Christian creed does not talk about evil or sin in an abstract way; rather, it refers to the 'remission of sins'. This use of language employs metaphor to point up the relationship between sin and redemption.

Ricoeur helps us to take metaphor and symbolic language seriously and without embarrassment. Christians need to avoid the temptation to reduce metaphor to a plain set of propositions. Take, for example, the doctrine of the atonement. Students of theology are usually taught that although there is a consistent Christian teaching that 'Christ died for our sins' in order that we might be reconciled to God, there is no one settled way in which this doctrine is expressed. Instead, there are a variety of metaphors in the New Testament and the history of Christian thought. The effect of Christ's death has been described in many ways, including a sacrifice for sin, a victory over Satan, a redemption from sin and death, the supreme example of self-giving friendship, a substitutionary punishment for the sins of the world. That these are metaphorical ways of talking about Christ's death does not mean that they are no more than human inventions; such metaphors can be seen as part of the gift that God gives in Christ.[89]

Memory and faithfulness

As we have seen, one of the effects of downplaying the significance of doctrine and tradition is to weaken the historical character of Christianity. On the one hand there is the tendency (found in a

---

88 Ricoeur, *Freud and Philosophy*, p. 38.
89 This is argued persuasively in Colin Gunton, *The Actuality of Atonement: A Study of Metaphor, Rationality, and the Christian Tradition*, T & T Clark, 1989.

number of so-called contextual theologies) to assume that each generation is at liberty to develop its own creed and to make of Christianity whatever it finds relevant and helpful. On the other hand there is the attitude (widespread among evangelical Christians) that sees little more than the text of the Bible and the present generation of Christian readers and interpreters. In both cases Christianity ceases to be a movement through history. If this is true then we can no longer expect to discern the Holy Spirit at work in the story of Christian doctrine and its development. Polanyi, Gadamer and Ricoeur all resist this anti-historical tendency in modern thought. What is especially interesting about Ricoeur is that he is not content with emphasizing the role of tradition, history and narrative in human knowledge and understanding. They are central to being human. Ricoeur sees them as intimately related to who we are as human beings and to our standing as moral agents. We are born into a historical tradition and we are who we are through a network of influences and relationships. Ricoeur speaks of a 'familial discourse' in which we are nurtured. He means that we grow up sharing the collective memory of our group or society. It is through this collective memory that we have access to the past, not as a set of brute historical facts, but as the story of our community. Ricoeur suggests that testimony and witness are key to bringing this collective memory alive and giving it credibility. People need to be able to say, 'This is what happened'.

In Christian doctrine, we might say, we share in the collective memory of the Church. Doctrine is, in a sense, part of our familial discourse. But it needs to come alive through the testimony of those who confess to its truth at first hand. Just as Jewish people testify to their collective memory as they recite the Shema or take part in the Passover Seder, so Christians, as they recite the creeds, take part in liturgy or testify to their personal faith, bear witness to something that is shared with others and in which they have been nurtured and shaped. It would be possible, too, to speak of the different sub-traditions of Christian doctrine (for example Reformed, Orthodox, Charismatic) as constituting familial discourses, but we would need to ask the further question: how can they each be part of a wider tradition? How, for example, can Irish Catholics and

Protestants, who have learnt rather different forms of the Christian doctrinal tradition, recognize that the other speaks the same language of faith, even if it is in a different dialect?

It is time to draw some conclusions from this selective sampling of recent philosophy. The aim has been to show that, in contemporary thought, 'the devil doesn't have all the best tunes'. We have seen that modernity tends to reject doctrine as both redundant and irrational and that postmodernity accuses it of expressing oppressive abuses of power. However, these three authors – Polanyi, Gadamer and Ricoeur – different though they undoubtedly are, lead us in a different direction. In looking at the ways in which human beings acquire knowledge, apprehend truth and interpret texts, they argue for the centrality of community, tradition and trust. At the same time they assure us that these values, so central to the concept of Christian doctrine, are compatible with critical thinking, with dynamic development and with a passion for truth. It would be disastrous if Christianity succumbed to those intellectual voices that call for tradition and doctrine to be abandoned. To do so would not only involve turning our back on the gift that God has given in the handing on of the story of Jesus Christ, it would mean rejecting a central part of what it means to be human.

5

How Christian Doctrine Works

The forests of truth: models and metaphors of Christian doctrine

This book began by offering two points of entry into the topic of Christian doctrine. One was an account of how traditional doctrine came about in the historical events of the early Christian centuries. The other was a defence of the centrality of doctrine for the biblical and early Christian understanding of what it means to be Christian. The guiding image for that discussion was that of doctrine as one way in which Christ is given to the Church and handed on by the Church. In following chapters I showed how doctrine has come, in recent centuries, to be seen more as liability than as gift, and then presented some of the voices that might encourage us to take doctrine more seriously again. In this chapter I am returning to the place of doctrine in the life of the Church and asking how we might give an account of the role of doctrine and of its development and diversity.

The method I have chosen for this chapter uses models and metaphors as a way of pointing out the differences between a number of different approaches to the role of doctrine in the Church and the way doctrine develops through time.[90] Such methods are nothing new. The nineteenth and twentieth centuries saw the development of a number of these models. Many of them have an organic theme and, in fact, the vogue for developmental and evolutionary think-

---

90 Two classic uses of models in recent theology have been written by the American Catholic theologian Avery Dulles: *Models of the Church: A Critical Assessment of the Church in All its Aspects*, 2nd edn, Gill and Macmillan, 1988 and *Models of Revelation*, Gill and Macmillan, 1983. The latter has an interesting section on the use of models in theology. See also Ian Barbour, *Myths, Models and Paradigms*, SCM Press, 1974.

ing in the nineteenth century saw a burgeoning of such ideas. One from the nineteenth century, which I discuss below in a little more detail, uses the image of the oak tree that develops from an acorn as a model for the history of Christian doctrine. This has prompted me to develop and describe a series of models of how Christian doctrine works, all based, even if sometimes rather loosely, on the life of different trees. They do not, I hope, presume too much knowledge of natural history, but rather take images that are familiar, at least in western Europe. Such models are, of course, limited in their application, but they do allow the use of the imagination in exploring this complex area. Students with whom I have tried them out have usually worked with them creatively, pointing to aspects of them I had not considered, and even coming up with new models of their own. Put at its simplest, different ways of describing doctrine and its development correspond to different approaches to the growth of trees, or the relationships between them.

Model 1: the artificial Christmas tree

Doctrine as settled and unalterable fact

My first model is not a real tree at all! It stays in its box in the attic until it is time to bring it out. Every branch, needle and berry has been there since the day it was made, and no more will ever grow on it. With many artificial Christmas trees, even the lights and decorations are supplied as part of the original purchase. Similarly, Christian doctrine can be seen as complete from the very beginning, unchanging and unchangeable. Vincent of Lerins (a fifth-century monk and scholar) had a famous definition of doctrine that expresses this view: 'That which has been believed everywhere, by everyone, at all times'.

The advantages – and disadvantages – of artificial Christmas trees are obvious. On the one hand there are no falling needles and no need to buy a new tree every year. You can be confident that what you have will stay as it is. Shape, size and colour are consistent and reliable. But it is a dead thing, with none of the vitality, or variation, of a living tree. Similarly, there are both advantages and disadvantages to Vincent's definition. Such a static understanding of Christian doctrine does at least bear witness to the stability and consistency of Christianity. We teach the same gospel as John Wesley, Francis of Assisi, Augustine of Hippo and the apostle Paul. In this view of doctrine God is consistent and dependable, not at the mercy of the changing fashions of human thinking. After all, we are assured that 'Jesus Christ is the same yesterday, and today and forever'.[91] And there was a sense in the early Church of a 'rule of faith' that was passed from generation to generation and shared between local churches throughout the world.[92] Furthermore it is useful to be reminded, contrary to the ethos of our time, that innovation is not necessarily a good thing and that what is new need not be an improvement on what has been handed down. Yet on its own the artificial Christmas tree approach is highly problematic, for at least two reasons.

First, it is guilty of a theological pessimism that fails to allow the Spirit of God a continuing and creative role in the life and thinking of the Church. Because of this it leads ultimately to a lifeless version of Christian doctrine, with no dynamism and no place for the ongoing work of the Holy Spirit. In the early Church the resistance to innovation was balanced by a careful development of Christian teaching. Where this static model of doctrine has been adopted without such a balance it has tended to produce an arid fundamentalism. This has particularly been the case over the last 250 years, since the heyday of the European Enlightenment. As the scientific revolution of that period promoted an understanding of truth as objective fact, settled once and for all, so many Christians wanted their doctrine to have the same unchallengeable claim to truth that was associated with those sciences.[93] However, that early phase

---

91 Hebrews 13.8

92 For a brief summary of the sense of the universality of doctrine in the early centuries, see Jaroslav Pelikan, *The Christian Tradition: A History of the Development of Doctrine: Vol. 1, The Emergence of the Catholic Tradition (100–600)*, Chicago University Press, 1971, chapter 7, 'The Orthodox Consensus'.

93 Among the many descriptions of the debt that modern fundamentalism owes to Enlightenment thinking it is possible to recommend the work of the American evangelical scholar Mark Noll in *The Scandal of the Evangelical Mind*, Eerdmans, 1994. He emphasizes the way in which American fundamentalism was based on the didactic, rather than the sceptical and revolutionary strands in the European Enlightenment.

of scientific thinking – and the philosophy that lay behind it – has not survived, except perhaps in the popular imagination. As more recent discussion of science has made clear, truth is never a matter of plain, unalterable facts. There are developments and changes of perspectives within science and no area of human knowledge is simply a matter of settled truth.[94]

In practice, most Christian theologians and Christian communities have wanted to talk about some development of doctrine. Even Vincent of Lerins wanted to affirm that the Holy Spirit leads the Church to unfold more of the meaning of scripture over time.

Second, this approach plays fast and loose with the known history of Christian doctrine. Even the canon of scripture took time to develop; the earliest list of New Testament books exactly as we know them today does not occur until 367, in a letter of Athanasius, Bishop of Alexandria. Similarly, the statement of faith we know as the Nicene Creed belongs to the late fourth century and was the product of debate, dissension and development. John Henry Newman (1801–90), one of the first people to give a detailed account of how Christian doctrine develops, was scathing about Protestants who denounced what they saw as the 'Catholic' developments of eucharistic doctrine or Christian priesthood, without recognizing that doctrines they held to be central – for example, the doctrine of the Trinity – had arisen through a long process of development.

Model 2: the rampant cypress leylandii

Doctrine as unchecked and harmful growth

Not all models of doctrine are positive. It is possible to see the doctrines of the various churches, the creeds, and even (to some extent) the New Testament itself, as an unwarranted and aberrant development from the historical figure of Jesus and from primitive Christianity. In the story I told earlier of the neglect of the gift of doctrine, we saw that much of the opposition to doctrinal teaching

---

94 As we have already seen, the scientist and philosopher Michael Polanyi developed an account of the relationship between science and the fundamental commitments of those who practise it.

comes from within the Church itself. For this reason, I have chosen the all-too-common cypress leylandii tree to represent a model that is highly critical of the process by which Christian doctrines came to be accepted. Leylandii, of course, are those conifers that are usually planted as small and ornamental shrubs but rapidly grow to a great height. Before long, their foliage has blocked out all light and their roots have so drained the soil of water and nourishment that nothing else is likely to grow around them. So tall and impenetrable do they become that they are often the cause of animosity and even litigation between neighbours.

Is that what Christian doctrine has become? A tall hedge to block out the light and divide neighbours? The great German liberal theologian Adolf von Harnack (1851–1930) thought so. For all his immense knowledge of the history of Christian doctrine (and his five-volume work on the subject was superseded only in the 1980s), he saw it as more of a degenerative disease than a healthy development. His book *What is Christianity?* seeks to find the live kernel in the dry husk of Christian doctrine.[95] The gospel for Harnack is a plant which 'if it is not to run wild from exuberance, or be choked by its own dry leaves, the reformer must come who purifies it and brings it back to itself'.[96]

Christian doctrine had, Harnack believed, run very wild indeed. He wanted to trim the tree of doctrine with severe pruning. He thought, for example, that the doctrines about the person of Christ – his having both divine and human natures and his sharing in the very being of God – were the product of the influence of Greek thought on Christianity and did not truly reflect the message of Jesus or the New Testament. He believed that it was possible to express Christian teaching much more simply, especially if you focused on the teaching of Jesus rather than what had been taught about him. Summarizing his own understanding of Christianity in what became an influential series of lectures, he presented the two

---

95 Adolf von Harnack, *What is Christianity?*, New York, 1908. The original German title, *Das Wesen des Christentums*, which translates as *The Nature of Christianity*, is much more accurate, as Harnack's main point is not so much about the content of Christian teaching as about the character of its origins.

96 Harnack, *What is Christianity?*, p. 270.

(to him) simple facts of 'the fatherhood of God and the brother-hood of man (*sic*)'.

His description of the corruption of the pure gospel of Jesus into the structure and doctrine of the developed Christian Church remains persuasive for many contemporary critics of Christian doctrine. A recent book by the former Anglican Bishop of Edinburgh, Richard Holloway, asked the question: 'What remains of Christianity?'[97] Traditional Christianity, Holloway suggested, has, through its unhealthy moral prescriptions and its incredible doctrines, become discredited. What is needed is a salvage operation that rescues something life-affirming out of the wreckage of the tradition. Many feminist theologians have also been critical of the way in which the doctrinal tradition has developed, pointing to ways in which doctrine has been employed to reinforce the dominance of those in power.[98]

There is no doubt that those who share Harnack's and Holloway's views point to something important, indeed something that is well represented in the Christian theological tradition itself. One strand of Christian theology, sometimes called apophatic, or negative, theology emphasizes the limitations of all human speech about God. We can, it urges, speak more easily of what God is not, than of what God is. Though present in the early centuries, apophatic theology has been especially characteristic of the Eastern Orthodox tradition, through such teachers as Gregory Palamas (1296–1359). This tradition has been less confident of building theological systems than the dominant western tradition, and although it has set great store by faithfulness to the early ecumenical councils, there is an emphasis on the essential mystery and unknowable nature of God. The leaders of the Protestant Reformation also wanted to put a check on the growth of doctrine in the medieval Church. They

97 Richard Holloway, *Doubts and Loves: What is Left of Christianity*, Canongate, 2001.

98 See, for example, Rosemary Radford Ruether, *Women and Redemption*, SCM Press, 1998. Like her earlier *Sexism and God-Talk* (SCM Press, 1983), this book offers a critique of the way in which doctrine has developed to the disadvantage of women. Commenting on how salvation is expressed in the early centuries of the Christian Church, she says: 'Salvation does not liberate women from domination here on earth, but teaches them to redouble their submission to their earthly lords' (p. 77).

sought to test the teaching of the Church by referring it back to scripture and to the earliest Christian writers. More recently, Karl Barth (1886–1968) – often thought of as a doctrinally conservative theologian – began his *Church Dogmatics* with the insistence that 'Christian language must be investigated as to its conformity to Christ'.[99] He saw a need for the Church, in every generation, to reread the scriptures and test out its traditional doctrines for faithfulness to God's revelation in Christ.

But it is one thing to say (as surely we must) that the health of Christian doctrine requires testing, criticism and humility; it is quite another to insist (as do Harnack, Holloway and others) that the whole structure of Christian doctrine needs to be dismantled. The truth is that, taken as the sole approach to Christian doctrine, the cypress leylandii model is destructive and unproductive. It shares with the artificial Christmas tree model a theological pessimism about the work of the Holy Spirit in the life of the Church. Can the history of Christian reflection, of the Church's teaching and biblical interpretation, be reduced to a series of power struggles and cultural influences? Of course, both have been factors in the doctrinal life of the Church, and naming and identifying them as such has been as necessary as it has been painful. But belief in a God who is active in human history and the life of the Church should deter us from such radical cynicism. The Holy Spirit's dynamic power has been at work, motivating, guiding and correcting the Church's development of its teaching. Growth, in doctrine as in plants, can be a healthy response to the environment and to nourishment, and not necessarily an aberrant departure from its true nature.

Model 3: from tiny acorn to mighty oak

Doctrine as natural development

Both of my first two models are suspicious of any change in Christian doctrine from one period to another. The third model aims to take account of such change and suggests that it is compatible with divine continuity and Christian faithfulness. It is based on

---

99 Karl Barth, *Church Dogmatics*, I.1, Edinburgh, 1936, p. 14.

the observation of natural growth and organic development. The mature oak tree looks nothing like the tiny acorn out of which it once germinated. Nevertheless, it derives all of its potential from the genetic material in that seed and will grow in response to both that blueprint and the conditions that surround it. Over several hundred years the growth of the oak tree expresses, in root and branch, in leaf and internal chemistry, the unique characteristics of the cells out of which it first emerged. There is continuity through change. Indeed, the oak that remained as an acorn, or even as a seedling, would not be fulfilling its proper destiny.

Similarly, it is possible to claim that while the historic doctrinal creeds and traditional dogmatic formulae often appear very different from the words of the New Testament, they have developed in a natural way from the person of Jesus and the Biblical witness. They are a proper, indeed necessary, result of the historic growth and development of the Christian community and its teaching. Such organic metaphors, and others borrowed from the world of nature, are not uncommon and began to develop in some of the Catholic theology of the nineteenth century. Johann Möhler (1796–1838) developed this organic approach to the development of doctrine and church structure in his *Unity of the Church*, while John Henry Newman used it as one of several metaphors and models in his *Essay on the Development of Christian Doctrine*.[100] Newman's was a view largely framed within the nineteenth-century confidence in progress, the same confidence that was reflected in the work of Spencer, Darwin and Marx. For Newman, the development of individual species provided an analogy to the development of Christian doctrine.

> The fledged bird differs from the rudimentary form in the egg. The butterfly is the development, but not in any sense the image, of the grub . . . if beasts of prey were once in paradise, and fed on grass, they must have presented bodily phenomena very different from the structure of muscles, claws, teeth and viscera which now fit them for a carnivorous existence.[101]

---

100 John Henry Newman, *An Essay on the Development of Christian Doctrine*, 5th edition, London, 1890.
101 Newman, *Essay on the Development of Christian Doctrine*, pp. 173f.

Newman, as a founder of the Anglican Oxford Movement and later as a convert to Roman Catholicism, had a high view of doctrine and was impatient of Protestant attempts to show that everything since the New Testament was a slide into excess. 'To be deep in history is to cease to be a Protestant' remains one of his most challenging conclusions.

The oak tree model of Christian doctrine helps to overcome some of the problems inherent in the approaches we saw in the artificial Christmas tree and cypress leylandii models, the one being largely static, the other largely destructive. Here is a view that can bring together change and continuity, faithfulness and maturity, in an account of Christian teaching. It also offers a way to test the faithfulness of a later development in doctrine to the origins of Christianity. An example will help to illustrate this point. In 325 the first Council of Nicaea met to discuss the doctrine of the person of Christ: could he be described in terms of divinity as 'one with the Father' or was he really a part of God's creation and only 'like the Father'? The Council wanted to affirm the divinity of Christ and did so through the use of the Greek word *homoousios*, meaning 'of one being'. To many (both in the fourth century and in more recent times) this seemed an unwarranted doctrinal innovation, putting at the centre of the Christian creed a word that was not found in scripture and had not been part of earliest Christian teaching. Modern Christians are often puzzled by the perceptible contrast between the Jesus of the Gospels, with his concrete teaching, his healing ministry and his death at the hands of the Roman authorities, and the seemingly abstract statements of later Christian doctrine. To these objections the supporters of Nicaea argued that the apparent innovation was needed in order to remain faithful to Christian teaching at a time when that teaching was under attack.[102] Throughout Christian history most have concurred with this view, seeing the Holy Spirit at work in the enquiry and

---

102 The story of this crucial period in the development of Christian doctrine is told in many standard textbooks as well as more specialist works. For example: J. N. D. Kelly, *Early Christian Doctrines*, 4th edition, London, 1968, chapter 9, 'The Nicene Crisis'; Jaroslav Pelikan, *The Emergence of the Catholic Tradition*, chapter 5, 'The Person of the God-Man'.

discernment of the fourth-century Christian leaders. Some more recent scholars have argued for a trajectory that leads from the New Testament to the Church's formal teaching. For example, N. T. Wright draws attention to the strong Christological claims implied by the Gospel portrait of Jesus.[103] Though different from the 'of one being with the Father' language of the later creeds, it is possible to tell a plausible story of development that links one to the other.

So here is a model of Christian doctrine that makes sense of some of the historical reality of change, asserts the presence of the Holy Spirit in the process of change, and provides some guidance for testing whether the doctrinal tradition is developing on the right lines. But it is still not a completely satisfactory way of picturing the reality of Christian doctrine. One problem is that it remains a highly linear model of doctrinal development – change is presented in the form of a single line of inevitable progress, and as having only one conclusion. It may account for differences in Christian teaching between, say, the time of Paul, the fourth century, the sixteenth and the twenty-first. What it does not do is account for the doctrinal diversity among Christians at any one point in time. It would, for example, mean that at the time of the European Reformation we would have to say that either the Protestant or the Roman Catholic version of Christian doctrine was the true development of the tradition, the genuine oak tree expressing the characteristics contained in the acorn. And, of course, even if we concluded that the Protestant version of Christian teaching was the correct one, we would be faced with the many forms – for instance Lutheran, Calvinist and Anabaptist – that version took. In contemporary Christianity we are faced with great diversity, not just of different denominational traditions and their particular teaching, but also doctrinal differences within churches and across different cultures. We need other models to help us appreciate how the Holy Spirit can lead us to creative difference as well as a common view.

---

103 N. T. Wright, *Jesus and the Victory of God*, SPCK, 1996, Part III, 'The Aims and Beliefs of Jesus'.

Model 4: the new graft on an old rootstock

Doctrine as response to a new situation

There are thousands of varieties of roses and more are produced each year as plant breeders seek out the characteristics they believe the market and climatic conditions require. Most are grown, like fruit trees, by grafting the new variety on to an existing rootstock. The rootstock provides the stability, the resistance to disease and the ability to absorb nutrients that are essential for healthy growth, while the grafted stem provides the blooms that delight the eye. There has to be compatibility between the rootstock and the new plant material – it is not possible to graft on something that is entirely alien. Yet for the new varieties there seems to be an unlimited diversity in colour, shape and scent.

This is quite suggestive of another model for Christian doctrine, one that sees it as an infinitely variable set of responses to the gospel of God's love in Christ. This model would still affirm the importance of the 'rootstock' of Christianity – though there will be disputes about how new insights and responses relate to the original teaching of Christianity. To refer back to my original description of doctrine as 'the gift of Christ', this model suggests that there can be any number of ways of 'gift-wrapping' the basic truth of the Christian gospel.

This approach has often been taken by Christians faced with the dramatic changes in European society over the last 200 years, and the associated challenge to traditional Christian doctrine. For Edward Schillebeeckx, a Roman Catholic theologian who has been a controversial figure within his own church, key Christian doctrines need to be re-expressed to take account of contemporary experience. His work often points to the way in which the Christian understanding of, for example, marriage or ordained ministry has been expressed in radically different ways in different periods of the Church's life – and claims that the contemporary Church should therefore not be afraid to offer new accounts of key teaching. His work on Christology drew particular criticism from the Sacred Congregation for the Doctrine of the Faith, the body that regulates doctrinal teaching in the Roman Catholic Church.

On the one hand Schillebeeckx[104] offers an account of the origins of the doctrine of the person of Christ, informed by recent biblical scholarship. On the other hand he tries to develop an account of what salvation means to the modern man or woman, which is different from what it meant to first-century people in the Middle East. What emerges is a new presentation of the doctrine of the person of Christ, grafted on to the rootstock of the biblical witness.

Similarly, writing to a friend from his Nazi prison cell, Dietrich Bonhoeffer (1906–45) developed an outline of a book he wanted to write after the war,[105] dealing with what he called 'a stocktaking of Christianity' and 'the real meaning of Christian faith'. Believing that Europe had lost its traditional religious basis, and that people now lived mostly without reference to God, Bonhoeffer looked for a new interpretation of biblical teaching and a 'religionless Christianity' based on Jesus Christ as 'the man for others'.

Another trend that uses this kind of a model is often called 'contextual theology'. How, it is asked, can Christianity be meaningful in an African setting, or among those seeking liberation in Latin America, or within a society with a Confucian outlook? Only, it is said, by adopting a form of Christianity (including a form of doctrinal teaching) that presents its basic truth in a culturally appropriate form.[106] In fact, what we call the doctrinal tradition may be a series of local forms which the gospel has taken in different circumstances.

I have suggested some of the merits of this model. It accounts for some of the diversity in Christian doctrine as it is found in different times and places, and between different traditions and groups. It emphasizes the need for any new expression of doctrine to be rooted in the scriptures and the ancient traditions of the Christian movement. Yet at the same time it raises questions of the truth of such new expressions. What are the limits of different varie-

---

104 Edward Schillebeeckx, *Jesus: An Experiment in Christology*, Collins, 1979; *Christ: The Christian Experience in the Modern World*, SCM Press, 1980.

105 Dietrich Bonhoeffer, *Letters and Papers from Prison*, SCM, 1971, pp. 380–3.

106 See, for example, Robert Schreiter, *Constructing Local Theologies*, Orbis, 1985.

ties that can be grafted on to the one stock? And can we easily tell whether one plant we are looking at shares the same root as another? The truth is that there are many forms of Christian expression that claim to be growing on the traditional root stock, but it is not always easy to establish that this is the case. Another problem with this model is that different grafted varieties become popular because of some fashionable characteristic (for example, the redness or scent of a rose, the sweetness of a fruit) rather than the basic qualities of their roots. As a model for doctrine this might encourage the idea that the religious equivalent of 'market forces' is all that is required to ensure which doctrines flourish and which are abandoned. Surely this is inadequate.

Model 5: The garden at the Chelsea Flower Show

Doctrine as freely chosen and creative

So far, our models have been based on particular plants and the way they grow. But what about the way in which plants relate to each other? Major flower and garden shows usually have specially designed gardens assembled in order to reflect the vision of the designer. Plants are gathered from many sources and are placed together just so long as the garden show is open. Once it closes they are dispersed, only to become part of new combinations that fit in with someone else's design. One might be a Japanese-style garden, another based on the theme of 'serenity', yet another on a combination of scents. This seems a good illustration of one aspect of the so-called postmodern culture: an emphasis on our human role as creators of meaning. History and nature, in this view, have no power to constrain the human imagination, which is itself the source of meaning. Individuals and groups are free to create new combinations of culture, architecture and ideas. One example would be music that brings together medieval plainsong, an Indian *raga*, Celtic folk music and electronic sounds. Another would be an office block with a mixture of architectural styles from the classical, gothic and modernist traditions.

Can Christian doctrine be treated in this way? Is it constrained by particular biblical concepts of God and by the accumulated tradition of Christian teaching, or do human beings adopt a much more creative role in relation to it? Can Christian doctrine be exactly what any individual or group want it to be? Sallie McFague, a contemporary eco-feminist theologian, argues for an approach to Christian doctrine that sees it primarily as a human construction, to be adapted, changed and rebuilt according to experience and need. Her approach to the language of Christian doctrine and theology is to see it as metaphorical rather than analogical.[107] If the metaphors of traditional doctrine (for example, the designation of God as 'Father', 'Son' and 'Holy Spirit') no longer resonate with our sense of human need, we are compelled to search for metaphors more appropriate for our experience (for example, 'Mother', 'Lover' and 'Friend'). The result (to change the metaphor for a moment) is a quilt constructed out of many squares of different fabric, rather than a rug in which a pattern is woven into a single article.

The popularity of McFague's approach to doctrine (and her more recent work has made the ecological crisis the central experience around which Christian metaphors need to be created and grouped) suggests that she has struck a chord with many who find traditional doctrine oppressive or irrelevant. But there are also problems with this way of construing Christianity. Perhaps the principal one is that it undermines the concept of doctrine as a shared understanding, based in some way on the revelation of God in Christ. If nothing is given in Christian faith (and the sense of 'givenness' was where this book began), it is more difficult to assert that doctrines refer to anything other than human needs and desires. Similarly, while McFague's approach does seek to account for variety in doctrine at any one time, it does not give us any grounds for judging between different doctrinal systems and may condemn us to live in different 'doctrinal gardens', unable to communicate with one another. The Chelsea Flower Show model certainly does not account for the development of doctrine through history, other than as the replacement of the outmoded and irrelevant by the fresh and immediate.

---

107 Sallie McFague, *Metaphorical Theology: Models of God in Religious Language*, Augsburg Fortress, 1982.

Although I have been critical of this model, there is an uncomfortable truth that most Christian groups or thinkers have exhibited more of the 'pick-and-mix' approach than we usually like to admit. For example, it is possible to see in John Wesley and the early Methodist movement an approach to doctrine that focuses on those doctrines that refer to personal salvation and holiness and neglects others (for example, those that deal with God's relationship to the wider creation). At the very least, this model should make all churches conscious of what leads them to give prominence to some doctrines, adapt others, and leave others in neglect.

Model 6: the field hedge

Doctrine as a diverse and hospitable environment

The models I have tried to describe all have important things to tell us about the way Christian doctrine works and how we should treat it. Some have been with us for a long time; others are more recent. It will have been clear that my sympathies lie more with those that stress continuity than with those that stress drastic breaks, but even those I find most uncongenial (the cypress leylandii and Chelsea Flower Show models) present necessary challenges. None of them, however, does justice to the diverse richness of Christian doctrine in history and in the contemporary Church. I want to offer a final model, not to replace the other perspectives I have given but to suggest aspects they fail to take into account.

The model I propose is based on an old field hedge, of the type that still exists around Britain despite the large numbers uprooted by modern farming practices. A hedge of this kind will have a number of species of trees and shrubs, appropriate for its environment. Probably it will have grown over several hundred years, but will have been managed during this time. Height and thickness will have been controlled by trimming and layering; gaps may have been created to allow access, some bushes will have been allowed to develop into full-sized trees. The result is a complex of trees and shrubs that, while they do not form an impenetrable barrier, act as a necessary boundary between fields, as a guard against soil erosion, and as a home for a great variety of species of animals and plants.

How would this provide a model for Christian doctrine? First, if this is an apt model, it will point to Christian doctrine as having deep historical roots, and intertwining branches. A hedge is, in effect, an ecological system – one in which each constituent part is interdependent and in which the whole has a life that depends on these relationships of interdependence. Removing one or more of the constituent parts – or introducing alien species – can have devastating consequences. Of course, it is important to emphasize that ecosystems are not static. Changes occur and species may rise and fall in significance. But ecosystems, we now realize, demand our respect. Cut down the hedge and soil may be eroded, songbirds will disappear and the landscape will become impoverished. An ecological model of Christian doctrine would remind us that truth is more complex than we are apt to recognize. Not only do the different areas of Christian doctrine interact with each other to form a living whole (there is, for example, no doctrine of redemption without a doctrine of creation), it is also true that the many different expressions of Christian doctrine, past and present, can be seen as interrelated and interdependent. Seen in this way, the doctrinal consensus of Chalcedon in 451, the decrees of the Council of Trent, the Reformed Confessions, and the declarations of churches committed to liberative justice, would all be necessary, like the different species in the field hedge.

This model can be related to recent debates about the nature of Christian doctrine. It has a certain amount in common with the cultural-linguistic model advocated by George Lindbeck,[108] with its emphasis on Christian doctrine as a living and developing complex.[109] While Lindbeck presents several useful insights through his model (he emphasizes, for example, the need for Christians to develop the skills needed to 'speak' the language of doctrine), there remains a certain arbitrariness about his understanding, with little

---

108 This is described in more detail in the next chapter.
109 George Lindbeck, *The Nature of Doctrine: Religion and Theology in a Post-Liberal Age*, Westminster John Knox, 1984.

sense as to how we can decide between one language (or cultural system) and another. In a later chapter, as I explore some of the historical and contemporary issues surrounding Christian doctrine, I will develop this ecological understanding of doctrine. It offers, I believe, a way of approaching doctrine that makes it neither a mere collection of propositions nor simply an account of human power struggles or religious experiences.

Second, it would suggest that Christian doctrine does mark out necessary boundaries. Hedges help to define space, they tell us whose field we are in. They do not, though, cut off the field from its surroundings: there is plenty of scope for interaction between the two. Christian doctrine, too, helps to define whether or not we are within the field of the Christian community. Without being an impermeable barrier that separates the Christian community off from all other ways of looking at the world, doctrine helps to define what is and what is not a Christian world-view.

Third, the hedge model expresses the generosity and hospitality of Christian doctrine. Hedges are places of richness and diversity. They serve the flourishing of the creatures that inhabit them. They give shelter and food; they are places where young are born and nurtured. A rich understanding of Christian doctrine encourages a concept of generous orthodoxy, an understanding of Christian doctrine that stresses its hospitality to different approaches and its tolerance of change, without removing the need for a sense of historical continuity or contemporary definition.

Finally, this model, alongside continuity, expresses change and management. Hedges work best when they have been around for a long time and have been managed with care and respect. Similarly, Christian doctrine works best when the Church appreciates its historical roots, but also looks to the careful and respectful development of structure. For John Henry Newman, 'chronic vigour' was one of the hallmarks of authentic development in Christian doctrine.[110]

---

110 Newman, *Essay on the Development of Christian Doctrine*.

Consequences

It is time to draw together some of the insights that have been gained through our explorations of the different tree and garden models for Christian doctrine – and to be more directly open about the understanding of doctrine that lies behind my evaluation of them. I realize that a number of key questions, including the way in which doctrine may or may not refer to a true state of affairs, have not been dealt with. That question will have to wait for a later chapter, though I am happy to affirm that doctrine should aim to teach what is truly revealed, though imperfectly grasped, through the gift of Christ. In the meantime I offer some general comments on the implications of my assessment of the models I have described.

First, Christian doctrine has as its aim the appropriate naming, by the Church, of the triune God whom it worships and serves. Its primary function is not the satisfaction of human curiosity, nor even the explanation of human experience. Rather it involves giving voice to that reality made known in creation, given to us in Jesus Christ and poured out through the Spirit. It is, in other words, a story-telling, a passing on of the gift that has called the Church into being. Through telling its story in doctrinal terms the Church seeks to tell the truth about God and about itself. My field hedge model tries to do justice to this sense of a shared narrative.

Second, doctrine is part of the life of the Christian people. It is not abstracted from it as a speculative system, nor imposed on it as an alien intellectual prison. On the contrary, it is intimately bound up with the Church's life of worship, its reading of scripture, its searching of creation for signs of God's action, and its life in the wider human community. Our journey with God and our turning towards the world *include* this naming, this handing over of the story. Because of this, and as I explain more fully in the next chapter, I cannot remain content with an account of Christian doctrine that describes it as essentially a second-order activity. Doctrine, in other words, is more than a stepping back from, a reflecting and commentating upon, the essential elements of the Church's life: worship, mission and service. There is a contemporary emphasis on orthopraxis (right action) as at least as strong a mark of Christian identity as orthodoxy (right teaching). This has much to commend it but it carries the danger that faithfulness to the apostolic faith may no longer be seen as intrinsic to the continuity of the Christian community.

Third, doctrine, having its origin in the living relationship between God and his Church, is itself a living thing. As such it will not always require exactly the same words – though it is appropriate that some words and formulae are given a special place as enduring marks of the Church's relationship with its Lord, and as the source of new doctrinal expressions. Its 'chronic vigour' is expressed in the Church's living commitment to the retelling of its doctrinal story and the handing over of the gift of Christ.

Fourth, an ecological understanding of doctrine implies that it will be nearest the truth in its wholeness and furthest away when it is analysed into minute particulars. This is another way of saying that Christian doctrine is ultimately a narrative whole. As such it cannot be broken down without some distortion. The doctrine of the Church cannot be described without Christology; neither can salvation be understood in a way that does not depend on creation and eschatology. The exposition of doctrine does require some specialization, but it cannot simply imitate the overspecialized analysis of secular sciences.

Finally, doctrine is historical. It follows from the last two points that doctrine is not only the telling of a story – the gifting to others of the gift we have received – it also has a story itself. To tell the story of the Spirit's way with the Church is, at least in part, to tell the story of the Church's doctrinal integrity, and failure. Attempts at such story-telling (the Roman Catholic dogma of infallibility is perhaps the best-known example) have obvious difficulties, but a witness to the Spirit's work in this aspect of the Church's life is still needed. Affirming the story of doctrine as *our* story also means taking responsibility for our history, especially those failures of charity and those abuses of doctrine as a tool of oppression that weigh heavy on the Christian conscience.

6

Recovering the Gift: The Rehabilitation of Doctrine in Recent Theology

In Chapter 4, I presented three leading thinkers of the twentieth century whose work suggests that tradition, faith and a common commitment to a story of human life are not necessarily the enemy of critical and honest thinking. Indeed, there is good reason to believe that they are all essential to a proper development of human thought and to the apprehension of truth. But we need to move on. How can we make the leap from the rather abstract reflections of philosophers to a theology that expresses a renewed sense of the importance of Christian doctrine? Is there evidence that Christian theologians and the Christian churches have taken account of these critics of modernity and produced more robust accounts of Christian doctrine?

Theology and doctrine: an uneasy relationship

The most famous Protestant theologian of the twentieth century, Karl Barth, was determined to do just that. Writing most of his theology before Polanyi, Gadamer and Ricoeur were well known, he challenged the prevalent view that doctrine could be described only in terms of its human origins and effects. He was determined to restore Christian doctrine to its right duty of speaking about God. Writing of his theological development at the beginning of World War Two, he said that:

I had to learn that Christian doctrine, if it is to merit its name and if it is to build up the Christian church in the world as she must needs be built up, has to be exclusively and conclusively the doctrine of Jesus Christ – of Jesus Christ as the living Word of God spoken to us men. If I look back from this point on my earlier studies, I may well ask myself how it ever came about that I did not learn this much sooner and accordingly speak it out. How slow is man, above all when the most important things are at stake![111]

It is no accident that Barth's great work, *Church Dogmatics*,[112] begins with a discussion of the doctrine of the Trinity. For him, Christian doctrine expresses in the life of the Church the revelation of God in Christ. Barth's challenge to modernity's doctrinal scepticism has not always been taken seriously in the Anglo-Saxon world. But in the last 25 years that has certainly happened – though not always in ways that Barth would have recognized.

In this chapter I intend to set out the way in which some recent theologians have developed a more positive account of Christian doctrine and its place in the life of the Church than the story of modernity might lead us to expect. Their methods vary, but they are united in wanting the contemporary Church to adopt a robust understanding of doctrine and to be more confident in proclaiming it against the strident secular philosophies of the age. It is worth noting that this approach marks something of a change of tack, at least for academic theology in Britain and the USA. We can illustrate that change by comparing some of the more influential theologians and theological books of the 1960s and 1970s with their counterparts in the 1980s and since.

Two of the great figures of British theology during this period were Maurice Wiles (1923–2005) and John Macquarrie (1919–2007). Both were appointed to influential chairs at Oxford in 1970:

---

111 Karl Barth, 'How my Mind has Changed', *The Christian Century*, September 1939.

112 Begun in the 1930s and running to four multi-volume parts, *Church Dogmatics* was still unfinished at Barth's death in 1968.

Wiles as Regius Professor of Divinity and Macquarrie (originally a Scottish Presbyterian) as Lady Margaret Professor. Neither, it has to be said, were at the very radical edge of theological thinking. Both regarded themselves as faithful servants of their church (the Church of England), sitting on its Doctrine Commission for several years. It is also fair to say that both developed a more sympathetic approach to traditional Christian doctrine in their later years. But their really influential work illustrates the difficulty that traditional doctrine presented for so many in the mainstream of theological thinking.

Wiles' *The Making of Christian Doctrine* (1967) was an account of the early development of key Christian doctrines. He argued that the way doctrine developed in the early Church was influenced by a range of motives (including philosophical reasoning and political expediency as well as religious devotion) and that it provided trajectories for Christian reflection rather than a settled system of beliefs. In *The Remaking of Christian Doctrine* (1974) he answered his own call (made at the end of *The Making of Christian Doctrine*) for a 'doctrinal revolution', and suggested the necessity of developing revised approaches to a number of key doctrines in the light of scientific development. More radical still was the contribution Wiles made to *The Myth of God Incarnate*, the controversial 1977 collection of essays edited by the philosopher of religion John Hick.[113] Here he went further than asking whether the doctrinal consensus of the early Church, however appropriate for its own time, needed contemporary revision; he argued that the classical doctrine of the incarnation might be seen as a mythological interpretation of the event of Jesus, not as the revealed truth about him.

Whereas Wiles was by training a historical theologian, an expert in the patristic sources of Christian doctrine, John Macquarrie was grounded in philosophical theology and a specialist in existentialism. His *Principles of Christian Theology* (1966) was written when the author was teaching at Union Seminary, New York,

---

113 Hick, John (ed.), *The Myth of God Incarnate*, SCM Press, 1977. Wiles' two essays (by no means the most radical in the book) are 'Christianity Without Incarnation' and 'Myth in Theology'.

before he was appointed to Oxford. This book was the first serious work of systematic theology that I read and I have to confess that it had a profound influence on me. It provides a rich grounding in the intellectual foundations of Christian theology and remains a stimulating and challenging read. However, it approaches the great themes of Christian doctrine only after a long journey through the disciplines of anthropology and the philosophy of language. Macquarrie had no wish to part company with the long tradition of Christian theology, but he was clearly nervous of the difficulties traditional doctrinal language posed for modern minds. The contemporary theologian must, he concluded:

> penetrate behind the possibly quaint and even alien language of the dogma to the existential issues that agitated the Church at the time of the dogma's formulation, and appropriate for our own time and in our own language the essential insight which the dogma sought to express.[114]

In other words, traditional doctrine and traditional doctrinal language simply will not do for the present.

If Wiles and Macquarrie were two of the most influential British theologians in this period, what was happening across the Atlantic in the United States? I will mention just two of the many possible candidates for inclusion in this brief survey.

Paul Tillich was originally part of the same circle of talented (and argumentative) German-speaking theologians that included Karl Barth and Emil Brunner. With the arrival of the Nazi regime in Germany he emigrated to New York, where he became a professor at Union Seminary. It is no exaggeration to say that within the traditional Protestant churches of the United States, no one was more influential than Tillich in setting the theological agenda for the second half of the twentieth century. No less a figure than Martin Luther King Jr, for instance, earned his PhD for work on Tillich's understanding of God, while Tillich's sermon 'You are

---

114 John Macquarrie, *Principles of Christian Theology*, SCM Press, 1966, p. 165.

Accepted'[115] must be the most frequently read of its time. Tillich's three-volume *Systematic Theology* was published between 1951 and 1963, and it is fair to say that in spite of the title it is not always systematic and frequently deviates from the subject of theology. What is consistent in this long work is a determination to look behind traditional language about the doctrines of Christian faith (for example God, Christ, humanity, sin, salvation) in order to find the deep human concerns they are intended to address. Tillich, it turns out, does not think that doctrine (or 'dogma') is a helpful word to use in modern theology:

> With the complete union of church and state after Constantine, the doctrinal laws of the church also became civil laws of the state, and the heretic was considered a criminal. The destructive consequences of this situation, the demonic activities of states and churches, Catholic as well as Protestant, against theological honesty and scientific autonomy have discredited the words 'dogma' and 'dogmatics' to such a degree that it is hardly possible to re-establish their genuine meaning . . . it makes use of the term 'dogmatics' impossible. 'Systematic theology', embracing apologetics, dogmatics and ethics, seems to be the adequate term.[116]

Tillich's exposition of theology is heavily slanted towards existentialist thought and the analysis of human culture. The result is a tendency to reduce the claims of Christian doctrines from being statements about God to being symbols that express human 'ultimate concern'. Take, for example, the doctrine of the Trinity. Tillich gives a total of only 13 pages to a discussion of what he calls 'Trinitarian symbolism'. As this is around the middle of the third volume of his *Systematic Theology*, it is clear that for him 'Trinity' is not the defining Christian doctrine of God. Instead, it

---

115 The sermon was published as part of the collection *The Shaking of the Foundations* (1948). It is easily accessible on the web <www.religion-online.org/showchapter.asp?title=378&C=84> and provides a very accessible introduction to Tillich's style.

116 Paul Tillich, *Systematic Theology*, Vol. 1, University of Chicago Press, 1951, pp. 36f.

turns out to be an intriguing but incomplete account of the human experience of the divine. He says in conclusion:

> The doctrine of the Trinity is not closed. It can be neither discarded nor accepted in its traditional form. It must be kept open in order to fulfil its original function – to express in embracing symbols the self-manifestation of Divine Life to man.[117]

The other American figure I want to cite is the Methodist theologian John Cobb. Cobb, whose teaching career was spent mostly at Claremont Divinity School, California, is one of the best-known practitioners of process theology. This approach to theology takes as its foundation the philosophy of A. N. Whitehead. Process theology is panentheist; that is, it sees God containing the universe and being influenced by it. The God of process thought shares with the rest of reality the same qualities of change and development, experience and suffering. Some traditional doctrines, such as the omnipotence of God, are obviously a problem within this framework. Others, such as creation or incarnation, have to get a radical reworking if they are to survive. The movement has been highly influential in North America, though less so elsewhere. Cobb's many books attempt to show that process thought is best equipped to help Christian theology meet the challenges of contemporary society: challenges such as environmental disaster and religious pluralism. He is by no means at the extreme edge of American theology; he has remained a major player in the life of the United Methodist Church and has worked on its doctrinal and theological standards. Yet he is clearly unhappy with the idea of Christian doctrine as it has been traditionally conceived:

> Finally, under the influence of the creed become dogma, Jesus became a sacred object. In relation to him no ordinary critical questions or inquiries were allowed. He could not be viewed as a historical figure or compared with others. He was to be worshiped rather than studied or even encountered. He was absolute,

---

117 Paul Tillich, *Systematic Theology*, Vol. 3, University of Chicago Press, 1963, p. 314.

and the religion that worshiped him was therefore the absolute religion. All other religions were supposed to be essentially misdirected or false.

This statement is harshly formulated. It is not intended as a comprehensive characterization of the Christianity of any period. It intends only to describe the tendency at work in Christianity in so far as it became a religion of dogma, whose key dogma was the Chalcedonian creed. It is intended to place in bold relief the contrast of the actual effects of this creed with the concerns that led to its formulation.[118]

Both Tillich and Cobb, then, see theological difficulties in trying to sustain traditional Christian doctrine in the contemporary world. Their strategy for dealing with this problem has two aspects: it is a matter of either looking behind the classical doctrines (to discover what came before them) or searching beneath them (to locate those experiences and concerns that gave rise to them). Both reflect a trend that had been typical of Protestant theology since the early nineteenth century.[119]

In their own day Wiles and Macquarrie, Tillich and Cobb[120] were hardly the most radical of theologians. Since the 1970s, Christian theology has produced several new movements (feminism and postcolonialism being two of the most important) that have, in their turn, expressed profound dissatisfaction with the doctrinal heritage of Christianity.

This consensus makes the theology described in the coming pages all the more surprising. Each theologian I mention wants to question the kind of philosophical, historical and cultural assumptions that have made their predecessors so negative about receiving classical Christian doctrine as a gift that hands on Christ to new

---

118 John Cobb, *Christ in a Pluralist Age*, Westminster Press, 1975, chapter 10.

119 For an excellent summary of this trend in Protestant thought (as well as its Catholic counterparts), see 'The Legacy of Modernity And the New Challenges of Historical Theology', in James Livingston and Francis Schüssler Fiorenza, *Modern Christian Thought: The Twentieth Century*, Fortress, 2006.

120 At the point of writing, John Cobb is the only one of this quartet still living. Though he remains active in theology, it is not unfair to see his main influence in the previous generation.

generations. If they have anything in common it is the conviction that the truth and purpose of Christian doctrine lies in its relationship to Christian practice. The first of them, George Lindbeck, requires an extended discussion. This is partly because his ideas have been around the longest (since the early 1980s) and partly because they have been so widely discussed. But mostly it is because Lindbeck invites us to pay particular attention to these questions: 'What is the nature and purpose of doctrine?' and 'How, in practice, do we go about learning doctrine and living it out?'

Doctrine as a set of rules: George Lindbeck and *The Nature of Doctrine*

Lindbeck is a veteran American Lutheran theologian, deeply committed to ecumenical theology, but also interested in the questions around which this book is shaped. He is usually thought of as a representative of the 'Yale School' or as a 'post-liberal'. This is an approach to theology that seeks to challenge the dominant liberal theological tradition without retreating into naive conservatism. Names associated with this movement would include Lindbeck's deceased colleague Hans Frei, as well as William Placher, Stanley Hauerwas and Gregory Jones. They share a concern for the particularity of Christian language and an unwillingness to allow criteria from other disciplines (such as philosophy or social science) to dictate what theologians can or cannot say. They tend to emphasize theology as a task of the Church, one that is undertaken within the Christian community and is accountable to that community. And they have a strong emphasis on narrative (the story of the Bible and the story told in Christian teaching) as the best way of expressing Christian truth.

Lindbeck's 1984 book *The Nature of Doctrine*,[121] though a mere 140 pages, proved to be one of the most discussed works of theology of the decade, with more than one journal giving over a special issue to articles commenting on and critiquing his proposals.

---

121 George Lindbeck, *The Nature of Doctrine: Religion and Theology in a Postliberal Age*, Westminster John Knox, 1984.

Most critical readers (and with hindsight, I suspect, even Lindbeck himself) have reservations about the rather crude way the book divides up approaches to doctrine and would want to refine Lindbeck's own suggestions. Nevertheless, it remains one of the most important approaches to doctrine in recent years, and a valuable way of entering the discussion of doctrine's place in the contemporary world. One reason is that it represents an early attempt to write theology in a way that is both faithful to the Christian community and sensitive to that shift in thinking that we have come to call postmodernism. Lindbeck's own concern is ecumenical: he wants to find a way to talk about doctrine that will enable different Christian traditions to make progress towards unity. This progress, he believes, can happen only if doctrine is both taken seriously and is subject to discussion and development.

According to Lindbeck, there are three ways in which the role of doctrine is currently understood within Christianity.[122] The first, which Lindbeck calls the 'cognitive-propositional' approach, treats doctrines as a set of statements that claim to describe the truth – what is, as it were, out there. According to this approach, doctrines provide objective information about the object of religious belief; they are straightforward descriptions of the way things are. The doctrine of the resurrection, for example, means precisely what it says: Jesus was dead and buried, but then was raised. His risen life is a fact about the universe independent of human thinking and experience. Doctrines that describe the way things are in this direct sense cannot be altered without denying their truth. It makes it very difficult to bring about reconciliation between different doctrinal systems if, for instance, the traditional Catholic dogmas concerning Mary and the Protestant repudiations of them are both regarded as fixed, rival descriptions of reality. Cognitive-propositionalism, says Lindbeck, is an approach characteristic of most traditional Protestant and Catholic teaching and provides the orthodoxies that vie for supremacy in inter-Christian or inter-religious conflict. It is problematic because it is wedded to a correspondent theory of truth – the view that statements are true only when they

---

122 Lindbeck focuses on Christian doctrine, but he sees his proposals as equally descriptive of other religious traditions.

are an exact description of the reality to which they refer. Such a view also runs into trouble because the power of human language to express the nature of God must be, to say the least, very limited. So, for Lindbeck, the cognitive-propositional standpoint, still characteristic of much Christian thinking, has both theoretical and practical drawbacks.

A second, more recent, way of looking at doctrine is to see it as symbolic of inner human feelings rather than as information about objective truth. Lindbeck gives this the name 'experiential-expressivism', a description that suggests doctrine is a way of giving voice to religious experience or expressing our orientation to existence. In other words, to speak of the resurrection of Christ might be, in an experiential-expressive approach to doctrine, to express an inner experience of the life and salvation identified with Jesus, or even a vague sense that there is hope in the midst of despair.[123] For Lindbeck, this is the view of doctrine characteristic of Liberal theology, from Schleiermacher onwards, and of the work of many recent Roman Catholic theologians such as David Tracy.

In passing, it is worth noticing that while a cognitive-propositional understanding may be characteristic of contemporary fundamentalism, those evangelical movements inspired by the pietist tradition are as likely to appear experiential-expressive in their use of doctrine. In any case, it is experiential-expressivism that Lindbeck finds most objectionable and that he is most determined to oppose. Why is he so keen to resist this understanding of doctrine, given that the experiential-expressive understanding does not have the problems associated with the cognitive-propositional version? After all, if doctrinal language provides us with symbolic truth, then there is nothing to prevent us from seeing different Christian doctrinal traditions, or even entirely different religious systems, as no more than different ways of using specific language to express some universal aspect of human experience. The doctrinal statements of Eastern Orthodoxy, Presbyterianism and Pentecostals could then

---

123 Rudolf Bultmann is perhaps the most famous representative of this approach to the resurrection in the twentieth century, though he is by no means unique. A more accessible version is found in the popular book by Harry Williams, *True Resurrection*, Mitchell Beazley, 1972.

be seen as complementary rather than contradictory; the Hindu and Buddhist doctrine of dharma might be merely a different way of talking about what Catholic teaching refers to as 'natural law'. But this, says Lindbeck, is to seek doctrinal reconciliation by robbing doctrines of any real significance, any independence from the experience and attitudes of those who articulate them. And it is to get the whole business of experience and language the wrong way round. The assumption of experiential-expressivism is that human beings first have an experience (for example, wonder, loss, dependency or joy) and then they try to figure out some way of giving linguistic and symbolic expression to it. In fact, says Lindbeck (and here he is drawing on the work of anthropologists such as Clifford Geertz as well as linguistic philosophers like Wittgenstein and Austin), it tends to be the other way round. The linguistic and symbolic world in which we are formed tends to shape the kinds of experiences that we have.

To take a rather obvious example: I am currently living in Belfast, a city whose Christian population is traditionally split along Protestant–Catholic lines. These communities (though they share more doctrinal language than they often acknowledge) tend to employ different forms of faith language and to speak of different kinds of faith experience. For those outside this society it comes as a shock to find people still talking about Protestantism and Catholicism as different religions rather than as different but closely related manifestations of Christianity. But it is not simply that everyone has the same kind of religious experience and then casts around for a form of words that lies conveniently to hand; rather, different faith languages and the symbols associated with them open people up to different kinds of experience. For instance, someone raised in the Shankill Road area of Belfast and nurtured within a Protestant community would be very unlikely to report an experience of a vision of the Blessed Virgin Mary! Their cultural and linguistic background will have encouraged different forms of religious experience – perhaps a dramatic personal conversion. Again, Lindbeck finds both theoretical and practical reasons to question a widely held understanding of doctrine.

Here, then, are two common approaches to the nature of doctrine, both highly problematic. In practice, as Lindbeck acknowledges, they are often combined, especially in contemporary Catholic theology.

If both cognitive-propositional and experiential-expressive ways of interpreting doctrine are so deficient, what is the alternative? The one that Lindbeck wants to commend he calls 'cultural-linguistic'. We do best, he says, if we think of doctrines not as literal descriptions of reality 'out there', nor as expressions of inner human experience, but as something rather like the grammar that sets out the rules for speaking the Christian language. Now grammatical rules tend to be one of two kinds. Either they describe the way a language should be used (every English sentence needs a main verb, avoid split infinitives) or they illustrate its use (for example, *amo, amas, amat* as a pattern for Latin verbs). But reciting the rules is not the same as using the language in everyday speech or formal writing, even though it may be an important part of becoming a proficient user of the language. These rules are therefore a second-order form of language. That means that they are guidelines for speaking well, and not the speech itself.

Similarly, for Lindbeck doctrines are second-order statements that reflect on how we should properly speak, think, pray and live within the Christian community. They should not be mistaken for the substance of religion itself. This may sound as if doctrine for Lindbeck is rather arbitrary, and that he has little sympathy with its traditional claim to represent vital truths. In a sense, Lindbeck pleads guilty to this charge. While doctrinal statements may turn out to be true, in the sense of corresponding directly with reality, that is not their essential function; they are not first-order propositions. Their claim to be true is primarily a matter of coherence with the other elements of Christian faith. They make a claim to what Lindbeck calls 'intrasystematic truth' rather than 'ontological truth'. In other words, they are true because they fit in properly with what it is to be Christian.

This is partly because Christian doctrine tends to be expressed in a narrative form, as in the Nicene Creed, rather than as a series of propositions and axioms. To take an example that Lindbeck himself uses, it is part of Christian doctrine that Jesus is called

'Messiah'. Why is that name so important? Partly, says Lindbeck, because it provides a reason for taking the Old and New Testaments together (as prophecy and fulfilment) as the Christian scriptures – a matter of practical importance in Christian worship, spirituality and ethics.[124] From this doctrinal rule of the Messiahship of Jesus, it would follow that Marcion, the early Christian teacher who argued that the Church should abandon the Old Testament because it represented a different God from the God of Jesus, can properly be called a heretic. Why? Because his proposals (and practice) are inconsistent with the affirmation of Jesus as the Messiah, the anointed one of Israel.

It is important to note, though, that Lindbeck does not altogether disregard the idea that doctrines express a more public truth. He suggests that the link is in the performance of Christian doctrine in the life of the Church. It is in their use that these doctrines acquire what he calls 'propositional force'. I think that what Lindbeck is saying is this: the truth of Christian doctrine does not rest on some universally agreed standard of objective truth. Its truth cannot be adequately judged from outside the Christian community, but only by those who are committed to the practice of Christian truth.

The value of Lindbeck's work is twofold. First, he provides us with an excellent way in to a serious discussion about the way doctrine works. To work through Lindbeck's discussion of his three categories is not necessarily to agree with them. But it does mean that the reader is forced to think quite hard about something they may have previously taken for granted. Rather more valuable, I think, is Lindbeck's insistence on the relationship between doctrine and practice. He is sure that right doctrine makes a practical difference; it is neither idle speculation nor intellectual oppression. In putting the emphasis on the way in which doctrinal language is used in the life of the Church he is reminding us that doctrine is embedded in the worship, witness and mission of the Christian community. Being Christian, he insists, demands that we are nurtured into a community's practice and develop the skills appropriate to a life lived according to the community's governing story of

---

124 Lindbeck, *Nature of Doctrine*, p. 81.

God's grace. As the letter to the Colossians says: 'As you therefore have received Christ Jesus the Lord, continue to live your lives in him, rooted and built up in him, and established in the faith, just as you were taught, abounding in thanksgiving.'[125]

I have given a lot of attention to Lindbeck's proposals and it will be clear that I find them valuable and constructive. But are there any problems with the approach he is suggesting? There certainly are, and they have been mercilessly exposed by critics and commentators. I will mention just three.

The first is that Lindbeck sets up 'straw men' in his description of cognitive-propositional and experiential-expressive approaches to doctrine. It really is not the case that everyone who believes that doctrine provides us with true statements and genuine knowledge is a crude fundamentalist. It is quite consistent to believe that doctrines have propositional force and add to our understanding of the way things are and at the same time accept that they are not a perfect fit with the reality they describe. The principle of analogy is what Christian theology has traditionally used when it wants to affirm that its language says something meaningful about God without the arrogance of claiming that it has God perfectly sorted out. It is not classical Christian doctrine, but the prevalent culture of modernity that has insisted that language either refers directly and totally to its object, or is a completely arbitrary, hit-and-miss affair.[126] Lindbeck has critiqued a caricature of the traditional approach to doctrinal language and failed to take account of the nuanced way in which it can be employed. Similarly, Lindbeck's criticism of experiential-expressivism, though it scores a number of hits, fails to acknowledge the close connection between religious belief and religious experience. You do not have to believe that doctrine is a mere function of religious experience to recognize the important link between the two. The role of Christian worship in developing doctrinal language would certainly support this.

The second problem concerns the relationship between Church

---

125 Colossians 2.6–7.
126 This is very well explained in William Placher's *The Domestication of Transcendence: How Modern Thinking about God Went Wrong*, Westminster John Knox, 1999.

and doctrine. As Kevin Vanhoozer has pointed out, referring doctrinal statements to the practice of the Church may not be enough of a step away from referring them to the lives and experiences of individuals. Doctrines need to be about God and God's action before they are about human action, even the action of the Christian community. Lindbeck clearly wants to free doctrine from the liberal tendency to equate it with human experience, but he is in danger of equating it with certain types of human action. Doctrine has to be able to criticize the Church and call it to account, and not simply describe the way it behaves.

Finally, there is something inadequate about picturing doctrines as rules. It can be argued that Christian doctrine needs to have a firm base in reality if it is to form a genuinely practical basis for Christian living. In other words, it can only function effectively as the second-order discourse that provides the grammar of Christian speech and action if it is also rooted in the first-order discourse of Christian belief. Lindbeck needs some of what he rejects in order to sustain the thing he wants to affirm.

Ellen Charry and the pastoral role of Christian doctrine

Doctrine makes no sense except in relation to Christian practice. If that is Lindbeck's main claim, it has been taken up by a number of other recent theologians. Our next theologian is perhaps rather more accessible than Lindbeck. Ellen Charry, who teaches at Princeton Seminary, is from a Jewish background and has embraced Christianity as a convert. She provides a distinctive overview of the history of Christian doctrine and its exposition in *By the Renewing of Your Minds*.[127] This is a tour de force, a survey that takes us from Matthew's Gospel and Paul's letters in the New Testament right through to John Calvin in the sixteenth century. Charry develops what she calls an 'aretological'[128] understanding of doctrine. By this she means that the pastoral function

---

127 Ellen Charry, *By the Renewing of Your Minds: The Pastoral Function of Christian Doctrine*, Oxford University Press, 1997.
128 From the Greek word for excellence.

of Christian doctrine is the promotion of Christian excellence, of lives that are renewed and shaped through contact with the truth that is God's nature and action.

> Christian doctrines aim to be good for us by forming or reforming our character; they aim to be salutary. They aim to form excellent persons with God as the model, and this in a quite literal sense, not as metaphors pointing to universal truths of human experience that lie beyond the events themselves.[129]

Charry pursues this thesis by taking key expositors of Christian doctrine, from the New Testament to the Reformation, and showing that the way in which each of them shaped their 'handing on of Christ' was determined by their conviction that God was seeking our transformation. So, for example, she compares the teaching of Thomas Aquinas and Julian of Norwich[130] on the doctrine of the cross. The main difference between them, she claims, is not that one was the extraordinarily well-trained professor of theology and the other a more down-to-earth woman. It is more to do with the different visions of Christian excellence they wanted to promote and the different audiences they addressed. For Aquinas the cross shows God redeeming us as he tempers justified divine anger with the supreme love of Christ's sacrifice. In this way he teaches us how we should live in such a way that our own anger (much less justified than God's) is dominated by loving, self-sacrificing mercy. Julian, on the other hand, sees the cross as evidence that in God there is ultimately no anger, but only love. When we understand the doctrine of the cross we begin to see ourselves not as disgusting wretches, worthy only of punishment and destruction, but as the objects of God's gracious and suffering love.

Charry ends her book with a plea for what she calls 'sapiential theology', a theology focused on the wisdom and goodness of

---

129 Charry, *By the Renewing of Your Minds*, p. vii.

130 Julian of Norwich was a fourteenth-century mystic who lived as an anchorite in a cell attached to a Norwich church. She is best known for *The Revelations of Divine Love*, in which she meditates on visions she received while seriously ill as a young woman.

God. For that to happen, she argues, Christians (especially those charged with theological reflection and doctrinal teaching) need to renew the ancient connection between what is true and what is good. Just as it is detrimental to Christianity if in its doctrine the head is separated from the heart, so it is disastrous if the rest of the body is separated from the hands and feet; if, in other words, Christian belief is separated from the practices that express the doctrine's truth.

This is a timely and important vision, and it reminds us of the necessity of revisiting the history of Christian reflection on the doctrines of the Church's faith. Going right back to our early consideration of Paul's admonition to the Corinthians about the manner of their celebration of the Lord's Supper, we can notice precisely this concern to connect the handing on of the truth of Christ with the Christian conduct that lives out that truth. The Corinthians are getting it wrong because their worship is a denial of the truth about Jesus and (because they practise gluttony for themselves and exclusion of others) a distortion of pastoral practice.

Ellen Charry is surely right in her call for this reading of the Christian doctrinal tradition and the reasons why handing it on is so important. But I want to sound a note of caution. While making the connection between Christian doctrinal truth and our Christian practice of human life is vital, it does not exhaust the purpose of Christian doctrine. If it did we would be in danger of reducing the nature and action of God to a human scale. As I try to show in the final chapter, doctrine is not simply about improving human life, ordering the language and life of the Church or giving a coherent account of Christian truth-claims to an unbelieving world. It is all these things, but it is also giving glory to God for who God is, not just for what God does for us. Naming truthfully the God we worship and adore will have a transforming effect on us, but only if the focus is on God rather than on ourselves.

Kevin Vanhoozer and the drama of doctrine[131]

Vanhoozer, an American Presbyterian theologian who has special-
ized in theological engagement with Paul Ricoeur and with postmodern interpretation, proposes a rather different approach to
doctrine from Lindbeck's cultural-linguistic proposal. He writes
from an evangelical, Reformed perspective and wants to argue for a
much more central place for scripture in doctrine. In fact, he wants
to rehabilitate the Reformation slogan of *sola scriptura* (scripture
alone) and show that it has a place in a contemporary, sophisticated reflection on the nature of Christian doctrine. This is not
quite as conservative as it sounds. For Vanhoozer, *sola scriptura*
does not mean turning our backs on the long history of Christian
tradition, nor ignoring the many ways in which human reason op-
erates in Christian thinking. What he means is that the Bible forms
the equivalent of the script for a play. Just as the text of *Romeo
and Juliet* must be the basis for all performances of Shakespeare's
play of that name, and nothing can replace the text as the norm
by which performances are judged, so the Bible is the basis for the
drama of Christian action. It is the supreme revelation of God's
dramatic acts in and towards creation. That means that Christian
action must be an acting out of the dramatic script provided by
scripture and must be guided by the direction of the Holy Spirit.
How, then, does doctrine fit in? The clue is in the word 'performance', which Vanhoozer rightly identifies both as a key term in
postmodern writing and as an apt way of describing the biblical
God. He puts it like this:

> The medium of drama is *acting*: people doing things with their
> words and bodies. The Christian theo-drama, similarly, is
> about God doing things with words, the Word and the Word's
> body . . .
> . . . *doctrine directs the church to participate rightly in the
> drama of redemption . . . one can participate rightly only if one
> has an adequate understanding of what the drama is about . . .*

---

131 Kevin Vanhoozer, *The Drama of Doctrine*, Westminster John Knox,
2005.

Doctrine proceeds from an authoritative script and gives di-
rection as to how individuals and the church can participate
fittingly in the drama of redemption.[132]

Vanhoozer calls his approach 'canonical-linguistic', to distinguish it
from Lindbeck's. He wants to see doctrine grounded more securely
than either a focus on tradition (Whose tradition do we follow?
he asks) or a focus on church practice (too flawed and variable to
be a helpful guide). Only the 'givenness' of the Bible can provide a
sound foundation: 'given' in both the senses we identified in Chapter 2. At the same time he wants to share Lindbeck's (and Charry's)
concern for the practical, living dimension of Christian doctrine.
He finds this is in the concept of 'theo-drama', a term associated
with the great Catholic theologian Hans Urs von Balthasar.[133]

All this means that, for Vanhoozer, Christian doctrine provides the rules for turning the theo-drama of scripture into the
performance of Christian life and community. They provide, he
says, 'a rule for storied practice'. This has four dimensions. First,
doctrine functions as a social demarcator (that is, it marks out
the cast of the dramatic performance). Second, it is generated by
and then interprets the Christian narrative; it is, to use the terms I
have developed, a handing on of Christ. Third, it is an interpretation of experience; it is not simply an expression of experience but
an interpretation that relates it to God's action. Finally, doctrine
makes truth-claims; it genuinely refers to a truth that is more than
internal coherence of Christian language. In this way Vanhoozer
hopes to take the positive insight of Lindbeck – that doctrine relates strongly to the lived practice of Christianity – while providing
a richer and more scriptural account of its basis and function.

Vanhoozer's project is much more complex than I can describe
in a few paragraphs; he uses the concept of performance to illum-
inate many aspects of the interpretation of scripture, the teach-

---

132 Vanhoozer, *The Drama of Doctrine*, pp. 77f. (Vanhoozer's emphasis).

133 Hans Urs von Balthasar (1905–88), who died the day before he was to have
been made a cardinal, produced a quantity of work to rival that of Karl Barth.
Among his last books was the series *Theo-Drama: Theological Dramatic Theory*,
published in five volumes (Ignatius Press, 1988).

ing of doctrine and the life of the Christian community. Perhaps most valuable is the way in which a dramatic account of doctrine helps to move away from a static, lifeless approach to the Bible or Christian teaching. It is central to his understanding that God the Holy Spirit is the director who enables the Christian community to perform the biblical drama and make it their own. Through their teaching of doctrine, theologians act as 'dramaturge', that is, they help the Christian 'performers' to shape their dramatic participation in God's action. This means that each situation calls for a fresh performance and a fresh interpretation of the biblical script. It will take care and sensitivity as well as creativity to discern what kind of performance is fitting, and what is not. The contrasting Christian 'performances' in Nazi Germany or apartheid South Africa provide stark examples of where such discernment is needed.

Here is another useful (if sometimes rather abstract) account of doctrine as embedded in Christian practice. Vanhoozer, like Charry and Lindbeck, helps us to see the embodied nature of Christian truth. Handing it on is about developing (or challenging) a performance tradition and not simply the teaching of items of belief. Yet Vanhoozer overplays the *sola scriptura* theme. The result is a mistrust of the doctrinal tradition of Christianity and an overemphasis on the text of scripture at the expense of the divine drama to which it bears witness. A Protestant obsession with the Word means insufficient attention to the sacramental drama of the Church's life, a point I come back to in the next chapter.

John Milbank and radical orthodoxy

Few recent developments in the understanding of Christian doctrine have been as forcibly expressed, or as controversial, as the movement known as 'radical orthodoxy'.[134] It has to be said at the outset that the writing of the group of people most associated with it (John Milbank, Catherine Pickstock and Graham Ward) is

---

134 A website that reflects the 'radical orthodoxy' approach is that of the Centre for Theology and Philosophy at Nottingham University, where John Milbank is currently Professor of Theology: <www.theologyphilosophycentre.co.uk/>.

challenging, to say the least. The reader is expected to move swiftly across the whole western tradition of theology and philosophy, as well as to be familiar with recent social thinking. The tone is highly intellectual and the writing largely reflects a background in the tradition of high-church, socially critical, Anglicanism.

Nevertheless, this movement represents an important attempt to define the place of Christian doctrine and theology in the context of postmodernity. *Radical Orthodoxy*,[135] the programmatic book edited by Milbank, Pickstock and Ward, begins with a series of essays on the relationship between Christian theology and its philosophical critics before going on to explore a number of fashionable postmodern concerns, particularly those around the erotic and aesthetic.

Why 'radical' and why 'orthodox'? The group claim to be orthodox in the sense of affirming the traditional Christian doctrines developed in the early centuries and summarized in the historic creeds. They also see orthodoxy as Christian belief in its richest sense, something that extends beyond the narrower confessions of Protestantism and Catholicism. Like the 'new theologians' of the last century whose work led to the Second Vatican Council, they see a future for Christian belief and practice only as it draws from the deep well of its past. The 'radical' part of the title is rather more complex. At one, very basic level, radical orthodoxy aims to restore the link between contemporary Christian belief and its roots in the patristic and medieval periods. But it wants to be radical in two other senses as well. It attempts to criticize contemporary society, especially its endemic violence, on the basis of this original Christian vision, but (in case this seems an entirely reactionary movement) it also seeks to rethink the Christian tradition and to ask whether there are aspects of Christian faith that have never been fully or properly expressed. It is nothing if not ambitious!

The programme may be overambitious, the writing often opaque and the claims sometimes arrogant, but there are still at least three reasons why radical orthodoxy in general, and John Milbank in

135 John Milbank, Catherine Pickstock, Graham Ward (eds), *Radical Orthodoxy*, Routledge, 1999.

particular, has something important to say about the place of doctrine in contemporary Christianity.

The first is the suggestion that we need to pay close attention to the way in which Christian theology has colluded with the forces that have been undermining it. Milbank's first substantial work, *Theology and Social Theory: Beyond Secular Reason*,[136] as well as some of his more recent essays,[137] takes the reader on a historical journey from the birth of modernity to contemporary secular liberalism. In doing so Milbank visits some of the trends we noticed in Chapter 3, trends which we saw eroding the place of doctrine in the societies of western Europe and America. In fact he sees the problems with systematic Christian thought beginning much earlier than the sixteenth century, putting the blame on developments in the later middle ages when thinkers like Duns Scotus were already challenging the link between faith and reason and developing a less subtle approach to the way in which language and meaning relate to each other. While classic Christianity invited shared belief in a common tradition, without necessarily being able to understand it fully and rationally, western modernity, he believes, has seduced us into looking for certainty in the human mind when no such certainty is possible. In this situation we need to open ourselves again to a God who is revealed in Christian tradition. In *Theology and Social Theory* Milbank does not so much dwell on doctrine itself, but rather looks at what happens when society (and the Church) exchanges a view of human life based on Christian teaching for one based on secular models. Milbank is particularly interested in the development of the discipline of the sociology of religion and its attempt to define religion within the terms set by a secular society. His conclusion is that recent theology has absorbed, in an uncritical way, many of the assumptions of modern social theory. He argues that these assumptions are not only inherently anti-Christian, they are also inherently violent. Christianity has a

---

136 John Milbank, *Theology and Social Theory: Beyond Secular Reason*, Blackwell, 1990.

137 For example, 'Faith, Reason and Imagination: The Study of Theology and Philosophy in the 21st Century', a programmatic address posted on the Centre for Theology and Philosophy website.

duty to reassert its own tradition of a story that links the origin of human society with the peaceful kingdom of Christ.

A second aspect of radical orthodoxy that makes it helpful for this study is its emphasis on the concept of gift and giving. In light of the fact that one premise of this book is that doctrine comes to us as gift, it is significant that gift is a recurring theme in Milbank's own theology. He attacks the contemporary assumption that gifts are either utterly free private gestures or really contracts in disguise, little more than a way of making sure that we keep on the right side of others. Instead, he wants to identify with what he sees as a biblical understanding of gift as a 'purified gift exchange'. Key Christian doctrines can be thought of as spelling out this gift. In creation, for example, God's gift is so absolute that it actually brings into being the ones to whom the gift is given.

A third and final aspect of radical orthodoxy that should claim our attention is a link with the other recent authors whose work we have visited in this chapter. Milbank and his colleagues highlight the necessary link between what Christians believe and their practical vision for society. He says:

> Christian belief belongs to Christian practice, and it sustains its affirmations about God and creation only by repeating and enacting a metanarrative about how God speaks in the world in order to redeem it. In elaborating the metanarrative of a counter-historical interruption of history, one elaborates also a distinctive practice, a counter-ethics, embodying a social ontology, an account of duty and virtue, and an ineffable element of aesthetic 'idiom', which cannot be dealt with in the style of theoretical theology.[138]

Any reader who finds Milbank's prose difficult to follow will be in good company! But for all the complexity and difficulty, something important is going on here. We have seen that Lindbeck keeps his doctrinal eye focused on the practice of the Church and does not want to be distracted by too much attention to the ques-

---

138 Milbank, *Theology and Social Theory*, pp. 422f.

tion, 'Is it really true?' Charry, we saw, is most concerned with the pastoral outcome of doctrines, how they form people into saints, while Vanhoozer has tried to return us to confidence in the Bible as divine revelation. The originality of radical orthodoxy is to insist, in a way that has become unfashionable during the modern era, on the metaphysical basis of Christian doctrine. In other words, it is grounded in the rational structure of all existence. Far from demonizing the Platonic influence on Christian theology, radical orthodoxy suggests that we return to the kind of Christian appropriation of that tradition that we meet in Augustine.

Here, then, are some of the voices in contemporary theology that point to a renewal of confidence in the Christian doctrinal tradition. Perhaps the main difference between these writers and the theologians I described at the beginning of the chapter is that the earlier generation saw inherited doctrine as a problem for a Church seeking to engage with the challenge of modernity. These more recent theologians have seen the question from the other end: how can a doctrinally aware Christianity become part of the solution for a modernity that is in crisis?

7

Using the Gift: Doctrinal Communities

In a previous chapter we looked at Christian doctrine as an aspect of life in the Christian community, a kind of grammar for speaking the Christian language, or rules for Christian living. I have suggested that this is a very helpful approach, however much it needs to be supplemented with a more robust understanding of doctrine's claim to truth. My desire to be rather more affirmative of the objective nature of doctrine is linked to a central concern with handing on the gift that has been given in Christ. Churches, and the Christian lives that take place within and through them, are shaped by doctrine whether they acknowledge (or indeed like) it or not. The particular form in which the Christian faith is handed on (which doctrines are emphasized at the expense of others, which side is taken in disputed doctrinal debates) affects the way in which churches worship, organize themselves and understand their mission. On the other hand, the form that a church takes will undoubtedly affect the way in which Christian teaching is handed on to new members and to following generations.

I want to look now at how, in the lives of real Christian communities, the tradition of handing on the gospel actually happens. What is the form of the doctrinal giving and receiving that takes place? How does it shape these churches and the Christians who are part of them? To respond to these questions we need to get closer to real examples of historical Christian groups. Too often studies of doctrine are concerned only with the grand sweep of Christian tradition and its transmission down the centuries, and not with the specific churches within which the doctrine lives. On the other hand, studies of church life often downplay the content of teaching and the details of belief in favour of an emphasis on structural elements, such as forms of leadership and patterns of membership.

In what follows I am looking at examples of what can be called 'doctrinal communities'. By that I mean that a church (in the form of a local congregation, a religious order, or a missionary enterprise) is a place where doctrine is taught and learned as part of becoming a Christian in a Christian community. It is a means of handing on Christ. A good analogy would be with a culture. We grow up as English, Irish, Maori, Xhosa and so on by being part of a family and community structure in which certain values, stories, ways of speaking and rules of behaviour are embodied. In some ways we become part of a culture by living as a member of it. But in many societies there is also a conscious attempt to teach those who are growing up the explicit world-view of the culture and to help them internalize it. This is the equivalent of catechesis (or whatever name it is called by) in a church community. In teaching and articulating the doctrines of Christianity, Christian churches are making explicit the deep implicit realities of Christianity. It is commonly said that it takes a village to raise a child; we might also say that it takes a church to raise a Christian.

Of course, it would not be difficult to find examples from Christian history of communities that have established themselves (and often split over and over again) around particular doctrinal understanding. But that has not been the norm. More often, Christian communities have been concerned with handing on the faith they themselves had received. Here, then, are some examples from Christian history of communities that receive and hand over doctrinal tradition.

Early Christian martyrs as communities of witness

In Chapter 2, I pointed out that those who handed over Christian scriptures to the Roman authorities in order to avoid persecution were called *traditores*; they came to be seen (and often saw themselves) as betraying their faith, symbolically handing Christ over for destruction. In doing so they were denying the teaching they had received as catechumens and which they had confessed at their baptism. But of course theirs was not the only response to the sporadic persecution of Christianity in the early centuries. Many neither disavowed their faith nor fled from persecution. Instead they embraced the role of confessor or martyr, 'handing on Christ' through the witness of their testimony in court and their unflinching acceptance of torture and even death. Such people (who could be men or women, lay or ordained, slave or free citizen) did not regard themselves as the passive victims of an unjust regime. Rather they, and their wider Christian community, saw themselves as the embodiment of the victory of Christian truth against pagan error and state power. The stories of martyrs (their own account of their suffering and the stories of their deaths) became key elements in the instruction and inspiration of new Christians. The sites of their burial became places of commemoration and worship; the well-known saying, 'The blood of the martyrs is the seed of the Church' was both figuratively and literally true.

Nowhere was the role of the martyrs in handing on Christ so prominent as in the North African city of Carthage. Here, in 202 CE, a young noblewoman, Perpetua, together with a number of companions, was arraigned before the Roman Consul for disobeying the edict of Emperor Septimus Severus that all must make sacrifice for the emperor's health. Thrown into prison to await death in the arena, they formed a tightly knit community of faith, sustained by spiritual visions and by the support of fellow Christians. When they were offered a free choice of a final meal, instead of the customary gladiator's feast, they opted for the Christian love-feast that included the Eucharist. It has to be admitted that the account of their deaths (involving attacks from various animals and a *coup de grâce* from a gladiator's sword) is a difficult read for those with modern sensibilities. In the popular description of the event, Perpetua and her friends come across as active participants in their own deaths rather than as merely the passive victims of the violence of others. But this is an important aspect of the role of martyrdom. These were people who believed themselves to be contending for the truth of Christianity against the forces that would destroy it. Their belief in the truth of Christian doctrine implied that the spectacle in the arena, far from being the ritual drama of Roman religious supremacy, was in fact the dramatic enactment of the truth of Christian belief.

Writing of martyrdom as a kind of public liturgy, Robin Young says: 'These deaths came about as the consequence of the necessity to give testimony to Jesus and what he represented, namely, the kingdom of God and its arrival, to which all earthly powers would be submitted.'[139] Just as the Christian community bore private witness to its key teachings through the celebration of the Eucharist, martyrdom provided a public witness that was a dramatic liturgy of Christian affirmation.

Tertullian's famous letter to a group of Christians waiting for the death sentence to be applied may well have been addressed to Perpetua's group. It speaks of the Holy Spirit training Christians for endurance and combat. Those who are to give their lives as martyrs are nurtured for their role by belonging to communities and groups where key Christian doctrines are shared.

It is, of course, true that most martyrs did not busy themselves with developing doctrinal treatises, though the second-century Ignatius of Antioch is a very notable exception. But they were often groups of people who formed what I am calling doctrinal communities. That is, they were very conscious of their role in handing on through word and action the Christian truth they had received in their Christian training and in the worship of the Church. So we see groups of martyrs receiving doctrinal teaching through the letters that are sent to them in prison (exhortations to martyrs becomes a well-known genre of Christian writing in the second and third centuries) and we see them confessing Christian teaching – handing on the gift of Christ – through their testimony before the courts and their steadfastness before torturer, wild beast, spectators and executioner.

---

139 Robin Darling Young, *In Procession Before the World: Martyrdom as Public Liturgy in Early Christianity*, the Pere Marquette Lecture in Theology, 2001, (Marquette University Press, 2001, p. 9.

The Dominicans as doctrinal communities: an example drawn from a medieval religious order

The later middle ages was a far more fertile period of Christian thought and practice than many (especially Protestants) give it credit for. The thirteenth to fifteenth centuries saw the development of the great European universities and the introduction of the 'new learning' as the works of Aristotle were translated from Arabic (where they had inspired Muslim philosophy) into Latin. Of the many forms of Christian community that were founded during these centuries, perhaps the most innovative were the orders of mendicant friars, so-called because they sought to live on free donations rather than through the financial control of land and property. The four main orders of friars, the Franciscans, Dominicans, Carmelites and Augustinians, were all founded in the thirteenth century. They provided a new vision of Christian community and ministry, just at the time when many urban centres were outstripping the traditional parish system. In today's terms they were 'fresh expressions' of Church.

The Dominicans were founded by Dominic (c.1170–1221), born in Spain but devoted for several years to a preaching ministry that sought to counter the Albigensian (Cathar) heresy in Languedoc. This sect, especially strong in the Pyrenees, had a theology reminiscent of the Gnostics and even had some similarities with the Manichees, the group in which Augustine had been involved before his conversion to Christianity. Their doctrines emphasized the opposition between the darkness and evil of the physical world and the light and truth of the spirit. For them there were two gods, the creator of the Old Testament and a higher god who sent Jesus as a messenger to reclaim the spirit lost in the material world. The elite among the Cathars (the name comes from the Greek word for purity) had a reputation for extreme aesceticism and holiness, and one of the problems faced by the Catholic Church was the poor reputation of many of its own clergy. Dominic's insight was to see the need for a strategy that combined an intellectual challenge to the dualist doctrines of the Cathars with a form of Christian life that rivalled their moral purity. As he began to gather a small group of companions around him, the defining features of his community emerged: preaching the true doctrines of Christianity through culturally appropriate and intellectually convincing argument, while also expressing those same doctrines through a life of simplicity and holiness.

From this simple beginning the Dominicans developed into a worldwide religious order. Like other orders it has a strong sense of family, of being a community that (like the Church of which it is a part) extends through centuries and is united across the continents. Whereas some religious orders have been suspicious of too much emphasis on the intellectual aspect of Christianity, the Dominicans have consistently supplied the Church with some of its most able and influential theologians and teachers of doctrine. In the thirteenth century, Albert the Great and (especially) Thomas Aquinas (1225–74) set a standard for theological excellence that continues to be a benchmark for the Catholic exposition of Christian doctrine. It might be said that Thomas' great *Summa Theologica* was an outstanding attempt to give intellectually able Christians an initiation into the doctrines of their religion. As he says in his preface:

> Because the doctor of Catholic truth ought not only to teach the proficient, but also to instruct beginners (according to the Apostle: As unto little ones in Christ, I gave you milk to drink, not meat – 1 Corinthians 3.1–2), we purpose in this book to treat of whatever belongs to the Christian religion, in such a way as may tend to the instruction of beginners ... we shall try, by God's help, to set forth whatever is included in this sacred doctrine as briefly and clearly as the matter itself may allow.[140]

It is true that those who have attempted to read this enormous work have usually found it rather more demanding and meaty than Thomas' modest introduction suggests, but that does not take away from his intention, which was the sustenance of a community that

---

140 Thomas Aquinas, *Summa Theologica*. The passage, as quoted, is from the online edition at <www.newadvent.org/summa/>. The most user-friendly book edition is the concise translation by Timothy McDermott, Christian Classics, 1989.

needed to be nourished and built up by faithful and contemporary teaching.

More recently, the Dominican order has continued to nurture the vocation to a life in community of a kind that articulates and hands on Christian truth in a challenging way. They have not always been thanked by their church for doing so. It was Dominican theologians, by and large, whose work provided the intellectual background to the Second Vatican Council. In communities of learning, for example the one at Le Saulchoir, members of the order looked at ways of making the Christian tradition more pastorally alive. This involved them sharing in what has come to be called the *ressourcement* movement. By looking at the foundations of Christian teaching in the Bible and Christian history, they found ways of challenging the stagnation of doctrine and life within the contemporary Church. Chief among them was the French Dominican Yves Congar (1904–95), who was made a cardinal shortly before his death and belatedly honoured as one of the great teachers of Christian theology in the twentieth century. Yet for much of his career, as he combined detailed research into the doctrines of the Church and Holy Spirit with a passionate commitment for the unity and compassion of the Church, he was forbidden to teach and regarded with great suspicion by the Roman Catholic authorities. Only with the pontificate of John XXIII and the calling of Vatican II did his work come into its own. He was able to help his Church make the link between *ressourcement* – the renewed awareness of its doctrinal sources – and *aggiornamento*, the renewal of its life, worship and witness. As well as being communities of prayer and service, the Dominicans provide one of the best examples of a network of doctrinal community.

An example from nineteenth-century Methodism

It may seem a strange leap from the eight centuries of Dominican teaching and preaching on Christian doctrine to the much more recent tradition of Methodism, but there are genuine similarities in the pattern of communal life and doctrine. While Methodism shares in the heritage of Pietism, with its emphasis on the inner experience of faith, the witness of the Holy Spirit and the journey towards Christian perfection, it has not been without a sense of the importance of doctrinal teaching. The first recorded question at an annual Methodist Conference was, 'What shall we teach?' and early Methodists were often caught up in doctrinal controversy, particularly over the tension between John Wesley's Arminianism and the strict Calvinism of some of his fellow evangelicals. As a 'grass roots' movement, early Methodism centred on small groups: the Society, the Class and the Band.

These were essentially schools for Christian nurture, communities dedicated to the development of what John Wesley called 'practical religion' and 'scriptural holiness'. These communities, often led by people who had little standing in the wider world and little formal education, were certainly concerned with encouraging the greatest possible spiritual fervour, with developing that experience of God which one contemporary author has called 'orthopathy' (right-feeling). They were dedicated, too, to the cause of 'scriptural holiness', developing a purity of life and character that would bear witness to the inner working of the Spirit. But the spiritual intensity and moral earnestness was accompanied by a distinct understanding of Christian truth, of what mattered most about the nature of God, the work of Christ and the path of salvation. These were also, I would argue, doctrinal communities, concerned to hand on a commonly held understanding of the Christian faith. The reading, discussion and exposition of scripture; the corpus of Wesleyan hymns written and sung both to warm the heart and to shape the understanding; the reading and dissemination of innumerable tracts and magazines, often summarizing classical expositions of the Christian faith: all these were part of a communal life that taught the language and practice of Christian faith.

A good example of this kind of doctrinal community is found in the early nineteenth-century rural Methodism of Lincolnshire and the effect it had on one of its outstanding products: the missionary John Hunt.[141] John Hunt's is a story that perfectly expresses the route of self-improvement which Methodism provided

---

141 The best account of Hunt's life is currently Andrew Thornley, *The Inheritance of Hope: John Hunt, Apostle of Fiji*, University of the South Pacific, 2000.

for many working-class people in the nineteenth century. Born in 1812, Hunt was a teenage farm-hand when he started attending a Methodist band meeting. In this school for holiness he gradually came to the evangelical commitment and spiritual assurance that was the hallmark of Wesleyan Methodism. A certain way of being Christian was handed on to him through the life and teaching of these groups. His account of a dramatic moment of personal commitment and joy, in the chapel of the tiny village of Thorpe-on-the-Hill, fits the pattern familiar to anyone acquainted with this Christian tradition. But this was never, even for the working-class teenager, simply a matter of religion fulfilling desperate emotional needs or steadying the urges of adolescent behaviour. Hunt was recognized as someone who had the potential, as a preacher and leader, to articulate the faith that was expressed in this fervent prayer and holy living.

A combination of supportive congregations and devout employers gave him an education and the confidence to preach. In 1835 he found himself in the newly established Methodist Theological Institute in Hoxton, north-east London. If the village chapel, with its classes and bands, combined an obvious aim of spiritual development, with a less explicit strand of doctrinal education, the Institute intended to provide students for Methodist ministry with a firm basis in Christian teaching within a community that was no less concerned with sustaining the personal holiness and spiritual fervour of its students. Sent to a new missionary District in the Pacific Islands of Fiji, Hunt had a remarkably energetic ministry of ten years before dying, worn down by hard work and a harsh climate, in 1848.

He left behind a growing number of Christian communities, and Methodism would soon become the dominant Christian tradition in the islands. He was the prime translator for the Fijian Bible; he wrote and translated hymns; he preached innumerable sermons. He was, in other words, a pivotal figure in the handing on of the gift of Christ from one culture to another. The new Fijian churches were modelled on those he had left in England, with classes for those who were baptized and committed and with the same focus on spiritual growth and holiness of life. And just as in the chapels of rural England, there was a keen stress on getting doctrine right, with a Bible translation that brought the words of scripture into the heart of Fijian culture, and preaching that would make clear the content of Christian belief and the particular emphasis placed on it by Methodism.

Alongside the churches, Hunt set up theological institutes to train Fijians as teachers and preachers, anxious that Christianity be shared as a vision of truth as well as an emotional experience and as a hope for material prosperity. His lectures on doctrine were accompanied by a new catechism in Fijian. If in today's post-colonial climate we find something either comical or sinister in this early Victorian planting of a European vision of education, it is as well to remember that Hunt refused to patronize his converts by sheltering them from the demanding aspects of Christian belief. Just as he had been drawn from a poorly educated, working-class background to a position of spiritual and doctrinal leadership, he saw no reason why recent Pacific Island converts could not do the same.

One of his particular concerns in doctrine was that distinctive (and to many rather puzzling) teaching of John Wesley on Christian perfection. Hunt's *Letters on Entire Sanctification* were written to a fellow missionary, published after his death, and became a mainstay of Methodist reading on the topic in the late nineteenth century. Not only had he succeeded in developing communities of doctrinal teaching in Fiji, he had made a significant contribution to the continuing doctrinal life of Methodism in Britain.

Some of his final words were in the form of a deathbed confession of faith that was surely meant to instruct those he was leaving behind, handing over the gift of Christ, as it were, with his last breath:

> Christ is our wisdom to enlighten us, our righteousness to atone for us, our sanctification to cleanse us, our redemption to deliver us from a great many temptations and he will deliver us in death and bring us to glory. These are the views that sustain me now.

Here is the evangelical version of Christian doctrine in a nutshell.

An example from the twentieth century: Christianity and Nazism

One of the most remarkable stories from that shameful period of European history that produced the Shoah (the Nazi-driven Jewish Holocaust) is of the small, impoverished French village of Le Chambon and its courageous decision to offer protection to about 5,000 Jews. In the midst of Vichy France, a puppet regime under the domination of the Nazis, this was a community that openly defied the order to hand over Jews for transportation to the camps set up for their destruction. There were elaborate strategies to keep the refugees out of sight when the authorities were searching for them. Not just a few brave individuals, but a whole local church shared in a resourceful but dangerous expression of their faith. *Lest Innocent Blood be Shed* tells this story from the perspective of a Jewish author inspired to find out the source of this bravery.[142] It is essentially the account of a somewhat dour Protestant congregation in an inhospitable environment and the remarkable pastor who came to be its minister in 1934 and remained there throughout the ensuing war. The pastor was Andre Trocmé, a passionate advocate of non-violence, whose teaching and example helped a whole community to understand what it means to live out the content of Christian belief.

There are interesting and perhaps surprising parallels between Trocmé and the better-known Dietrich Bonhoeffer. Bonhoeffer was the outstanding young German theologian who became part of the Christian resistance to Hitler and was executed by the Nazi state at Flossenbürg concentration camp on the eve of its defeat in 1945. Although he was only 39 when he was killed, Bonhoeffer left behind a substantial body of work, including theology, devotional writing and poetry. His life and work have inspired innumerable books, articles and even films. Like Bonhoeffer, Trocmé came from a privileged background, though (unlike Bonhoeffer) he turned away from it and lived in austerity for much of his life. Like Bon-

---

142 The story of Andre Trocmé and his ministry in Le Chambon is told in Philip Hallie, *Lest Innocent Blood be Shed: The Story of the Village of Le Chambon and How Goodness Happened There*, Harper and Row, 1979.

hoeffer he studied in Union Seminary, New York, and had an early commitment to peace, though unlike Bonhoeffer, he never came to believe that a Christian might have to take up the sword in a situation that was spiralling downwards into an abyss of evil.

There is another parallel. Both Bonhoeffer and Trocmé were committed to the expression of Christian truth through life in community. For Bonhoeffer that is illustrated primarily in the illegal theological seminary he developed at Finkenwalde in the 1930s, and in the writings on Christian community that he produced at that time. For Trocmé, it was found in the development of a congregation and community that was as open to the Jewish stranger as it was open to the person of Christ.

At first sight, Trocmé seems an unlikely advocate of doctrinal Christianity. His emphasis appears to be on its ethical dimension: the Jubilee teaching of the Old Testament, the teaching and example of Jesus, the vision of the kingdom of God. I suspect that he would have been impatient of some of the classic doctrinal debates and rarely thought of himself as a doctrinal preacher. Yet as a student Trocmé had been deeply dissatisfied with the American version of the social gospel, seeing it as an activism without sufficient spiritual and theological basis. His published writings show a concern for the content of the Christian gospel and the way it is shared: 'every time the church doubts its election, every time it plays down the "scandal of particularity", its capacity to witness to the gospel also diminishes'.[143]

What is clear is that Trocmé did not wait until the persecution of Jews began in France and then organize a congregational discussion on what should be done. He had prepared the congregation through years of teaching and worship, so that when the challenge came the response was a natural outcome of Christian faith rather than an agonized response to a particular ethical dilemma. Here was a church that through its teaching and its understanding of Christian truth became adept at the performance of Christian faith. In the same way, Dietrich Bonhoeffer, though he could be very critical of inherited ways of talking about Christian belief,

---

143 Andre Trocmé, *Jesus and the Nonviolent Revolution*, expanded edition, Orbis, 2003, p. 5.

was in no doubt that the Church was to be a living expression of the person of Christ. As Christ was understood to be 'the man for others', so the Church was to live out its doctrine in terms of service.

Learning from doctrinal communities

The four examples sketched above seem a rather disparate group. Only one, the Dominican order, seems to be concerned with doctrine in an obvious way. In others the teaching of doctrine appears a secondary consideration, at most. But I hope it has become clear that all of them represent a convincing picture of the relationship between doctrine and the practice of Christian community. There are a few things to be said by way of conclusion.

The first is that Christian doctrine is taught, handed over as we have been calling it, within the context of the whole of the life of the Christian community. This is represented in the nature of its worship, its vision of holiness, its sense of mission and its search for divine justice.

Second, doctrine is related to the tasks of developing, sustaining and expanding the Christian Church. There is, in other words, a relationship between doctrine and mission. Each of the examples I have chosen shows doctrinal teaching alongside, and in the service of, the mission to which the Church was being called at that time and place. This is something I pick up in the next chapter.

The third point, which follows on from the last, is that each Christian tradition or manifestation of the Church has its own particular emphases in doctrine. For the martyrs of the early Church it was the doctrine of the kingdom of God. Christians asserted that they were citizens of, and owed allegiance to, the God who is revealed in Jesus Christ – their obligations to the Roman state could not compromise their priority to serve Christ. Early Dominicans, it might be said, had as their doctrinal focus the true nature of the Christian God. Was God to be understood in the dualistic manner of the Cathars, with light and darkness, good and evil, equally matched in twin divinities? Or could God be described, as in the classical Christian tradition, in terms of unity and Trinity, love and incarnation? For nineteenth-century Methodists, the central doctrinal concern was the evangelical understanding of the order of salvation as a universal human need and possibility. All, without regard to wealth or standing, needed, and could attain, the experience of salvation that Christ offered to every person. In the 1930s the confessing Church focused on the doctrinal assertion that Christ alone, and not Hitler or the Nazi state, was Lord of the Church. 'Jesus is Lord' was for them the primary confession for Christians. The teaching at Le Chambon, on the other hand, promoted the doctrine of the Church as the people of God called to exhibit the justice and *shalom* of God, and to live as disciples of the Jesus whose Sermon on the Mount was a radical call to nonviolence and hospitality.

Finally, if each community has its doctrinal emphases and, by implication, its doctrinal blind spots, it must be true that few Christian churches in history have had what we might call a perfect balance of doctrine. Sometimes this has been understandable and healthy. Particular circumstances, like the rise of Nazism or the dominance of apartheid in South Africa, call for a strong affirmation of some aspects of Christianity rather than others. But in other situations the imbalance is unhealthy, especially if (as often happens) the context changes without a corresponding adaptation of doctrinal teaching. We may admire the early martyrs for their fortitude in confessing Christ, but feel uneasy about their contempt for the body and their enthusiasm for a grisly death. The early Dominican emphasis on the true nature of God did not always have a corresponding sense of the dignity of humanity. The Methodist focus on the doctrines of personal salvation was accompanied by a corresponding neglect of the bigger picture of God's desire for the transformation of all creation. Even the confessing Church, for all its courageous proclamation of the Lordship of Christ, never adequately managed to affirm the doctrine of God's continuing covenant with the Jewish people.

Christian doctrine is embedded in the life of concrete Christian churches. It is not merely a matter of creeds and confessions, nor is it only found where bishops speak *ex cathedra* or where theologians debate. It is part of the nurturing of Christians into communities of faith. It is expressed in the actions through which churches respond to whatever challenge they face in a particular historical epoch or cultural setting. The handing on of Christ happens through the worship, teaching, life and mission of what I have called doctrinal communities. This earthing of doctrine in the local and specific is important, for Christianity is not only a matter of abstract truths. Nevertheless, we have seen that each of these specific communities never engages fully with the whole sweep of Christian teaching. They may affirm the historic creeds, but in practice their teaching and practice will be only a partial engagement with what it represents. That is why it is vitally important to affirm the universal nature of the Church. We speak of the 'one, holy, catholic and apostolic' Church because each community needs to see itself in relation to the whole. Doctrine is universally shared, however much it is expressed in particular communities and actions. To return to Lindbeck's metaphor of doctrine as culture and language: if Christian doctrine is a language, it is one with many different dialects and accents. Different situations see the development of new expressions and idioms. But it is important that those who share a common language can still communicate with each other. A form of Christian speech and action that other Christians could not recognize as Christian would be necessarily suspect.

8

Unearthing the Buried Treasure: Rediscovering Neglected Doctrines

In Chapter 5, in discussing models of doctrinal development I argued that systems of religious doctrine have something in common with ecological systems such as rainforests and coral reefs. There is a relationship between all the different elements in the system. You cannot change one without changing (and perhaps undermining) the whole. Introduce an alien species without proper thought and native species can be dominated or wiped out. We might think of the cane toad in Queensland or Japanese knotweed in the British countryside, both of which have wrought havoc unsuspected by those who brought them in. By the same token, remove key elements (for example by logging hardwood trees or spraying to kill certain insects) and a whole edifice of biodiversity can collapse. It is not a matter of preserving the ecological system from any change whatsoever; that would be neither possible nor desirable. Rather, it concerns the ignorant interference that has unforeseen and perhaps disastrous results. In other words, a failure to give proper attention to the interdependence of all elements in an ecological system will, as likely as not, mean that the health and the future of the whole system is in peril. While the rainforest or coral reef will always be in a state of flux, changing according to climate and other factors, it always needs a proper balance between its different elements in order to flourish and continue. It is no good studying just one element of the system (perhaps a single species of plant or animal); understanding and appropriate action come only when the system is seen as a living, organic whole.

There is at least a partial analogy between this picture of an eco-logical system – and the potential dangers of failing to see it as such – and the living network of Christian doctrine. Doctrinal teaching does indeed develop in response to changing situations. We have seen that static models of doctrine are unhelpful compared to those that give a dynamic account of its development. We have noted that what is emphasized in one situation (for example, doctrines relating to personal salvation during a period of evangelistic revival) may have less prominence in another. But without a balance between its different parts, the system of teaching, as well as the commu-nity that shares it and lives it out, will come to suffer. The great Christian theologians, from Irenaeus in the second century to Karl Barth in the twentieth, have recognized the interconnectedness of Christian doctrine; the way that you cannot (for instance) say any-thing meaningful about the person of Christ without an awareness of what that implies about the Christian understanding of what it means to be human. Now there are, of course, drawbacks in pressing this point too far. There are (as other theologians, such as Søren Kierkegaard, point out) real dangers in presuming to make a watertight system out of Christian belief, as if we could understand everything there is to know about God. Where that has happened (and Kierkegaard thought it happened disastrously in the writings of the German post-Enlightenment philosopher George Friedrich Hegel) human rationalism has tended to triumph over an openness to God's self-revelation. Nevertheless, while taking that warning to heart, I would urge the importance of seeing Christian faith not as a series of disconnected propositions but as a living organism.

In this chapter I highlight some examples of how, in the last few decades, elements of Christian doctrine that have been neglected for many years have been recovered. We will see both the conse-quences of that neglect: the damage, as it were, to the doctrinal ecosystem, and the benefits of recovering those doctrines that have become (to change the metaphor) buried treasure. In doing so, I want to show that the Christian Church needs to value the whole of its faith-story if it is to be responsive to the challenges it faces in new situations.

The forgotten Trinity

Given that it is a term used in any number of religions and cultures, what do Christians really mean by the word 'God'? The classical answer to that question is given in the doctrine of the Trinity. It is true that this doctrine is hardly spelled out in the text of the New Testament, but over the early Christian centuries the Church came to believe that it represented the only way of being true to the story that the Bible tells. Through the second, third and fourth centuries, Christians began to use the language of three persons, Father, Son and Holy Spirit, who share the same divine nature and are inseparable in their work of creation, redemption and consummation. This was, they believed, the only way to be faithful to scripture. It has been suggested that the Trinity is present in the New Testament much as a salt is present in solution: it permeates the whole narrative of Jesus and the Church. The Nicene Creed makes it clear that the Son and the Holy Spirit are to be seen as one with the Father; together they are worshipped and glorified as the one God.

Early in the fifth century, Augustine of Hippo, in his great work *On the Trinity*, developed vivid metaphors for thinking about this difficult concept. Father, Son and Holy Spirit, he said, were like a lover, the one who is loved and the love that is shared between them. He even believed that God had left the imprint of the divine nature in the structure of the human mind, so that through contemplating the Trinity we may come to share in its life. The eastern Christian tradition, following the Cappadocian fathers,[144] speaks of the mutual indwelling (*perichoresis*) of each member of the Trinity with the other. The whole goal of God's saving relationship with the world is for us to come to participate in the Trinitarian life of the Godhead. It is a teaching represented in the well-known Russian icon attributed to Anton Rublev and called both 'The hospitality of Abraham' and 'The Trinity in the Old Testament'. Three figures, representing those entertained by Abraham in Genesis 18,

---

144 Three great theologians of the fourth century who came from the Cappadocian area of what is now eastern Turkey: Basil of Caesarea, Gregory of Nyssa and Gregory Nazianzus.

sit around a table, their eyes making contact with each other, with one side of the table open, as if ready to receive a guest. To hand on the Christian story is inseparable from speaking of the relations and actions of Father, Son and Holy Spirit.

Yet, when I began the study of theology in the mid 1970s there was very little mention of the doctrine of the Trinity. 'God' tended to be described in much more general terms, and not as the Father, Son and Holy Spirit of the classical Christian confessions. In part, this was the result of the kind of environment in which British, continental and American theology had been conducted during the twentieth century. The whole idea of God was under intellectual threat. Nietzsche had proclaimed the 'death of God' and influential 'masters of suspicion' like Freud and Marx had interpreted belief in God as evidence of an underlying pathology in personal and social life. Linguistic philosophy (particularly influential in Britain and America) had insisted that any talk about God was inherently meaningless, that it was literally nonsense. In this environment it must have seemed enough of a challenge to defend the very concept of a divine being, without getting drawn into debates about whether God was one person or three, or how the members of the Trinity related to each other. Perhaps it was no wonder that the 1960s produced some robust defences of Christian theism (for instance the early work of John Hick) and some popular reworking of Christian belief (most famously John Robinson's *Honest to God*) but little that reflected the distinctive Christian Trinitarian understanding of God.

But in fact the neglect of the doctrine of the Trinity has much deeper roots than that sketch of recent history would suggest. It is not simply a case of the acids of modern rationalism so eroding the Trinitarian doctrine of God that we have been left only with a shadowy, undifferentiated divine being. Trinitarian amnesia has a longer history than that. There has been a western Christian tendency (some would say beginning as far back as Augustine) to give such priority to the oneness of God that God's Trinitarian nature is at best an afterthought. Colin Gunton, writing as part of a British Council of Churches study in 1989, summarized this interpretation of theological history:

A truly Trinitarian framework for our worship and life has rarely been found in the life of the Western Church; ... we have forgotten because we never really remembered. The result is that on the face of it – and it is the suspicion of so many Christian professional and lay alike – the doctrine of the Trinity is a piece of abstract theorizing, perhaps necessary as a test of Christian belief, but of little further interest.[145]

But if there has been (as Gunton persuasively argues) a long-term Trinitarian forgetfulness, and if (to use another of his arguments) western Christianity has never properly acquired the skills to speak, worship and live in a Trinitarian way, we now live in a time of intense Trinitarian revival. Since the publication in 1981 of Jürgen Moltmann's *The Trinity and the Kingdom of God* there has been a spate of books, popular as well as technical, focusing on the nature and implications of belief in a Trinitarian God. In fact, the recovery of the doctrine of the Trinity has been one of the outstanding features of recent Christian theology, both in the writings of professional theologians and in the life of the churches themselves. Why is that? I want to suggest several reasons for the rediscovery of the Trinity, not simply as an item in a confession of faith, but as doctrine living in the practice of the Church.

The first is the increasing influence of the Eastern Orthodox tradition on Christians in the West. In 1054 there was an acrimonious schism between eastern Christianity (the Orthodox churches of Greece, Russia and Eastern Europe) and the West. The split was based partly on doctrinal issues – the Orthodox objected strenuously to the introduction of the phrase 'and the Son' to the Nicene Creed – and partly on cultural and political tensions. Since then there has been little theological understanding, and a great deal of misunderstanding, between the traditions. However, the last 50 years has seen the spread of Orthodox churches around the world through a combination of emigration and evangelism. At the same time, the very significant involvement of the Orthodox in

---

145 British Council of Churches, *The Forgotten Trinity*, Vol. 1, BCC, 1989. Gunton's essay is reprinted as chapter 1 of *Father, Son and Holy Spirit: Toward a Fully Trinitarian Theology*, T & T Clark, 2003.

the ecumenical movement has broken down their theological isolation. One result is a deeper appreciation by other Christians of the centrality of the Trinity to the Orthodox understanding of God's nature and action. The communion (the Greek word *koinonia* has a rich range of meaning, not easy to translate into English) of the Father, Son and Holy Spirit is a relationship of loving action in which the Church is invited to participate.

A second factor in the revival of Trinitarian doctrine has been the recovery of the central place of the Holy Spirit. Again, this is something better preserved in the eastern churches than in the West. For example, the 1662 Church of England *Book of Common Prayer* has notoriously very little mention of the Holy Spirit except in cursory formulae. God is addressed almost exclusively as the Father and Son. The result is an absence of a sense of the Holy Spirit as the dynamic, gracious power of God at work in the Church and the world. Here is another symptom of the impoverished understanding of God that comes when the doctrine of the Trinity does not shape our understanding and spirituality. But the Holy Spirit is no longer the forgotten member of the Trinity. Revival movements, especially the recent Pentecostal and charismatic ones, have provoked the whole western Church to a fuller recognition of the Spirit of God.

Third, there has been a development in recent theology that responds to the cultural situation in the contemporary world. The two words 'narrative' and 'relationship' are prominent in contemporary books and articles, and not only in theology. Relationship has become prominent because of the recognition that modern western society – and by extension, modern western Christianity – has been too individualistic. Relationship, in which there is intimacy in and through difference, can now be recognized as central to human well-being. Our identity is shaped by the relationships in which we live. Narrative, too, reflects a recognition that human life, especially life in community, is shaped and expressed by the story that we construct. In response to a modern tendency to live only in the present and ignore history, an emphasis on narrative draws attention to the connectedness of human life, and to its purpose. The ethicist and philosopher Alistair McIntyre, for example, has argued that any meaningful ethical system has to be based on our belonging to a 'narrative community'.

What has happened is that those seeking a theological approach to both relationship and narrative have found it in a Trinitarian understanding of God. For Jürgen Moltmann, Christian belief expresses the 'Trinitarian history of God'; the story of God's actions in creation and providence, in the life, death and resurrection of Jesus and in the Spirit-filled Church, is the story of the Father, Son and Holy Spirit acting together. Similarly, the liberation theologian Leonardo Boff speaks of the Trinity as demonstrating that the heart of reality is not the independent individual, still less an example of domination, but rather a relationship of equals.[146] The Greek Orthodox theologian John Zizioulas is particularly well known for his insistence that the communion-in-otherness of the Father, Son and Holy Spirit is the model for that *koinonia* to which the Christian Church is called.[147] He brings the traditional Trinitarian theology of the eastern Church, especially as it is expressed in the Cappadocian fathers, into discussion with postmodern thought. Only this Trinitarian understanding of personhood constituted by relationship can, he believes, give a positive response to the postmodern concern with 'otherness' as the great challenge to our human identity.

Mention of postmodern thought brings me to a final reason for the resurgence of interest in the doctrine of the Trinity. We have already seen that the modern era has witnessed a sustained attack on traditional Christian doctrine. At the heart of this is the debate about whether it is at all meaningful to refer to the reality of 'God', or whether it is better (for intellectual honesty as well as human flourishing) to abandon such belief. Of course, atheism was not invented in the modern era, nor is it the preserve of post-Enlightenment thinking. The Jesuit author Michael Buckley has traced the roots of modern atheism deep into the development of western thought from the middle ages onwards.[148] But it was from the late eighteenth

---

146 Leonardo Boff, *Trinity and Society*, Burns and Oates, 1988.
147 John Zizioulas, *Being as Communion*, St Vladimir's Seminary Press, 1985; *Communion and Otherness*, T & T Clark, 2006.
148 Michael J. Buckley, *At the Origins of Modern Atheism*, Yale University

century that atheism became a real option for all but a few of the people living in Europe and North America. Much of this atheism drew its credibility from the modern confidence in naturalistic explanations of the way the world is ordered. God became less necessary and less credible for those who saw the universe as governed by the immutable laws of physics and the world and its inhabitants as the products of long geological and evolutionary changes.

The other main strand of atheism, what Moltmann calls 'protest atheism', objects to belief in God on the basis of the harm that it does to human development. Karl Marx, Sigmund Freud and Friedrich Nietzsche are perhaps the most famous representatives of this approach. Each of them attacked belief in God as a distraction from the real business of human progress. The remarkable thing is that both atheists and their believing opponents were pretty much in agreement about who God was. The issue was whether God existed, not what God was like. Thus William Paley's *Evidences of Christianity*, required reading for English university students in the early nineteenth century, argues from the ordered nature of the cosmos to the existence of a divine designer and creator. Believers and unbelievers tended to see themselves sharing the same history, the same sense of what is reasonable and the same culture.

If postmodernism has done anything, it has shattered that consensus. As Alistair McIntyre observes in *Whose Justice, Which Rationality?*, our understanding of what makes a reasonable argument is very dependent on where we start from and which community we belong to. Theologians such as Moltmann and his fellow German Eberhard Jüngel argue that Christians allowed themselves to be backed into a corner where they defended a picture of God that was not truly Christian at all. Christians have to get rid of some ideas about God, not because belief in God is no longer credible but because they owe more to classical models and modern rationalism than they do to the story of the Christian gospel and the basic affirmations of Christian doctrine. The time has come

---

Press, 1987. His further reflections have been published as *Denying and Disclosing God: The Ambiguous Progress of Modern Atheism*, Yale, 2004. A more popular study, Alister McGrath's *The Twilight of Atheism*, Doubleday, 2004, has (from the Christian perspective) a rather optimistic account of atheism's decline.

for Christians to be much more upfront about their particular belief in God. God, for Christians, is neither a managing director
in the sky nor a vague spiritual force that pervades the universe.
The Christian God is the God who in Christ is emptied of power
and privilege in order to serve a stricken humanity. The Christian
God is Father, Son and Spirit, a community of love, the origin and
destination of human life.

Well, you may say, this may be a fascinating story of how theological fashions come and go, but why is it important to regain a
sense of the Trinitarian richness of the Christian understanding
of God? I hope I have already given some of the answer to this
question. When we fail to hand on Christ and the 'Christ-shaped'
God we meet in him, we lose out in two ways. On the one hand we
allow our minds to be conformed to the age and culture in which
we live, and not transformed by the renewal that comes from life in
Christ.[149] Our vision, our spirituality and thinking are all cramped
and confined. On the other hand, we miss out on the richness of a
Trinitarian vision of God and its capacity to challenge and transform human life.

One more thing. I have been arguing all along that the handing
on of doctrine is one (though only one) of the ways in which the
Christian Church reflects the generosity of God. One twentieth-
century theologian, Karl Barth, proposed that the doctrine of the
Trinity provides us with the most basic model for God's gracious
nature.[150] The divine Trinity of Father, Son and Holy Spirit exists
as the total openness of each person to the other, a total self-giving
and revealing. It is in God's revelation in Jesus Christ that we encounter that open-handed giving that is part of the triune nature.

Learning how to live in God's world: the neglected creation

The Nicene Creed opens with the words, 'We believe in one God,
the Father Almighty, Maker of heaven and earth, and of all things

---

149 Romans 12.2.
150 See the discussion on the Trinity in Barth, *Church Dogmatics*, I.1, *The
Doctrine of the Word of God*, chapter 9, ' God's Three in Oneness'.

visible and invisible.' With those phrases echoing in Christian worship it might be hard to imagine that the doctrine of creation could be, in any sense, counted as a neglected area in need of re-discovery and fresh emphasis. After all, some of the most famous religious disputes in modern centuries have revolved around issues to do with creation. In 1633, for example, Galileo was formally condemned by the Roman authorities for refusing to disown the proposition that the sun was the centre of the planetary system. To many in the seventeenth century the idea that the earth orbited the sun, rather than the other way round, implied that neither the earth, nor its human inhabitants, could lay claim to being the pin-nacle and original purpose of God's creative activity. I know of no Christians, however conservative, who would draw that conclu-sion today. In fact, the case of Galileo has for many people (and rather unfairly) come to represent the sheer effrontery of Christian doctrinal teaching. At the very least it should warn us against the abuse of power that intimidates those who deviate from a particu-lar interpretation of doctrine.

More recently, in the nineteenth century Charles Darwin's sem-inal work *On the Origin of Species* gave an account of the gradual evolution of life to produce the various species that have appeared on earth, and seemed to imply that humanity was not unique in its origin but had evolved in the same way as all other creatures. His work was widely held to imply an attack on the traditional Christian reading of the opening chapters of Genesis, and even today many contemporary evangelical Christians, especially in the United States, want to promote so-called creationism as an alterna-tive and contradictory explanation to the prevalent scientific evolu-tionary standpoint. So at least a certain understanding of creation seems to have been sustained through the period when the doctrine of the Trinity has been more obviously neglected.

But appearances can be deceptive. At least two trends prominent in modern European thought have, I believe, undermined the cen-trality of the Christian doctrine of creation. It has taken consider-able effort, and a number of false starts, to bring creation back into the prominence that Christian teaching requires. Why is that? Partly because it is so very easy to forget the interconnectedness of

Christian belief, what I suggested at the beginning of the chapter was like an ecosystem of mutually dependent living organisms. It has, for example, been all too common for Christians not to spot the essential link between the doctrine of creation and the doctrine of the Trinity. It is easy to imagine that for Christianity the world is simply the product of the Father's action, as indicated by that line from the Nicene Creed with which this section began.

You can see how far this is taken for granted in the way some people attempt to get away from any exclusive, gendered, language about God. They refer to 'creator, redeemer and sustainer' instead of 'Father, Son and Holy Spirit', as if each member of the Trinity had their own one-word job description. But that is to ignore the way in which the creed goes on to speak about the role of the Son and the Holy Spirit in the activity of creation. The Son is the one who shares the life and action of the Father: 'through him all things were made'. He is the divine Word, the *Logos*: 'All things came into being through him, and without him not one thing came into being.'[151] Similarly, the creed calls the Holy Spirit 'the giver of life'. In other words, creation according to Christian teaching is a Trinitarian action. The universe we inhabit is an expression of the love that exists between the Father, Son and Holy Spirit, and it comes into being through the mutual action of that Trinity of love. To speak of creation is both a way of saying how there is something that exists outside of God, and a way for us to begin to learn how the world can be in relationship with that triune God. If we forget that Trinitarian link, there is always the danger that the understanding of creation will become less than Christian. And that, in fact, has been a good part of the problem with the history of the doctrine of creation.[152]

But we need to return to those developments that I suggested had tended to obscure the significance of the doctrine of creation. The first of these trends began in the late middle ages and was intensified by the Reformation. It concerns the relationship between God, creation and human beings. In the early Christian centuries,

---

151 John 1.3.

152 One way of accessing that history in more detail is through a major work on Christian doctrine and theology. I would particularly recommend the account in Wolfhart Pannenberg's *Systematic Theology*, Vol. 2, chapter 7.

Christians had got used to speaking of creation as *ex nihilo*, out of nothing. They wanted to emphasize that the world owed its being entirely to God; it is neither the inherently flawed product of a lesser being (as some Gnostics taught), nor the result of God taking over some already existing 'stuff'. There were only two kinds of being – God and God's creation.

For Thomas Aquinas, writing in the thirteenth century, this doctrine of creation was central to a Christian understanding of God. He taught that the universe we live in reveals something of the God who has created it. God is rational rather than irrational, and the universe God has created expresses divine reason in its order and regularity, as well as in the way it discloses the 'natural law' of human behaviour. What is more, the human mind, perhaps the zenith of creation, is uniquely fitted to appreciate that order and so look towards the God who has created it. Not that Aquinas believed that human qualities were exactly the same as those found in God, or that human beings could have a saving knowledge of God through their own intellectual efforts. But he did teach that there was an analogy between the creaturely life of humans in the world and the divine life of God. His famous 'five ways', which discuss the links between our experience of the world (for example, causation or movement) and the nature of God, are not meant to be proofs of God's existence. Instead, they illustrate how as human beings we can dare to talk about God in the first place.

Here, then, is a way of speaking of creation that links it directly with other aspects of Christian belief and practice: the nature of God, what it means to be human and the pattern of life that God desires. All of this is set within the overarching story of Christian belief in the God who has shared created existence in the person of Jesus Christ and who, through Christ, enables humanity to return to its source.

But towards the end of the scholastic period this intricate and closely argued way of thinking came under fire. William of Ockham (*c*.1287–1347) was one of the more famous thinkers whose work challenged the Thomist system.[153] He wanted to loosen the

---

153 'Thomism' is a convenient way of referring to the theological method inherited from Thomas Aquinas.

link between human reason and a divinely ordered universe. For him, there were no universal qualities that formed part of the eternal blueprint for the things of earth. There was, for example, no such thing as 'redness', only a number of instances of red objects. This had consequences for how he understood the relationship between God, creation, and human reason. Because he emphasized the supreme will of God and the direct revelation of God, he had little time either for the concept of divine reason, or for creation as its expression. And because he so emphasized the doctrine of creation out of nothing, and made little effort to link creation with either the person of Christ or the work of the Holy Spirit, he encouraged a way of thinking that kept God and the world apart rather than in relationship.

Although Luther and many of his fellow Reformers were firm in their belief in God's Trinitarian action, they shared Ockham's desire to disentangle reason from creation. One result was that while the Catholic theological tradition has always taught that God is revealed through the created world, Protestants have been more wary of such an idea. God and the world are kept more rigorously separate. The universe is no longer seen as a reflection of God or even as an instrument of God's revelation, but rather a separate sphere governed by its own internal laws, laws that did not need the constant intervention of God. It is possible to see in this Protestant tendency to make the world less sacred the origins of modern science. It implies that only when the earth is not sacred can we dare to examine it and classify it according to the light of human reason.[154] It can also be seen to contribute to the eventual development of atheism; a world through which we cannot learn anything of God increasingly became a world that could get along

---

154 Colin Gunton developed this understanding of the problem of neglecting an emphatically Christian understanding of the doctrine of creation in his Bampton Lectures (*The One, the Three and the Many: God, Creation and the Culture of Modernity*, Cambridge University Press, 1993), in *The Triune Creator*, Edinburgh University Press, 1998 and more briefly in his essay on creation in *The Cambridge Companion to Christian Doctrine* (Cambridge University Press, 1997). While I am sympathetic to his general argument, I believe that he exaggerates the extent to which Augustine can be blamed for the problems of western Christian and post-Christian thought.

well without any reference to God or to divine action.[155] Taking the doctrine of creation away from the rest of the Christian story and our human experience of it made creation more a matter of philosophy than theology and opened the door to that conflict between science and faith that has had such a detrimental effect on the credibility of Christianity. As Colin Gunton points out, the development of modern science and philosophy took a direction that left little room for a doctrine of creation.[156]

The other tendency that has hindered Christians from a full appreciation of the doctrine of creation is rather easier to explain. Western Christianity, especially in its Protestant form, has tended to make the doctrines of atonement and salvation the centre of its teaching. This was as true in the middle ages, with its vivid depictions of the cross and the last judgement in stained glass, wall-painting and wood-carving, as it has been in evangelical Protestant preaching, with its dramatic appeal to the sinner, caught between the two ways that lead either to salvation or to damnation. It is not that the western tradition has forgotten the doctrine of creation, it is more a case of so emphasizing other doctrines that creation has retreated to the background, almost hidden from view. The result is that Christianity appears only to be about the personal salvation of certain individuals who respond to God's call and follow Christ. The created order – everything that is animal, vegetable or mineral apart from humanity – exists as a mere backdrop to the real business between God and human soul. Sometimes salvation is said to be escape from the material world, as in the evangelical chorus:

Turn your eyes upon Jesus,
Look full in His wonderful face,
And the things of earth will grow strangely dim,
In the light of His glory and grace.

---

155 The story is developed with immense learning by Michael Buckley SJ in *At the Origins of Modern Atheism* (Yale University Press, 1987) and *Denying and Disclosing God: The Ambiguous Progress of Modern Atheism* (Yale University Press, 2004).

156 Gunton, *The Triune Creator*, pp. 125ff.

I have often challenged students by saying that if they can show me a Charles Wesley hymn with a positive attitude to the created order, I will buy them a drink. I am still waiting to be taken up on the offer!

It is easy to see how this over-concentration on one aspect of doctrine could combine with the long-standing tendency of Christians to downplay the goodness of the material world as inherently inferior to the spiritual. This was something it inherited from the Platonic philosophy that was so prevalent during the early Christian centuries. According to Plato, in his famous parable of the shadows in the cave, the things of this world are mere shadowy imitations of the eternal realities that lie beyond it. This is, of course, hardly a reflection of the picture painted by the Bible, where there is strong affirmation (especially in the Psalms) of the beauty and value of created things. But it had a profound and not altogether healthy impact on Christianity down the centuries.

The point of this diversion into history is to sketch how Christianity came to be so ill-prepared for some of the most challenging issues to emerge in the late twentieth century. One was the massive change (at least in the West) in attitudes towards human sexuality. Christian churches, it has to be admitted, have rarely been wholehearted in affirming the enjoyment of sexual relationships as part of God's creative gift. It is not surprising, then, that they have often struggled to respond in a credible and constructive way to the questions raised by the sexual revolution in the 1960s, or by the more recent tendency to place same-sex relationships on an equal footing with heterosexual ones.

What has been even more serious has been the belated response of churches to the many aspects of the environmental crisis. It is no coincidence that I found it natural to begin this chapter with an analogy drawn from ecological disaster. The precarious situation of life on earth has become inescapable in recent decades. This extends from the dawning awareness, in the 1950s, that human beings could not pour chemicals onto the farmland and forests of the earth without wreaking destruction on both the environment and themselves, right through to the present panic about the effects of climate change. According to many opinion-formers,

Christianity (in this as in many other things) is part of the problem rather than part of the solution. It seems to teach that human beings are lords of the earth, free to exploit it without any sense of responsibility. Critics have pointed to Genesis 1.28:

> God blessed them and God said to them, 'Be fruitful and multiply, and fill the earth and subdue it; and have dominion over the fish of the sea and over the birds of the air and over every living thing that moves upon the earth.'

Surely, it is said, that must mean that the world exists only for the sake of human beings, that there is no need to have any thought for the value of things in and for themselves. Only in the last two decades or so have Christians seen the need to respond to this challenge.

Unfortunately, many of those who took on this task did so with the assumption that traditional Christian doctrine was indeed an obstacle to a proper Christian environmental ethic. There was a tendency for theologians to see a key problem in the traditional distinction between God and creation. John Cobb, whose process theology has already made an appearance, was an early advocate of a Christian ecological theology. His firm belief is that in the matter of ecology, as in other pressing issues, the Church has to leave inherited doctrine behind and embark on a theological journey, seeking truth from whatever quarter it can be found.

> If the 'theologies of' become 'doctrines of', I fear that the church as a whole will not be freed from its basic alliance with the dominant bourgeois class, its patriarchalism, its suspicion of the body, its individualism, or its anthropocentrism. Slightly improved doctrines about the oppressed, about women, about the body, about community, or about the whole of creation will not change the church much. In many, many respects the church will continue to be part of the problem rather than the bearer of good news. Can we envision a more promising scenario?[157]

---

157 John Cobb, 'The Role of Theology of Nature in the Church', in Charles Birch, William Eaken and Jay B. McDaniel (eds), *Liberating Life: Contemporary Approaches in Ecological Theology*, Orbis, 1990.

His approach puts a strong emphasis on panentheism – what he also calls 'mutual immanence'.[158] God and the world are mutually determined. Cobb makes some valuable points about the distortions in the Christian tradition that have prevented the Church from affirming more fully the immanence of God and the value of non-human creation. But he does this at the expense of any real continuity with the biblical and traditional doctrine of creation. He is, for example, more at home talking about 'nature' than he is about 'creation', for he does not want to imply any radical separation between God and the world. In fact, he would rather put the emphasis in his theology of nature on Christ, rather than on God. Again, the word God carries for him too much inherited bias towards a being separate from other reality.

Another influential writer on these themes has been Matthew Fox, originally a Roman Catholic Dominican priest but now an Anglican. He is best known as the founder of 'creation spirituality' and as the author of *Original Blessing* and *The Coming of the Cosmic Christ*. Like Cobb, his theology could be called panentheist. However, Fox is really developing a form of mysticism rather than building on philosophical ideas. Again, like Cobb, he provides some important correctives to the world-denying aspects of Christianity. Yet it is clear that his world-affirming spirituality (I suspect its Californian origin is no coincidence!) comes at considerable cost. The distinctions between God and the world, between Christianity and other religions and between creation and redemption are all blurred. Jesus becomes much more of a cosmic source of energy than a historical person. Both Cobb and Fox respond to the ecological crisis of the world, but they do so in a way that detaches them from the doctrinal tradition of the Church, with its emphasis on the transcendence as well as the immanence of God and with its balanced affirmations of the goodness of creation and the reality of sin.

And they are not alone. The movement known as Christian eco-feminism has produced arguments that dissolve the transcendence

---

158 It is important to distinguish between pantheism, the belief that all reality is divine, and panentheism, which believes that all reality is in some sense within God.

of God into an immanent world-spirit.[159] The result is an affirmation of the world and a heightened sense of human responsibility for it, but it comes at the expense of the wider Christian teaching. Having inherited a fractured Christian theology, in which creation, Trinity, Christ and redemption have been separated, they have felt compelled to import leading principles from other religions and world-views. The result reminds us of the Gospel parable: it is new wine in old wineskins that is destructive, not old wine in new wineskins.

But the truth is that only a rediscovery of the full range of Christian wisdom can help us. Fortunately, there has been just that kind of rediscovery in a lot of the recent writing on the doctrine of creation. Can there be a Christian response to the ecological situation that is more integrated with that wider teaching? Putting it another way, are there resources in the traditional doctrine of creation that enable that response to be made? One key attempt to do just that was made by Jürgen Moltmann. A theologian whose major works all seem to respond to urgent challenges in the contemporary world, he produced one of the first large-scale attempts to work on the Christian doctrine of creation in relation to ecological issues. True, *God in Creation*[160] does flirt with some of the more questionable trends we have found in Cobb and Fox; Moltmann develops his own version of panentheism, for example. But the overall framework is of the Trinitarian history of God. Creation is related to the entire work of God, including its fulfilment in the kingdom of heaven. True to his long-standing concern with Christian hope, Moltmann looks to biblical visions of the kingdom and to the overall pattern of Christian belief in the future. Only an Easter faith, one focused on resurrection, can see the renewal of the earth.

The past 20 years have seen a spate of books on the relationship between the Christian doctrine of creation and the ecological crisis.[161] For example, the Irish Catholic author Sean McDonagh

159 See, for example, Rosemary Radford Ruether, *Gaia and God: An Eco-Feminist theology of Earth Healing*, SCM Press, 1993.

160 Jürgen Moltmann, *God in Creation: An Ecological Doctrine of Creation*, SCM Press, 1985.

161 An idea of the range of work can be found in these books: Colin Gunton, *The Triune Creator*; R. J. Berry (ed.), *Environmental Stewardship*, T & T Clark,

was spurred to reflect on the theology of creation through his experience of working as a missionary in the Philippines. His work draws on the biblical roots of the doctrine of creation and its historical outworking, especially among religious orders. In a helpful example of doctrinal connectedness, he links the doctrine of creation with the doctrine of the sacraments, finding in both an affirmation of God's commitment to the world of physical matter and to the creatures that inhabit it. From a very different Christian tradition, the popular evangelical author and speaker Tony Campolo has an accessible guide to the doctrinal and ethical issues in *How to Rescue the Earth without Worshipping Nature: A Christian Call to Save Creation*. Though not a work of technical theology, Campolo shows himself well aware of the kind of problems we have seen in Cobb and Fox, where the distinction between God and the world is all but eliminated. Celia Deane-Drummond, one of a number of research scientists who have turned into professional theologians, has written *Creation Through Wisdom: Theology and the New Biology*. Her work tackles the particular issues of a human treatment of creation (for example, in the new genetics) as well as the wider issue of humanity and the future of the world. Though she examines the work of those who have moved beyond received Christian doctrine, she makes a persuasive argument that the biblical concept of divine wisdom enables us to bring creation and resurrection, humanity and Trinity, into a relationship that is productive for responsible living in a threatened world.

> with eyes fixed on the Wisdom of God we can begin to discover the meaning of creation. Such a discovery brings with it a sense of homecoming, a reintegration of humanity in the world. For it is in humanity that Wisdom in the guise of the Spirit of Christ

2006; Celia Deane-Drummond, *Creation Through Wisdom: Theology and the New Biology*, T & T Clark, 2000; Sean McDonagh, *To Care for the Earth: A Call to a New Theology*, Chapman, 1986 and *The Greening of the Church*, Orbis, 1990; Jeff Astley, David Brown and Ann Loades (eds), *Creation: Key Readings*, T & T Clark, 2003 (a brief but helpful anthology offering traditional and contemporary material); Tony Campolo, *How to Rescue the Earth without Worshipping Nature: A Christian Call to Save Creation*, Word, 1992.

becomes most evident. Yet wisdom seeks to integrate the anthro-
pological with the cosmological.[162]

The recovery of hope: a fresh look at the Christian doctrine of the last things[163]

The discussion about the future of creation leads to my third and
final example of important but neglected areas of Christian doctrine that have begun to come back into renewed prominence.
According to the Nicene Creed, Jesus Christ 'will come again in
glory to judge the living and the dead, and his kingdom will have
no end', and Christians 'look for the resurrection of the dead and
the life of the world to come'. These short phrases summarize the
area of Christian doctrine known as 'eschatology': literally, 'talk
about the last things'. They are the beliefs that concern the final
destiny of human beings and the world: death, judgement, heaven
and hell, the kingdom of God. Eschatology is about Christian hope
in a future that is of God's making. Here, too, there is a story of an
area of doctrine relegated to the storeroom of Christian teaching,
only to be rediscovered and freshly valued in recent decades.

The Christian doctrine of hope is rooted in the person of Jesus
and the writings of the New Testament. In fact, it is impossible to
read the New Testament without sensing its powerful orientation
towards the future. Prophecy is alive and well; the time is short;
the present order is on its way out and a new one is waiting in
the wings. Of all the Gospels, Matthew has a special emphasis on
eschatology. Like the rest of the New Testament, Matthew was
written at a time when many Jewish people had a strong sense that
God was about to intervene in human history in a final and decisive way. That intervention would vindicate God's chosen people
the Jews, defeat their enemies (currently the Romans) and usher in

---

162 Deane-Drummond, *Creation Through Wisdom*, p. 248.

163 In addition to the works referred to in the text, the following provide help-
ful summaries of the discussion of eschatology in recent Christian theology: Hans
Schwarz, *Eschatology*, Eerdmans, 2000; Robert C. Doyle, *Eschatology and the
Shape of Christian Belief*, Paternoster, 1999; Wolfhart Pannenberg, *Systematic
Theology*, Vol. 3, T & T Clark, 1998, chapter 15.

God's final and perfect kingdom. Jesus seems to have intensified and radicalized this belief through his teaching and actions.

According to Matthew, his ministry begins with the proclamation, 'Repent, for the kingdom of heaven has come near' (Matthew 4.17) and it ends with his final words to the disciples, 'Remember, I am with you to the end of the age' (28.20). Matthew's Jesus is more than an eschatological prophet – he is, after all, the Son of the living God – but an eschatological prophet he certainly is. Between the story of Jesus' entry into Jerusalem and his arrest, trial and crucifixion, the Gospel is dominated by parables and sayings that speak of the end of the present age and the coming judgement. The world is already going through the terrible trials that will usher in a new age. There is an urgent need to watch and keep ready, for God's kingdom will come like a thief in the night. Even the Jerusalem temple is not safe; its destruction will be one of the signs of the end of the present age and the coming kingdom. At the last there will be a great judgement and the men and women of the earth will be separated like sheep and goats, according to their compassion for Jesus and his people.

No wonder, then, that the early Christians lived with a sense of urgent expectation, a belief that they were living 'between the times', with the final victory of God already shaping the present. Similarly, Paul's letters are full of what has been called the tension between 'the already and the not-yet', between the new present reality that Jesus' resurrection has brought into being, and the final fulfilment of God's purposes for all creation. As he puts it in Romans:

> We know that the whole creation has been groaning in labour pains until now; and not only the creation, but we ourselves, who have the first fruits of the Spirit, groan inwardly while we wait for adoption, the redemption of our bodies. For in hope we were saved. (Romans 8.22–24)

No wonder Karl Barth, commenting on this passage, says: 'If Christianity be not thoroughgoing eschatology, there remains in it no relationship whatever with Christ.'[164]

---

164 Karl Barth, *The Epistle to the Romans*, Oxford University Press, 1933, p. 314.

And, of course, the final book of the New Testament, the inspiring yet perplexing Revelation to John, directs us to the scene of God's final victory over evil and to the life of worship, peace and healing that is characteristic of the new heaven and new earth.

For the early Christians, then, handing on Christ meant handing on the hope of his return and his kingdom. So how did something so central come to be so neglected? The first reason is the most obvious. Jesus did not, in fact, return as quickly as many early Christians expected. It was hard to keep up an intense belief in the imminent end of the present world generation after generation. Christians got used to playing the long game of living in the world as it is while aspiring to be citizens of God's heavenly kingdom. St Augustine's great work *City of God* is in part an explanation of how God still works through the worldly city, even as Christians are called to live in the hidden reality of the city of God.

As the centuries went by, Christian thinking about the end focused more and more on the personal destiny of individual human beings, on their final judgement and their welcome into heaven or their condemnation to hell. My eternal destiny and what decides it came to be much more prominent than God's final victory and rule. This is a world-view wonderfully expressed by the Italian poet Dante Alighieri (1265–1321) in *The Divine Comedy*, with its vivid descriptions of hell, purgatory and heaven. In the middle ages it was common to see 'doom paintings' over the chancel arch of a parish church. Like a giant game of snakes and ladders, these depicted Christ in judgement, warning worshippers to behave in such a way that they ended up on the side of those ascending the ladder that leads to heaven, rather than with those sliding down into the fire of hell. Michelangelo's famous scene of the last judgement, painted in the Sistine Chapel in the heart of the Vatican, continued that tradition. Here, bishops are among those entering the jaws of hell, a warning that even people who thought themselves at the centre of the Church could find themselves alienated from God. This trend may have focused people's minds on their own responsibility to live lives of obedience and holiness, but it also led to destructive fear and (with the development of indulgences) an abuse of power by the Church.

Just as the concentration on the doctrine of personal salvation left the doctrine of creation to recede into the background, so the concentration on personal judgement led to a neglect of the doctrine of the kingdom of God. Eschatology, at least in the western half of traditional Christianity, was reduced in scope and shorn of its cosmic dimension.

It often happens that when an important truth is neglected by the mainstream of church teaching it appears in an extreme or distorted form elsewhere. This has certainly happened with this area of doctrine. One result of the neglect of the Christian vision of the kingdom of God was the persistent development of what I can only call 'crackpot eschatology', the tendency of individuals and groups to produce their own version of how 'the end' will come about. This is often expressed in one or another variety of millennialism, the belief in a 1,000-year period of blessing either before or after the second coming of Christ. The medieval mystic Joachim of Fiore (1135–1202) was one millennialist; he divided the history of salvation into seven epochs and looked for a new messianic leader who would bring about spiritual renewal. Another was the Reformation radical Sebastian Münster (1488–1552), who saw the German peasants' revolt as the beginning of the end-time. In the nineteenth century both the Jehovah's Witnesses and the Latter-Day Saints (Mormons) developed their own eschatology in ways that took them a considerable distance from traditional Christian teaching.

More recently, the dispensationalism of John Nelson Darby (1800–82) and his successors has become enormously popular in some Christian circles. Dispensationalism claims to find in the Bible evidence for a series of seven dispensations, periods of human history that reveal the failure of humanity and the judgement of God. These ages culminate in the millennium kingdom of Christ, preceded by the 'rapture' in which believers are taken up directly into heaven to meet the returning Jesus. This kind of eschatology has been promoted by Hal Lindsey in his bestseller *The Late, Great Planet Earth*,[165] and in the *Left Behind* series of novels by

---

165 Hal Lindsey, *The Late, Great Planet Earth*, Zondervan, 1970.

Tim LaHaye and Jerry B. Jenkins.[166] It is difficult to overestimate the extent to which these books, and their spin-offs of films, video-games and music, have influenced the popular imagination in America. There has even been a parody of the genre in an episode of *The Simpsons* with the title 'Thank God It's Doomsday', a sure sign that it has percolated popular culture.

More seriously, this eschatology, based very loosely on a reading of the biblical books of Daniel and Revelation, plays into the hands of an extreme right-wing approach to world politics. In the words of one commentator:

> It seems to accommodate affairs and events of the modern world to prophetic scriptures ... It also places a benediction on the 'world's mess' which only Christ can correct in visible power. It eliminates social responsibility other than the Christian's duty in citizenship. And it provides joy in every sign of approaching calamity, for calamity demands parousia.[167]

This dispensationalist theology is not the only dire result of the widespread neglect of traditional eschatological doctrine. When hope is eliminated from Christian thought, it often re-emerges elsewhere. Secular versions of Christian eschatology have cropped up with increasing regularity. In the last century none has been more influential than Marxism, with its vision of a world transformed and a humanity restored to harmony and equality. It is not diffi-cult to see in Marxism a godless version of Christian eschatology, with hope for the economic transformation of this world replacing the Christian hope for a new heaven and a new earth. Even some Marxist thinkers have seen the importance of the link between the Christian story and the communist vision. Ernst Bloch, for ex-ample, produced a three-volume history of movements that have promoted human hope for a better future.[168] He is very critical of

---

166 The first novel in the series of 16, *Left Behind*, was published by Tyndale House in 1995. Collectively, the books have outsold all other series of novels, with sales running into several million.

167 Hans Schwarz, *Eschatology*, Eerdmans, 2000, p. 333.

168 Ernst Bloch, *The Principle of Hope*, Oxford University Press, 1986.

Christians, accusing them of ignoring their own biblical emphasis on the future and their own history of visionary hope and social challenge.

Now that we are all too aware of the human cost of the regimes that have tried to implement the Marxist eschatological vision it is vital that Christians take their own tradition of future hope more seriously. There are signs that this is exactly what is happening. Part of the initiative has come from New Testament studies. For example, the mammoth study of New Testament theology by N. T. Wright, written (unlike many of its predecessors) from a doctrinally robust orthodox Christian perspective, has highlighted the centrality of Jewish eschatology for understanding the ministry and message of Jesus.[169] Like Albert Schweitzer 100 years ago,[170] Wright shows Jesus focused on the future, a figure whose message and ministry points to an imminent apocalyptic transformation of this world. But unlike Schweitzer and many of his contemporaries he sees this dimension of the New Testament as a foundation for Christian doctrine and not as an embarrassment to be explained away. In Jesus, God's purpose for the universe is coming to fruition. A very different contemporary New Testament scholar, Christopher Rowland, has made a particular study of New Testament eschatology. In its vision of God's plan for radical change he sees the roots of a Christian teaching that can bring hope to those who, like many in the first century, still find themselves oppressed by the violent and destructive powers of the world.[171]

As in the doctrine of the Trinity, the increasing contact with the thinking of eastern Christianity has helped western Christians rediscover truths they were in danger of forgetting. There is a thread in Eastern Orthodox theology that takes its inspiration from such passages as Colossians 1.19–20: 'For in him all the fullness

---

169 The volume I have particularly in mind is N. T. Wright, *Jesus and the Victory of God*, SPCK, 1996.

170 Schweitzer's book is known in the English-speaking world as *The Quest of the Historical Jesus* (A & C Black, 1910) but was published in German in 1906 with the more prosaic title *Von Reimarus zu Wrede*. It is a measure of Schweitzer's importance that his book has remained in print for the last hundred years and has recently been reissued in a new English translation (SCM Press, 2000).

171 See, for example, his commentary on *Revelation*, Epworth Press, 2003.

of God was pleased to dwell, and through him God was pleased to reconcile all things, whether on earth or in heaven, by making peace through the blood of his cross', and Ephesians 1.10–11, which speaks of God's 'plan for the fullness of time, to gather up all things in him, things in heaven and things on earth'.

For a writer like Maximus the Confessor (c.580–662),[172] this hope for God's gathering up of everything in Christ is best expressed through the Greek word *apokatastasis*. By this he means that God's work of salvation, though rooted in Christ and addressed to humanity, is universal in scope. Ultimately, we can be confident that God's grace will draw the whole cosmos into the state for which it was created, a perfection that shares in the glory of God. This tradition, which has been rediscovered by a number of recent theologians, shows how eschatology can bring together the doctrines of creation and salvation. It is not that salvation takes us out of the world and into the presence of God, but that salvation draws us, and all that God has made, towards its true end and purpose.

In contemporary theology no one has done more to help Christians rediscover the doctrine of hope than the German theologian Jürgen Moltmann. In 1964 he produced one of the first full-length treatments of eschatology in recent times, *Theology of Hope*.[173] What Moltmann was saying was something like this: because eschatology has been thought of as the 'last things', it has usually been the last thing Christians have thought about. What a difference it would make if we looked at eschatology first, and then found how this altered our whole understanding of the Christian faith. Just as looking at a familiar building from an unfamiliar angle gives us a fresh impression of it, so taking 'last things first' in Christian faith gives us fresh insights into the meaning of Jesus Christ. In terms of Christian belief, Moltmann thinks this will give

---

172 There is an accessible selection of Maximus' theology, together with a modern commentary, in *On the Cosmic Mystery of Jesus Christ: Selected Writings from Maximus the Confessor*, translated by Paul Bowers and Robert Louis Wilken, St Vladimir's Seminary Press, 2003.

173 Jürgen Moltmann, *Theology of Hope: On the Ground and the Implications of a Christian Eschatology*, SCM Press, 1967.

us a new emphasis on the resurrection of Jesus as the utterly new and startling fact that reveals who God is and what God is doing. Here is the God who makes all things new, who brings life out of death and hope out of despair. In Jesus' resurrection God is making the future break into the present so that we can begin to live by the light of what is coming, rather than live according to what is old and dying. The world is not a vicious cycle of cause and effect, for God has broken that cycle through the wholly unexpected and unforeseeable way in which resurrection followed crucifixion. Moltmann was quick to draw out some of the implications of his eschatology for the way in which Christians should approach the challenges of the contemporary world. They should, he said, be an Exodus people, living out of the promised future that God has prepared, and not worried too much about the passing of what has been familiar and comforting.

Thirty years after *Theology of Hope*, Moltmann returned to the theme of eschatology in a book that tries to bring together the many different aspects of the Christian hope: death and eternal life, resurrection and judgement, the kingdom of God and the new heaven and earth. Some of his closing words show how much he has learned from the way eschatology has been handed on in the Orthodox tradition:

> Do believers have this joy for themselves in a world hostile them and to life? No, for them the transfiguration of liege in Easter joy which they experience is no more that a small beginning of the transfiguration of the whole cosmos. The risen Christ does not come just to the dead, so as to raise them and communicate to them his eternal life. He draws all things into his future, so that they may become new and participate in the feast of God's eternal joy.[174]

Summing up this section, what can we say to the question, why do we need eschatological doctrine? After all, Christianity constantly battles against the mistaken impression that it offers nothing more

---

174 Jürgen Moltmann, *The Coming of God*, SCM Press, 1996, p. 338.

than 'pie in the sky when you die'. We need it for a number of important and timely reasons.

The first is that eschatology is intrinsic to the Christian story. To leave it out is to dissect from the Bible and Christian doctrine one of its vital organs. Christianity looks to the future and interprets the present in the light of what God has promised. A Christianity without eschatology is two-dimensional, and robbed of vision.

Second, Christians need an eschatology to remind them that the future belongs to God and comes from God; it is not something that we construct through our own efforts, however well-intentioned they may be and however sacrificially they may be carried out. There is a key difference between living out the life of the kingdom that God has begun in Jesus and will bring to completion in the future, and imagining that we are somehow building that kingdom through our own projects and institutions.

Third, we need Christian eschatology because the non-Christian alternatives have proved so costly, destructive and disappointing. Utopian visions presented as alternatives to the Christian teaching of the kingdom of God have a habit of promising liberation but delivering violence. While this is obviously true of Marxism and Fascism, it is also the case with the ideology of progress to which western liberalism is still addicted.

Finally, we need good Christian eschatology because so much of what passes for a Christian vision of the future is a dangerous distortion of both the Bible and the Christian tradition. The dispensationalist teaching that is rampant in some parts of contemporary Christianity turns the Bible into an esoteric code for interpreting contemporary events, it denies God's universal concern for the world and its peoples, and it makes the conflicts of the world little more than God acting like a child playing with toy soldiers. The biblical vision of God's final victory, judgement and healing of the nations is grander, more generous, and more hopeful than this perversion suggests.

The 26-year-old Dietrich Bonhoeffer, lecturing on the doctrine of creation in the University of Berlin in 1932, began with words that were especially relevant for the turbulent times in which he lived, but which have an enduring quality:

The church of Jesus Christ witnesses to the end of all things. It lives from the end, it thinks from the end, it acts from the end, it proclaims its message from the end . . . The church speaks within the old world about the new world.[175]

What I have wanted to show in this very selective dip into recent developments in Christian theology is that doctrinal amnesia in one age can seriously impede the life and witness of the Church in another. But I have also tried to show that gifts set aside or lost are not necessarily irretrievable. If they are part of the 'faith once delivered to the saints' they remain available to renew Christian thinking, prayer and action. After all, the *ressourcement* movement in Roman Catholic theology in the mid twentieth century led to the *aggiornamento* of renewal in the Second Vatican Council.

Ultimately, the Christian Church has something to give the contemporary world only if it is aware of what it has been given. Once again, this is not a plea for the Church to do no more than repeat in exact words the doctrinal formulae of past generations. It is a confident belief that the Holy Spirit continues to give gifts through the teaching that it inspired in the past, and that it continues to lead the Church in expressing and developing those gifts.

---

175 Dietrich Bonhoeffer, *Creation and Fall*, Fortress Press, 2004, p. 21.

9

Handing on Christ: The Future of Christian Doctrine

So what? Just what sort of difference is it likely to make if the argument of this book is accepted and doctrine is taken more seriously in the life of the contemporary Church? We have seen that there is a widespread suspicion, as active within the Church as among its critics, that doctrine and theology are at best irrelevant distractions from the proper practical business of Christianity and at worst indulgent word-games that exclude and oppress the uninitiated or the critical. In this chapter I want to show how a renewed appreciation of doctrine can make a significant difference in a number of areas that are central to the matter of bearing faithful Christian witness in an increasingly faithless world.

What I want to emphasize is the connection between confessing the faith of Christ and living faithfully as Christian disciples, in other words the correspondence between belief and practice. One word that seems to fit this correspondence well is 'performance'. Of course, 'performance' can have highly negative connotations. To talk of 'putting on a performance' may imply an element of falsehood and unreality about an action. We are all too aware of the salesperson who is glibly plausible but cynically insincere, or of the footballer whose dive to the ground is an act to get the referee's attention rather than the result of a foul. But I want to use the word in a different sense. By performance I mean a set of actions (which may or may not include words) that express or achieve something significant.[176] At its best, a theatrical performance is not an attempt

---

176 In emphasizing performance, I am partly reflecting the idea of 'performative utterance' developed by the philosopher John Austin (1911–60) and taken up

to deceive us into believing that the actors on stage are really different people, or that they are genuinely getting angry, making love or killing each other. Instead, a dramatic performance means a combination of action and words that takes us into a new way of looking at reality, one that makes us part of the story that is being told and enables us to share in the emotions and arguments that it embodies.

Sometimes this kind of performance, in theatre, dance or music, is based on a printed script or a musical score; sometimes it is based on an orally transmitted set of words or music. It can even be improvised at the moment of performance by, for example, jazz musicians who know the way they want to move through a progression of chords. Indeed, we might say that all significant performance has an element of improvisation. It is never merely the repetition of a set of words or dance steps or musical notes. These form the basis of the performance; they are not the performance itself. A choir in which I once sang spent week after week rehearsing a complex and difficult piece. Eventually the conductor said to us: 'You know the words, you know the notes and you know the rhythm. Now we can start turning it into music.'

I want to suggest that one of the ways in which doctrine is related to the practice of the Christian community is similar to the way a script is related to the performance of a play or a score to a musical performance. This is by no means a new idea, though it does run counter to the deep suspicion that the Christian tradition has often held towards public theatre. The early Christian writers were unanimous in their belief that Christians should not attend the spectacles of Roman games or public plays. It is not too difficult to see why. The Roman arenas were scenes of Christian martyrdom and brutal gladiatorial battles; to attend them would mean

---

by a number of theologians (for example Anthony Thiselton in *New Horizons in Hermeneutics*). I am also taking account of the many ways in which performance has become a key category in recent theology, beginning with Barth and von Balthasar and now further developed under the influence of postmodernism. To take a few examples: Frances Young, *The Art of Performance: Towards a Theology of Holy Scripture*, Darton, Longman and Todd, 1990; Stanley Hauerwas, *Performing the Faith*, Baker, 2004; and the already discussed Kevin Vanhoozer, *The Drama of Doctrine*, Westminster John Knox, 2005.

becoming accessories to murder. Similarly, to watch plays involving adultery would risk being shaped by the values of pagan gods, rather than by those of Christian virtue and godliness.[177] And alongside these suspicions was the belief that acting was somehow a form of lying, reflecting that negative meaning of performance we noted above. It is interesting that the word 'hypocrite', found so often in the teaching of Jesus, has its origins in the description of actors in the Greek theatre.

In spite of this history of suspicion, I still think that performance is a good word to describe the relationship between doctrine and Christian life. As a matter of fact, my reasons for doing so are very similar to the early Christian objections to the theatre. They assumed that no one could ever be a mere spectator to a dramatic performance. They must participate in it in some way. They will become part of the performance themselves, informed by the beliefs that lie behind the drama and transformed by sharing in its action. Just so! But if the violence and immorality of pagan drama has the power to seduce us into sharing its beliefs, values and action, how much more powerful must be participation in the drama that is the true story of God's loving redemption of the world? This view has become much more prominent in recent years. It has been encouraged by the contemporary emphasis on shared narrative as the basis of human community; the Christian Church is shaped by the common story that is summed up in Christian doctrine. It also echoes the insight that the biblical God is a performing God, a God of drama whose action in history shapes reality and who invites the human audience to become part of that action.[178]

In *The Art of Performance*, Frances Young uses the analogy of performing a musical score to indicate ways in which the Bible can be interpreted, while, as we have seen, Kevin Vanhoozer's recent

177 This teaching is widespread among the writers of the early Christian centuries. Extended denunciations of the theatre are found in the work of Tertullian (*The Shows*) and Augustine (*The City of God*).

178 I am thinking particularly of the work of the Roman Catholic theologian Hans Urs von Balthasar and his five-volume *Theo-Drama: Theological Dramatic Theory* (Ignatius Press, 1988). Von Balthasar explores the relationship of Christian theology to the history of drama, but also develops an understanding of the divine Trinity as author, director and actor.

The Drama of Doctrine argues for the connection between theatre and church life. In what follows I explore how Christian doctrine is both a performance in its own right and a contribution to the performance that is the effective life of the Christian community in time. Performing doctrine is linked to the processes of both informing and transformation. I have chosen to explore three key areas of the Church's life – worship, teaching and mission – to illustrate this perspective and show that it can be fruitful.

Doxology: doctrine and worship

Corporate worship is central to the performance of the Christian faith. But Christian worship is in trouble. It has, at least in the West, fewer regular participants than for many centuries. What is more, churches themselves are deeply conflicted over what worship is and how it should be conducted. Whether it is the question of style or content, words, music or leadership: all come under intense scrutiny and cause controversy. The traditional, 'mainline' churches, Protestant and Catholic, have been through an unprecedented series of liturgical revisions, yet for all their development of vernacular services, inclusive language and greater participation, their worship has been progressively less well attended since the mid 1960s. On the other hand, churches with charismatic and Pentecostal worship, unconstrained by traditional forms, have developed a worldwide base which current estimates put at between 150 and 200 million members.

So what is Christian worship? One definition (which I admit might not be shared by all those participating in it) is that it is a set of communal activities within which the Christian God is named and praised and through which worshippers are formed into the Body of Christ. Worship is essentially performance. Not in the sense that the leaders of worship are performing to the congregation (though of course that does happen, with both good and bad results). What I mean is that Christian worship is a performance in which both God and God's people are performing for and with each other. For the Christian congregation, worship is a performance that informs them and others of the reality of God and transforms them into the living likeness of Christ.

We noted in Chapter 1 that one classical way of relating doctrine to worship has been through the term *lex orandi, lex credendi*, 'the rule of prayer is the rule of faith'. Christian history is full of examples of the way in which doctrine and worship have developed through interaction with each other. We can see worship reshaped in the light of a fresh understanding of Christian doctrine in the composition of the *Book of Common Prayer* by Thomas Cranmer during the reign of Edward VI. Its order for Holy Communion, for example, uses language that tries to rule out any sense that the Eucharist can be a repetition of the sacrifice of Christ on the cross. On the other hand, the way in which doctrine is perceived in the Orthodox tradition is derived from participation in the Holy Liturgy. As one contemporary Orthodox writer puts it:

> Precisely during the liturgy Christ is transmitted, handed down to us (*trado, paradido*). In fact, what occurs is a mutual handing over: 'Thine own of thine own.' Orthodox spirituality would affirm Irenaeus's words that 'our whole life should conform to the Eucharist, and the Eucharist should confirm our whole life.' There is, in the context of liturgy, a virtual identity between Christ and tradition, between Christ as past, present, and future (compare Rev 4:8), between the One who has already come and who is yet to come. This constitutes the heart and center of the Christian faith.[179]

This echoes one of the starting points for this book; I suggested that 1 Corinthians 11 was a key text for understanding the centrality of Christian doctrine as sharing the gift which is Jesus Christ. Paul's account of the handing over of Christ for our salvation and the handing over of the story of the Lord's supper are connected both by a subtle play on words (*paradidomi*) and by the need for story and action to be integrated in any act of Christian worship. Worship and doctrine are inseparable. We worship because of

---

179 John Chryssavgis, 'The Prayer of Liturgy in the Orthodox Church', *Theology Today*, October 2001.

what we believe, but our belief is shaped by the worship we share. A closer attention to doctrine would make Christian worship more effective as performance.

Worship and the performance of doctrinal teaching

Language changes things. We are so used to the idea that language describes a state of affairs or expresses our ideas that we forget that language can also perform actions. 'I name this ship . . .'; 'I pronounce you husband and wife'; 'I admit you to the degree of this university': these are all examples of what has been called performative utterances. Christians should not need reminding that the Bible begins with exactly this kind of language: 'Then God said, let there be light, and there was light.' This performative role is especially apparent in relationships. I once worked with a colleague whose relationship with me was sometimes strained. Things changed for the better after an occasion when I publicly praised him for the work he had done. I was saying no more than the truth, but saying it was more than reporting on what I thought; it was a significant development in our colleagueship that established how I regarded him.

That performative role of language is especially relevant to the words used in Christian worship. The language of worship is both an account of what worshippers believe to be true (it is doctrinal) and an action that develops their relationship with God. Christian worship addresses God: 'O Lord, open our lips, and our mouths shall proclaim your praise.' It uses words to set forth God's praise, and those words have both a doctrinal and a devotional content. In worship, doctrine is also doxology.

The word 'doxology' comes from the Greek *doxa*, meaning 'glory', and it therefore refers to what happens when Christians celebrate the praise and glory of God.[180] That is why 'orthodoxy' is not just about believing the right things, but about giving glory

---

180 The most extensive treatment of the relationship between worship and doctrine is in Geoffrey Wainwright, *Doxology: The Praise of God in Worship, Doctrine and Life*, Oxford University Press, 1980.

where it is properly due – to the God who is Father, Son and Holy Spirit. Sometimes a formal set of words is called a doxology, as in:

Glory to the Father and to the Son and to the Holy Spirit,
As it was in the beginning, is now and shall be for ever. Amen

Traditionally said or sung at the end of a Psalm or Canticle in Christian worship, this is both an act of praise and an affirmation of the nature of God as it has been handed on in the Christian community. Similarly, the so-called great doxology, traditionally part of the liturgy for Holy Communion, combines the language of prayer that glorifies God with the affirmation that this is the God who is given us in Jesus Christ.

Glory to God in the highest, and peace to his people on earth.
Lord God, heavenly King,
almighty God and Father,
we worship you, we give you thanks,
we praise you for your glory.
Lord Jesus Christ, only Son of the Father,
Lord God, Lamb of God
you take away the sin of the world:
have mercy on us;
you are seated at the right hand of the Father:
receive our prayer.
For you alone are the Holy One,
you alone are the Lord,
you alone are the Most High,
Jesus Christ,
with the Holy Spirit
in the glory of God the Father. Amen.

Notice that this, too, is a combination of the language of doctrinal affirmation ('Lord Jesus Christ, only Son of the Father') with the language of praise and prayer ('we worship you'; 'receive our prayer').

In worship the language of doctrine is part of the performance of praise. Does what I have said about it imply that Christian worship needs to stick to these traditional words and these only if it is to be doctrinally sound? Not entirely. I do believe that a doctrinally aware church will value these traditional forms of Christian praise; after all, they have been a significant part of the handing on of Christ as a living reality in our worshipping life. But I do not want to imply that no new forms of words can offer glory to God or share the content of Christian belief. What I would want to make clear, though, is that the language of worship (whether it is in a formal, written liturgy or in a more extemporary form) needs to be rooted in what Christians have received and want to hand on about the truth of their faith. Here I will mention just two examples of what I mean and then go on to handle a contemporary challenge to the argument I am making.

First, because the Christian understanding of God is Trinitarian the language of Christian worship needs to speak of God as Father, Son and Holy Spirit. This means that there will be places where a Trinitarian form of words is used. In baptism, for example, the words, 'I baptize you in the name of the Father, and of the Son and of the Holy Spirit', form a good example of what I mean by the performative character of the language of worship. But it will also mean that the language of prayer should more generally reflect the richness of this Trinitarian belief. I sometimes give students an exercise in which they are asked to reflect on the language used in worship in their local church and check how far it is genuinely Trinitarian and how far it refers to one member of the Trinity at the expense of others. Some report that prayers are so focused on the person of Jesus that the acknowledgement of transcendence and mystery that comes with addressing God as Father and Holy Spirit is lost. Others point to a lack of any real invocation of the Spirit in the language of prayer.

The second point is that worship needs to reflect the fact that Christian doctrine has a narrative quality about it; it forms what is today called a metanarrative, an overarching story that makes sense of the whole of life. One danger in worship is that it easily focuses on one aspect of that story in such a way that we lose sense of the whole, for example when the only hymns and songs sung are ones referring to Christ's death on the cross. A particular problem arises when the language of worship concentrates solely on the personal experience of those taking part (however important that is), without reference to the whole drama. One way of addressing this is through prayers of thanksgiving. The thanksgiving prayer in the service of Holy Communion is a model example of how the great story of God's action in creation and incarnation, redemption and consummation is linked with the faith and worship of those taking part. So, for example, the eucharistic prayer for Pentecost in the *Methodist Worship Book* begins by setting the scene for the story of salvation:

In the beginning
your Spirit swept across the face of the waters,
bringing order out of chaos.
You formed us in your own image
And breathed into us the breath of life
Though we turned away from you,
Your love remained steadfast.[181]

The prayer goes on to recall the Spirit-filled life and ministry of Jesus Christ, his death and resurrection and the gift of the Holy Spirit poured out on those called to continue his mission. As it ends, it looks to the participation of the worshippers in the perfect kingdom of God's love:

Unite us with him and with one another
in mission to all the world;
and bring us with the whole creation to your perfect kingdom.

But before we leave this aspect of doctrine's relationship to worship, I need at least to acknowledge one contemporary area of difficulty. The feminist critique of traditional Christian doctrine and the language of worship has raised questions about the continuing use of traditional formulae and prayers. It has done so out of

---

181 *Methodist Worship Book*, Holy Communion for the Day of Pentecost and Times of Renewal in the Life of the Church.

the conviction (which I have already set out) that language really does change things; it shapes our sense of reality and our relationships, for better and for worse. If this is so, it is said, how in our worship can we use the language of 'Father' and 'Son', or 'Lord' and 'King', and how can we employ pronouns like 'he' and 'him'? Surely to do so reinforces a patriarchal understanding of God and puts worshippers (especially women) in a relationship with God more reflective of distorted human class and gender systems than the loving intimacy that should be ours in Christ. What is needed, such critics go on to say, is a new set of formulae and prayers, ones that are more inclusive of all worshippers and free of sexist and classist language.[182] Furthermore, there are rich resources in the language of scripture to enhance worship through fresh metaphors for God. So it has become common for new liturgies to eliminate at least some of the gendered pronouns for God and to employ a variety of metaphors to enrich the language of praise. A Church of England communion prayer speaks of God with the words 'as a mother tenderly gathers her children . . .'.[183]

Rather more controversial is the beginning of a eucharistic prayer in the *Methodist Worship Book*: 'God, our Father and our Mother . . .'.[184] The capitalization of Mother is significant; it seems to imply that Mother is a way of naming the Christian God that has the same doctrinal standing as Father.

In other liturgies, for example those of the Anglican Church of Aoteoroa/New Zealand, the traditional Trinitarian formula of Father, Son and Holy Spirit is often replaced with a non-gendered alternative, most commonly, 'Creator, Redeemer and Sustainer'.

Do these innovations represent a creative and valid development of doctrinal language in worship, or do they hinder the setting forth of the praise of God? I hope I have already indicated that

---

182 The literature on this topic is immense, and not entirely good-natured. A good example of a constructive feminist approach to doctrine and the language of worship can be found in Ruth C. Duck and Patricia Wilson-Kastner, *Praising God: The Trinity in Christian Worship*, Westminster John Knox Press, 1999. The book includes interesting examples of liturgies framed in accordance with the authors' theological understanding.

183 *Common Worship*, Eucharistic Prayer G.

184 Holy Communion, Ordinary Season 2.

Christian doctrine is not entirely static; there is growth and development alongside faithfulness and tradition. So, it seems to me, the task we face is one of discernment: are these developments (the adoption of new language as well as the omission of old) appropriate for the faithful handing on of Christ in Christian worship? My response would be that some are and some most definitely are not. On the positive side, the feminist critique has alerted us to the limited palette of language with which Christian liturgy has often worked. There are good reasons to look critically at the relationship between Bible, doctrine and culture in the form and words of worship; many prayers by individuals such as Janet Morley and Ruth Duck, as well as those in revised liturgies, are good outcomes in this process. For some years I have tried to avoid gendered pronouns for God as far as possible.

But not all developments are helpful or innocent. For example, the 'creator, redeemer, sustainer' formula, often used as an alternative to 'Father, Son and Holy Spirit', represents a distortion of the doctrine of the Trinity, defining the members of the Godhead solely in terms of functions rather than referring to their relationships. This is a serious loss. I would argue that the language of 'Father, Son and Holy Spirit' is 'given', both in the sense that it is not ours to drop and in the sense that it comes to us from God's revelation in Christ and the Church. It is not simply a metaphor devised by human beings in a culture that was inescapably patriarchal. But if it is genuinely gift, then it needs to be acknowledged in the language of praise and worship. And if it is a vital part of handing on Christ, then Christian teaching and learning (to which I will come in a later section of this chapter) have to help this language escape from the sexist interpretation and sexist use in which it is so often trapped.

Worship and public confession

In worship doctrine is the language of God's glory, but it is also the language of Christian witness, the confession of the faith before the world. It is clear that in the early Church the desire for a common confession of faith was driven in part by a need for a common Christian witness. This was necessary in times of perse-cution, when Christians needed to know what they were standing firm on, and it was needed in the response to pagan attacks on Christianity. But above all it was needed to provide a common confession for those entering the Church in baptism, and for those meeting as the Christian community in worship. Hence the creeds developed out of the baptismal confession made by new members of local congregations. Gradually these became more uniform and the Apostles' Creed became the common creed for baptism, espe-cially in the West.

Taking doctrine more seriously means giving a regular place to the confession of faith in worship. Though still common in many churches, creeds tend to be missed out in others, and for a variety of reasons. There may be a worry that not everyone in the congre-gation can say them with a good conscience; there may also be a concern that they are 'boring' or 'irrelevant' in a context where dif-ferent age groups and people of different backgrounds are present. And for some congregations, of course, anything that has been written down is inherently poorer than a spontaneous outpouring of words.

But these fears need not deter churches from this kind of cor-porate affirmation. Singing the creeds has a great tradition and there are plenty of settings easily picked up by the whole congrega-tion. There are question-and-answer forms that break up the text. For example, the question, 'Do you believe and trust in God the Father?' elicits the response, 'I believe in God the Father, maker of heaven and earth . . .'. Nor are creeds and affirmations of faith alternatives to spontaneous accounts of God's grace. Worship that included both the formal confession of faith and the testimony of its members as to how God is working in their lives today would be doubly enriched. And (against those who worry about the scruples and doubts of congregation members) the point about creeds and communal confessions of faith is that they are not meant to repre-sent what any individual, left to their own devices, would write as the summary of the Christian faith; they are testimony to what is shared, an act of solidarity with others. This means that they can earth the act of worship in the beliefs of the whole Church.

This is especially the case with the Nicene Creed. Saying 'We believe' does more than refer to all who are present in that service at that time: the 'we' includes all Christian congregations in all parts of the world and in all traditions. It even extends through time and includes the worshipping church of the present with those who have gone before and who are now part of the communion of saints. As, through their witness, Christ has been handed on to us, so we, with our confession, seek to offer Christ to the world we inhabit. I have often joined in saying the Nicene Creed with a sense of relief just after hearing a sermon that has flatly contradicted it! But it will also witness the faith of this congregation before their fellow Christians and before reciting the creeds or an affirmation of faith.

Just as the development of the language of worship is vital, but needs a discerning eye, so the development of any new affirmations for public worship need critical examination; it is all too easy to distort the Christian confession through excessive leaning towards this or that contemporary fashion. That is one reason why it is helpful to distinguish between the creeds (those ancient Christian confessions handed down from the early centuries) and affirmations of faith, more recent ways of summarizing Christian confession for contemporary worship. The latter are best when they are simple and do not take to themselves the role of preaching. The perils can be seen in this recent Canadian example, called by its church 'A New Creed'.

> We are not alone,
> we live in God's world.
> We believe in God:
> who has created and is creating,
> who has come in Jesus,
> the Word made flesh,
> to reconcile and make new,
> who works in us and others
> by the Spirit.
> We trust in God.
> We are called to be the Church:

to celebrate God's presence,
to live with respect in Creation,
to love and serve others,
to seek justice and resist evil,
to proclaim Jesus, crucified and risen,
our judge and our hope.
In life, in death, in life beyond death,
God is with us.
We are not alone.
Thanks be to God.[185]

This seems so intent on not offending anyone that it fails to affirm the distinctive Christian belief in God as Trinity, Father, Son and Holy Spirit being conspicuously absent, and it deletes the historical reference to Jesus being 'born of the Virgin Mary' and having 'suffered under Pontius Pilate'. In their place, the affirmation 'we are not alone' is eerily unsubstantial.

The theologian Karl Barth was fond of saying that the best apologetics is good dogmatic theology. I would want to say that the best evangelism is good Christian worship – and that means worship which at the very least confesses Christ unambiguously before the world.

Worship and transformation

Finally, I want to come back to the statement I made earlier about the nature of worship – that it is an activity through which worshippers are formed into the Body of Christ. Worship is the performance of the Christian drama of God and it informs Christians and others what the faith is all about, but it also aims at the transformation of worshippers into a new people. Worship is an arena of the Holy Spirit and it cannot leave its participants unchanged.

---

185 'A New Creed' of the United Church of Canada. If anyone thinks I am taking this unfairly out of context, let them visit the church's website and see its recently adopted 'Song of Faith', which can only be described as a several-pages-long exercise in collective theological thought-association: <www.united-church.ca/en/beliefs/statements/songfaith>.

Returning to the crucial New Testament passage of 1 Corinthians 11, and picking up my discussion of Ellen Charry's arguments about doctrine and Christian excellence, I can make these points.

First, becoming a Christ-like community is linked to the right remembering and handing on of Christ. That is why Paul is so anxious about what is going on in the Christian community in Corinth. Because it is not properly receiving what has been handed on about Jesus (particularly the teaching about the inauguration of the Lord's supper) it is hindered from reflecting Jesus in its pattern of life. He tells the Corinthians that to become transformed into a community of Christ-like hospitality and reconciliation (rather than to remain conformed to the patterns of exclusion in the surrounding culture) means taking seriously the tradition that has been handed down to them through him and taking it as their guide to the performance of worship.

While many people would agree that transformation (both of individuals and communities) is a core purpose of worship, there is a tendency to downplay the role of doctrine. For example, a congregation might ask, 'How will our worship transform us into a more inclusive and welcoming community?' Tempting answers could well include some of the following: 'If our building is more attractive, if the language in our worship is more accessible, if we are more fervent in our prayers.' These may all be important aspects of the process, but I want to suggest that there needs to be a doctrinal element to this desire for transformation. So some useful questions might be: does our worship reflect belief in a God who loves and desires all those whom God has made? Do we worship as a community that accepts the universal need – and possibility – for forgiveness? Is the Holy Spirit named and claimed as the source of communion with God and with each other?

The Orthodox theologian John Zizioulas, whose Trinitarian theology was mentioned in the previous chapter, makes a direct link between the doctrinal understanding of the Church and the transforming power of its worship. For him the liturgy of the Eucharist is rooted in the doctrine of the Church as the communion of those who are being drawn into communion with God through the work of the Holy Spirit. Worship that is truly faithful to this understanding of God and of the Eucharist will transform those who take part and forge them into a true community of faith.

Second, we need to attend to the doctrine of the Holy Spirit if we are to develop Christian worship into a more transformative activity. Here, the word 'gift' is vitally important. Christians commonly speak of the gifts of the Spirit manifested in worship: prophecy, wisdom, healing, tongues, and so on. These are the gifts listed in 1 Corinthians 12. And there is a contemporary trend to talk about the 'giftings' the Spirit gives to Church members, equipping them for speaking and leading. But alongside these there needs to be set those doctrines that link the Holy Spirit with what the Church receives and hands on. We might, for example, speak of scripture as the gift of the Spirit. Written under the inspiration of the Holy Spirit as a faithful witness to God's word and action in Jesus Christ, it is the means through which the Holy Spirit hands Christ on to successive communities of worshipping Christians.

Furthermore, the Holy Spirit inspires those who attend to the words of scripture, so that they become the Word of God for that particular situation. How would these doctrinal beliefs make a difference to what happens in worship? Well, first it would mean making proper space for scripture to be read and heard in Christian worship. I am constantly surprised by the number of so-called biblical churches that provide very little scripture in worship, often treating it as little more than fuel for the preacher's rhetoric rather than a word through which God may be saying challenging and alien things. It would also mean surrounding its reading and interpretation with prayer and treating the task of preaching as the discernment of what the Spirit is saying through scripture. In this way the worshipping church can be a community of the Word, open to transformation by the living Spirit and not simply treating the Bible as a dead letter or a set of inspiring stories.

Teaching and learning of Christ

Worship, however central, is not the only activity of the Church. Teaching and learning are also central, and although they should be part of what happens in worship they are by no means confined to it. To be a Christian is to be a disciple, in other words, a learner – someone open to teaching. In the Gospels, the disciples of Jesus frequently address him as 'rabbi', 'teacher'. The rabbi–disciple relationship was much more than a matter of going to hear a gifted speaker; disciples shared the life of their rabbi, following him where he went and serving him. There was an aspect of perform- ance in the roles of rabbi and disciple and this is easy to see in the Gospels. Jesus' disciples pluck grains of corn on the Sabbath (Mark 2.23); they are sent out to announce and enact the mis- sion of Jesus (Luke 10); they prepare for his entry into Jerusalem and their final meal together (Luke 19 and 22). But this perform- ance also included a change in understanding. Jesus taught in a way that informed his disciples about such things as the life of the kingdom of God, the fulfilment of God's law, the true way to pray and the nature of servant leadership. In the relationship between Jesus and his disciples there was informing as well as performing – and both aimed at transforming the lives of disciples so that they formed a new kind of community. Augustine, himself an outstand- ing teacher, captures the sense of this relationship between inform- ing and performing:

> He who reads to an audience pronounces aloud the words he sees before him: he who teaches reading, does it that others may be able to read for themselves. Each, however, communicates to others what he has learnt himself. Just so, the man who ex- plains to an audience the passages of Scripture he understands is like one who reads aloud the words before him. On the other hand, the man who lays down rules for interpretation is like one who teaches reading, that is, shows others how to read for themselves.[186]

What applied to the relationship between the first disciples and Jesus applies to discipleship in the Christian community today and, as Augustine suggests, a key element is learning how to learn and not simply learning this or that piece of information. A Christian

---

186 Augustine, *On Christian Doctrine*, Book 1.

church is a community of discipleship, and so learning should be at its centre. And modern-day disciples, no less than their first-century forebears, should expect to be informed, to be involved in performance, and to become transformed through their learning. So a church that has a future as a doctrinal community (by which I mean a community that receives and hands on Christ) needs to think carefully about the place of learning and teaching.

In the last few years there has been something of a revolution in thinking about learning. The emphasis has shifted, from the passing on of information that will increase the learner's stock of knowledge to a process of formation that enables people to learn for themselves. The stress has moved from the teacher and his or her techniques of communication to the learner and to the different ways in which he or she might find it helpful to learn. In formal education this has meant that traditional forms of teaching, for example the lecture, have been disparaged in favour of a learning system that is much more participative and open-ended.

Within my own field of theological education and ministerial training there has been a similar move away from pushing information at people. It is not enough for students to know the history of the Church or the vocabulary of New Testament Greek. We now speak of a three-fold process of learning in which developing understanding (of the Bible and Christian teaching), increasing skills (of pastoral leadership, worship and preaching) and forming character (as a Christian disciple) are all woven together. Contemporary programmes of ministerial training should involve an integration of these three streams of learning, with each shaping and informing the other. This is absolutely right, indeed I often find myself battling to take this process further in the situations where I work. But I have also seen the result of taking this process too far, in the sense of promoting formation and skills without reference to the development of Christian understanding. It is possible to overstress the experiential aspect of learning to the exclusion of any meaningful communication. Yet teaching and learning does involve handing things over; it is a matter of informing as well as transforming. Education without any content produces frustration and ignorance. I once found myself taking part in an experimental course in which the staff were instructed to impart no information whatsoever, but simply help the members experience learning for themselves. The results were predictably disastrous, with frustration for staff and students alike.

Yet this is a process that often happens by default within contemporary churches; Christians are left to find their own way through the maze of confusing and contradictory messages that our culture throws at them. I have even encountered resistance to taking young people through confirmation classes on the grounds that they need to be left to make up their own minds – as if our minds were not constantly being shaped by the consumerist and violent world in which we live. The truth is that there is little present danger of people being 'brainwashed' by exposure to traditional Christian teaching; most of us are already brainwashed by its alternatives. It is one thing for the Christian Church to abandon, as it surely must, an arrogant approach to teaching that simply says, 'Here are a series of truths for you to memorize and assent to, but never ever question.' It is quite another for it to lose all confidence in having anything distinctive to hand on. Fear of being accused of indoctrination has led too many churches to be tentative and neglectful in the matter of teaching.

One result of this is that in an increasingly multi-faith society, Christians are often ill-equipped to discuss their faith with those from a different religious background. This is especially the case with Muslims, who have generally been taught not only the doctrines of their own faith but also the reasons why (from an Islamic point of view) Christian doctrines (particularly the Trinity) are dangerous and wrong. Furthermore, the impact of evangelists for atheism such as Richard Dawkins, whose *The God Delusion* was in the bestseller lists for months on end, has been all the more destructive for those Christians who have little grounding in the doctrinal basis of their faith and practice. Only those who have had handed on to them a robust Christian understanding of God as Father, Son and Holy Spirit will be in a position to see that writers like Dawkins are usually addressing a caricature of Christian belief rather than the real thing.

This suggests a positive need for programmes of teaching that are integrated with the practice of Christian life. In the last few years there has been an explosion of these programmes. The best known among them is Alpha, designed at the charismatic Anglican Church, Holy Trinity Brompton, and reflecting that church's doctrinal emphasis on the Holy Spirit. But there are many others offering slightly different emphases on the basics of Christian belief and its relevance for life in the contemporary world. 'Christianity Explored', 'Emmaus' and 'Star' are just a few of those currently used by churches in the UK, while the Roman Catholic RCIA courses tend to follow a similar pattern.[187] Although their aim may be to introduce non-Christians to the Christian faith, in practice many long-standing church members have found them a place where their Christian understanding and Christian performance have been transformed. What they all have in common is a form of learning situated within a small group committed to friendship and open service. Meals are normally part of each session of the course. The success of Alpha and its competitors is based on a combination of content and context that promotes a form of learning that is both experiential and informative. They are, in short, close to what I mean by doctrinal communities, consciously handing on Christ both through performance (Christian hospitality and friendship) and the informed sharing of belief. In this way they mark a return to something like the process of catechesis that developed in the early church.

But such courses can only be part of the picture: being a disciple is a life-long commitment for the Christian, and so is Christian learning. Is it too much to hope that programmes for Christian education, be they for children, young people, new Christians or those mature in the faith, will consciously ask, 'How will this help people to make the connection between receiving the basic teachings of Christianity and what is happening in my life and the world right now?' In this, ordained ministers are called to be examples. It is notorious that this is often not so. A study of the reading habits of American pastors suggested that, at least among those from

---

187 RCIA stands for Rite of Christian Initiation of Adults.

more conservative churches, there was very little engagement with serious doctrinal and theological literature.[188]

Doctrine and mission: acting out and handing on the gospel

I have been arguing throughout this book that at the heart of Christianity is the story of a God who gives by handing over to the world the very being of God in the person of Jesus Christ. The traditional word for this dynamic and costly movement of God is mission, from the Latin *missio*, meaning 'to send'. The Father sends the Son as the expression of divine love; the eternal Word becomes incarnate in the life of Jesus of Nazareth. God's mission in Jesus Christ is therefore nothing less than the revelation of the unseen God and the transformation and restoration of human life in God's image. God's mission, the *missio Dei*, embraces the whole of God's action in relation to humanity and creation: guiding, caring, challenging, saving, reconciling, sanctifying. It is a mission that *informs* us what God is like (God, for Christians, is always Christ-like). It is a mission that *performs* the work of God through the redeeming work of Christ. It is a mission that *transforms* those who respond to God in Christ. In the same way, the Holy Spirit is sent (though western and eastern Christians differ as to whether this is by the Father and the Son or by the Father) and exercises the mission of God in the Church and the world. The Spirit, too, has a mission that informs (the Spirit leads into all truth), a mission that performs (according to Paul, the Spirit 'intercedes with sighs too deep for words'[189]) and a mission that transforms, as those who live by the Spirit show forth in their lives the Spirit's fruit of love, joy and peace.[190] Notice that there is always a link between the doctrine of God (the message) and the way that doctrine is expressed (the medium). The manner of God's revelation – God's performance, we might say – is not incidental to its substance, just as the means

---

188 J. W. Carroll, 'Pastors' Pick: What Preachers are Reading', *The Christian Century* (23 August 2003). Accessed at <www.pulpitandpew.duke.edu/pastorspicks.html>.
189 Romans 8.26.
190 Galatians 5.22.

God uses are always consistent with God's aims. So, for example, the Christian doctrine of the incarnation is both an account of who God is and the story of how God's nature is expressed in the life of the world. It is medium and message rolled into one.[191]

So God's mission includes both teaching and performance, and the Church participates in that same mission of God. The Church, too, is sent to inform, perform and transform in the name of Jesus Christ and in the power of the Holy Spirit. For many Christians this sending is best summed up in what has become known as the 'great commission', the risen Jesus' final words to the disciples in Matthew 28.18–20:

> All authority in heaven and on earth has been given to me. Go therefore and make disciples of all nations, baptizing them in the name of the Father and of the Son and of the Holy Spirit, and teaching them to observe everything that I have commanded you. And remember, I am with you always, to the end of the age.

Handing on Christ is, then, basic to the idea of Christian mission. It is a sharing of the good news of who God is and what God has done in Christ, as well as an acting out of the drama of salvation.

How might closer attention to doctrine help the Church in its sharing in the mission of God? First, it would help churches develop a more holistic model of mission. By and large, different groups of Christians tend to major on divergent aspects of mission, often suggesting that their priority represents the only activity that is truly mission. For some, mission is essentially the proclamation of the gospel message of redemption and the summons to repentance, conversion and Christian commitment. For others, mission is service in the name of Christ, particularly to the poor and vulnerable. For yet others it is the prophetic challenge to all that threatens God's gift of abundant life, be it a racist government, an unfair employer or an unequal distribution of the world's resources. But if I am right in suggesting that mission is the Church's active participation in the saving actions of God, then mission has to embrace all of

---

191 It is surely no coincidence that the author of the famous slogan, 'The medium is the message', Marshal McLuhan, was himself a committed Roman Catholic with a particular interest in the doctrine of the Trinity.

them. What these partial approaches to mission have in common is that they operate out of too narrow an understanding of who God is and what God does.

Closer attention to the whole doctrine of God should make it impossible to narrow the concept of mission to only one aspect of the Christian understanding of God. The doctrines of creation and humanity, of incarnation and Trinity, of salvation and hope all contribute to the Christian understanding of God's loving action and so they all inform Christian mission. For that reason, Christian mission needs close attention to its doctrinal roots. This does not mean that all churches will at all times be engaged in every possible aspect of mission with equal force. In any one situation there will be priorities for mission, but the discernment of those priorities needs to be accompanied by the recognition that those who are differently engaged are also in mission.

One example of this discernment can be found in the 1985 *Kairos Document* produced by theologians and Christian leaders in apartheid South Africa.[192] *Kairos* is a Greek word implying the right time for action, a sense of urgency. The document engages with the biblical narrative of God's actions and the Christian tradition of teaching about God, and it asks: 'What, in the light of this tradition and present situation of South Africa, is the priority for the Church's speech and action?' How, in other words, are we to perform, once we have been informed by our contextual reading of the Bible and doctrine? Its conclusion is radical: in the light of the biblical teaching about God's justice and judgement, the Church is called to confront the powers of evil in apartheid South Africa rather than seek reconciliation with them. One commentator at the time claimed that the *Kairos Document* represented the contemporary struggle between orthodoxy and heterodoxy.[193] In other words, it was about getting doctrine right and not just about defining how the Church should act.

---

192 The document can be accessed at: <www.sahistory.org.za/pages/library-resources/official%20docs/kairos-document.html>. Since 1985, a number of other 'Kairos Documents' have been produced in different situations.

193 Dorothy Sölle, '"The Moment of Truth": The Kairos document from Africa', *Concilium*, 192, 1987.

A counter-example, illustrating how often the Church and a Christian society get it wrong, comes from the Virginia Slave Law of 1667:

> Whereas some doubts have risen whether children that are slaves by birth, and by the charity and piety of their owners made partakers of the blessed sacrament of baptism, should by virtue of their baptism be made free, it is enacted and declared by this Grand Assembly, and the authority thereof, that the conferring of baptism does not alter the condition of the person as to his bondage or freedom; that diverse masters, freed from this doubt may more carefully endeavour the propagation of Christianity by permitting children, though slaves, or those of greater growth if capable, to be admitted to that sacrament.[194]

Here is a community that calls itself Christian desperately misunderstanding both the doctrine of Baptism and the nature of Christian mission. Of course, it is relatively easy to spot examples like this from the distance of history, but much more difficult to discern them in the life of the contemporary Church.

So, engaging more fully with doctrine is essential for developing Christian mission. But the engagement works in two ways. Yes, the Church needs a doctrinally informed understanding of mission, but it also needs a missiologically informed understanding of doctrine. As David Bosch says in his definitive work, *Transforming Mission*, 'We are in need of a missiological agenda for theology rather than just a theological agenda for mission; for theology, rightly understood, has no reason to exist other than critically to accompany the *missio Dei*.'[195]

I would not want to go quite so far as to say that Christian doctrine only exists for the purpose of mission; after all, we have seen that worshipping God in adoration and praise, not just doing things for God, is central to Christian life. Nevertheless, Bosch points to an important fact: thinking about doctrine needs to have

---

194 <www.swarthmore.edu/SocSci/bdorsey1/41docs/24-sla.html>.
195 David Bosch, *Transforming Mission: Paradigm Shifts in Theology of Mission*, Orbis, 1992, p. 494.

a mission focus. It is not an abstract set of truths but truth received for a purpose: handing on Christ in such a way that the kingdom of God may flourish. In the eighteenth century John Wesley coined the phrase 'experimental divinity'. By that he seems to have meant that reflection on Christian doctrine needs to be driven not by human curiosity or speculation but by the missionary needs of the Church. There is, as we would say now, an intimate link between orthodoxy and orthopraxis. It would be the practical effects in fruitful mission that would help to discern where the emphasis and development of doctrinal teaching needs to go.

In the late twentieth century no one was more effective in linking the development of doctrinal teaching with the missionary needs of the Church than Bishop Lesslie Newbigin. Some time before the resurgence of formal theological interest in the doctrine of the Trinity, Newbigin had published a significant book on the relationship between the doctrine of the Trinity and the mission of Church.[196] It was not simply that a study of the Trinity had led Newbigin to missionary conclusions: his immersion in the practical business of directing mission as a bishop in South India had convinced him that the Church needed to draw on its doctrinal heritage as a way of facing up to its missionary task. That meant taking the doctrine of the Trinity more seriously than was fashionable and understanding it in a missiological way. Newbigin believed that the doctrine of the Trinity had developed in the early Church not so much as a speculative philosophical account of belief in God but as a response to a concrete situation in which many rival gods were promoted. A mission-focused understanding of Christian doctrine, then and now, has to be Trinitarian. It is the nature of the missionary task – especially in relation to societies that have never before encountered the Christian faith – to give a proper account of how Christians understand the nature of God. For that reason there is, Newbigin believed, real danger in emphasizing the doctrines of the person and work of Jesus Christ at the expense of the full-blown Trinitarian account of God's work.

---

196 Lesslie Newbigin, *Trinitarian Faith and Today's Mission*, John Knox Press, 1964.

Conclusion

I cannot, of course, claim that this chapter has shown how doctrine can solve all the practical problems currently facing the churches and those who exercise ministry in them. What I hope to have shown is that in key areas of the Church's life and work – worship, teaching and mission – a renewed attention to the gift of Christian doctrine can be part of Christian renewal and effectiveness. It simply is not the case that doctrinal orthodoxy, generously understood, is a dead weight preventing the Church from moving forward, or a straitjacket to stifle creativity. Jaroslav Pelikan's oft-quoted aphorism still holds: 'Tradition is the living faith of the dead: traditionalism is the dead faith of the living.'[197] The living faith of the dead is a gift that hands on Christ to those who are today living and struggling with the call to be both faithful and effective.

---

197 Pelikan, *The Christian Tradition*, Vol. 1, p. 1.

Index of Subjects and Authors

Aquinas, St Thomas 129, 143, 164

Arnold, Matthew 51

Atonement 60, 92, 166

Augustine of Hippo, St 44, 54, 61, 78, 97, 137, 142, 152, 155, 156, 165, 174, 184, 198

Barth, Karl 12, 110, 114–17, 132, 154, 161, 173, 183, 195

Bible 11–12, 18–20, 23, 26–8, 31, 34, 36–8, 40, 42, 53, 57, 61, 63, 64, 67, 69, 70, 76, 83–4, 90, 93, 98, 101, 103, 106, 112, 121, 126, 131–3, 137, 139, 144–7, 155, 167, 175, 180, 183–4, 197–9, 204

Bonhoeffer, Dietrich 66, 106, 148–9, 180–1

Bultmann, Rudolf 82–3, 123

Catechism 15, 16, 18, 147

Charry, Ellen 22, 128–33, 137, 196

Christology 23, 26, 53, 90, 104–6, 113

Church (doctrine of) 113, 151, 196

Cobb, John 119–20, 168–71

Councils 3–6, 11, 13, 15, 17–18, 30, 39, 52–3, 71, 81–3, 100, 103, 110, 134, 144, 156, 181

Creation 26, 45, 63, 70, 854, 103, 109, 110, 112–13, 119, 131, 136, 151, 155, 159, 163–73, 175, 178, 180–1, 190, 195, 202, 204

Creeds 12–15, 18, 20–2, 28, 30, 35, 37, 39, 42, 66, 69–70, 85, 88, 91–3, 98, 102–4, 119–20, 125, 134, 151–2, 155, 157, 161, 163, 172, 193–5

Da Vinci Code, The 31, 40

Development (of doctrine) 44, 97–8, 102, 108, Ch. 5

Dominican order 144, 150–1, 169

Doxology 185, 187–8

Eschatology 113, 172–80

Ethics and Christian Doctrine 55, 70, 75, 118, 126, 136

Evangelicalism 58, 60, 62, 67, 70, 93, 97, 123, 131, 146–7, 151–2, 166, 171

Feminist theology 100, 108, 120, 169–70, 190–2

Gadamer, Hans Georg 75, 82–9, 93, 114
Grotius, Hugo 52–5
Gunton, Colin 92, 156–7, 165–6, 170

Harnack, Adolf von 53–54, 69, 99–101
Hermeneutics (interpretation of bible and doctrine) 30, 43, 75, 82–3, 85, 88–91, 101, 105, 116, 131–3, 156, 162, 183, 192, 197–8
Holy Spirit 13, 17, 29–30, 38–40, 50, 53, 58, 62–4, 66, 70, 84–5, 93, 97–8, 103–4, 108, 112, 131, 133, 141–2, 144–6, 152, 155–9, 161, 163, 165, 170–1, 181, 186, 188–91, 194–7, 200–3
Hunt, John 145–7

Judaism 10, 21, 23–4, 26, 35, 36

Kairos Document 204
Kant, Immanuel 59, 65–7, 76, 86

Lessing, Gotthold Ephraim 67

Liberal theology 21, 53, 55, 59, 69, 109, 110, 121, 123, 128
Lindbeck, George 79, 110, 121–8, 132–3, 136

Macquarrie, John 115–17, 120
McFague, Sallie 108
McIntyre, Alistair 158, 160
Meiderlin, Peter 55
Metaphor 20, 91–2, 108, 152, 154, 192
Methodism 7, 11, 18, 44, 46, 49, 58, 61–3, 70, 109, 129, 144–7, 151, 190–1
Milbank, John 133–6
Ministry 5, 21–3, 29, 38–40, 46–7, 57, 69, 103, 105, 142, 146, 148, 173, 177, 190, 197
Mission 40, 41, 71, 112, 126, 138, 150, 152, 185, 190, 198, 202–7
Moltmann, Jürgen 157, 159, 160, 170, 178–9

Newbigin, Lesslie 81, 206

Orthodoxy 3, 5, 15, 17, 19, 23, 27, 30–1, 43–7, 55, 64, 79–81, 93, 97, 100, 11, 113, 123, 133, 137, 177, 187, 204, 206, 208

Paine, Thomas 66–7
Pagels, Elaine 30–1, 39, 90
Pannenberg, Wolfhart 163, 172
Paul, St 9, 17, 21–4, 29, 33–8, 48, 83, 97

Performance 35, 126, 131–3, 182–8, 195, 196, 198–203

Pietism 54–4, 69, 72, 77, 123, 144

Postmodernism 41–2, 8, 89–90, 94, 107, 122, 131, 134, 159–60, 183

Polanyi, Michael 74–81, 84, 86, 88, 89, 93–4, 98, 104

Power and Christian Doctrine 17, 40, 94, 101, 111, 140, 162, 174, 176, 184, 196, 203

Radical Orthodoxy 133–4, 136–7

Rauschenbusch 69–70

Reception 37–8, 40, 42, 43, 113, 127, 129, 139–41, 171, 189, 206

Resurrection 12, 22, 29, 33, 39, 67, 82, 122–3, 159, 170–3, 179–80

Ricoeur, Paul 75, 87–94, 114, 131

Schleiermacher, Friedrich 59, 61, 62, 123

Scripture *see Bible*

Social gospel 69–71, 149

Spener, Philip 57, 63

Theodoret of Cyrrus 1–7, 17

Tillich, Paul 117–20

Tradition 4–5, 7–10, 14–15, 23, 27, 32–3, 39–43, 45–6, 49, 50, 52, 59, 61–4, 68, 74, 76, 80–8, 92–4, 97, 100, 103, 104, 108, 130–9, 144, 146, 151, 157, 169, 171, 174, 178–80, 193, 196, 204, 207

Trinity (doctrine of the) 61, 75, 98, 118–19, 155–63, 170–1, 184, 189, 191–2, 195, 200, 203–3

Trocmé, Andre 148–9

Vanhoozer, Kevin 128, 131–7, 183–4

Vincent de Lerins, St 96, 98

Violence and Christian doctrine 49–56, 58, 134, 140, 148, 151, 180

Wainwright, Geoffrey 43, 72, 187

Wesley, John 18, 32, 35, 54, 62–4, 85, 97, 109, 145–7, 206

Wesley, Charles 58, 63, 167

Wiles, Maurice 115–17, 120

Worship 8, 13–15, 18–20, 24, 24, 29, 31, 38, 43–4, 50, 52, 58, 77, 112, 126–7, 130, 140–1, 149–50, 152, 157, 162, 185–97

Zizioulas, John 159, 195